Bob Cass had a reputation for being a story-getter, breaking many exclusives involving the top names in the game. He built up an extensive list of contacts working as a football writer first with The Sun but latterly the Mail on Sunday. After a long battle with cancer, Bob passed away aged 78 in November 2016 to tributes from the likes of Gary Lineker, David Beckham, Sir Alex Ferguson, Alan Shearer and Niall Quinn.

Bob Cass

By the Way

AUSTIN MACAULEY PUBLISHERS™

LONDON • CAMBRIDGE • NEW YORK • SHARJAH

A CIP catalogue record for this title is available from the British Library.

ISBN 9781786936790 (Paperback)
ISBN 9781786936806 (E-Book)

www.austinmacauley.com

First Published (2017)
Austin Macauley Publishers Ltd™
25 Canada Square
Canary Wharf
London
E14 5LQ

To my wife, Janet, for her long suffering patience and understanding. Also to my son, Simon, for his invaluable help in the technicalities in putting the book together.

FOREWORD
BY SIR ALEX FERGUSON

Having first become acquainted with Bob Cass all those years ago when I was managing Aberdeen and he was a much younger journalist, I think I have a good enough knowledge of him, both as a sports writer and a friend, to write this foreword.

In the modern world of football, relationships between managers and journalists have become fragmented over the years. Older, experienced writers have quit or been replaced by young bucks.

Maybe it is a generation thing, or maybe journalism has just deteriorated, but I found it very difficult to trust sports writers, although I do understand the difficulties they face—pressure from editors or sports editors hardly inspires confidence that they can write good articles on the game of football.

I came to recognise that, which is why I never held long-term grudges, particularly if they apologised for some inaccurate reporting. There was an occasion when Bob's name was on an article which turned out had been generated from his office.

It all ended in hilarity when he turned up at the next press conference, uninvited, and asked how long was his life ban to last! What a character!

I was in a rage for a few days but it was a rare exception in a relationship which, for over a long period, was based on trust.

I can also safely vouch for all the other managers and people in football who feel the same. I think, at the end of the day, he could stand alongside some of the best of his profession in the country. I believe it emphasises the strength of Bob's honesty and integrity that he has retained his friendship with all the managers he has dealt with.

For bit of devilment I was tempted to say this book was a figment of his imagination but, seriously, it is a carefully crafted chronicle of his time dealing with delicate issues, always handling situations without betraying confidences or revealing sources to his bosses. It must have been very difficult.

How he managed it, is down to the relationship he had with his contacts; the trust they had in him to know how far he could take the information. You have to wonder whether any of his younger colleagues would be able to benefit from similar experiences should they want to record their own memoirs.

Having now retired for almost two years, I can honestly say I miss the old bugger. I have had good relationships and some friendships with a few journalists such as Glen Gibbons and Hugh McDonald in Glasgow, Hugh McIlvaney, Paul Hayward, Bill Thornton and John Bean in England.

But there is only one Bob Cass. And for that many will say: thank God!

PROLOGUE
THANK GOD FOR
GRANNY HARBURN

So, who *was* Granny Harburn? Well, great Granny
Harburn was a remarkable old lady who was steeped in
class—working class. When God created Granny
Harburn, the mould was stored in heaven among giants
of humanity; although a giant in stature she certainly was
not. But if she was physically frail her astonishing
strength of personality and character belied her barely
five feet from tip to toe.

Granny was 92 when she died, bequeathing nothing
but inspiration and example to her family and anyone
who had the good fortune to know her. She left this
world without a penny to her name but never owing one
either. Her character was chiselled out of living through
the best and worst of what the human race contrived to
do to itself. But, as well as being the matriarchal head of
a forever spreading family tree, she still found time—a
lot of time—to develop an incredible sense of political
awareness.

Feed her stats into a computer and it's a certainty
you would come up with someone whose politics would

be a shade to the left of Lenin. But this lady was a one-off. A diehard royalist, she was also until her dying day an unflinching Tory who fought tooth and nail to facilitate the election of people who lived their lives in a different social stratosphere.

Inevitably, her passionate anti-Labour convictions spawned generations of like-minded true blues, and I for one have never contemplated denying that heritage, especially since she was directly responsible for saving the life of an inconspicuous little runt almost as it began in the squat little front room at 37 Barton Street; a two-up two-down terraced house on Albert Hill in Darlington on May 27th, 1938.

I should point out that unlike today when modern pragmatism denies kids their childhood fantasies such as babies delivered by storks or found under gooseberry bushes, the tooth fairy, or belief in Santa Claus, the birds and bees were not part of the curriculum at either of the Darlington Catholic schools I attended; St Williams and St Mary's Grammar. And since sex and matters relating were also taboo in the home, you somehow came across the facts of life by eavesdropping on the graphic conversations of older kids. Hey, don't forget, there was a war on and with my dad, like thousands of others, doing his bit to help win it, my mother had enough on her plate making sure there was food on the table for her kids.

Anyway, I reached an age when it was finally presumed I had grasped previous information about babies being sold by a local character by the name of Granny Welsh along with the bundles of second-hand clothing she lugged, red-faced and perspiring, around the seven streets of terraced houses that constituted the 'Hill' was total bollocks. Almost instantly I became fair game for any family member who felt compelled to relate to me, usually in the most lurid detail, that early morning front room drama. It was as if they had all been waiting desperately for an opportunity to let me know how fortunate and grateful I should be for simply being alive.

I was the first issue of a marriage between Sarah Alice Park, a Darlington lass of some beauty and principle, and Robert Stanley (Bob) Cass, an airman she had met while he was stationed at Catterick in North Yorkshire. It was a union that bridged the length of the country; Dad was born and bred in Windsor and worked for a time cleaning the clergy's footwear in St George's Chapel before enlisting in the RAF, where he eventually became an accomplished photographer whose war-time jobs included sitting alongside the tail-gunner on a Lancaster bomber either taking pictures of targets on reconnaissance flights, or to assess bombing damage when the raids were over.

Anyway, the arrival of the first born to the eldest daughter of Emma and Billy Park, a wire drawer at Darlington Wire Mills, a furnace of a place on the Hill where a lot of the kids headed after leaving school, was a long-awaited event. As it happened, had my arrival been a week premature, I would have been born a Scot. Dad had been stationed at Abbotsinch, the RAF base which is now Glasgow Airport and Mam had been with him in Paisley. But they packed their bags and travelled south a few days before I was due (I have to think the reason had more to do with Mam wanting her nearest and dearest around her on the big day than me having the necessary birth right to achieve sporting fame in an England shirt).

At the first signs of labour, the family, headed by the dowager, the aforementioned Granny Harburn, gathered dutifully in the front room. The scene wasn't quite Neanderthal but working class mothers-to-be like Alice Cass did not enjoy the finest obstetric luxuries either. Things could go wrong, and on that May morning they certainly did. In truth, I was an awkward little sod from the word go.

The problem was my head was just too big to allow me to propel myself smoothly into the world, and no matter how much my poor mother puffed and pushed I just would not come out. Things would have been a lot different today, of course; scans would have highlighted the fact that something close to an alien form had appeared in the womb and no doubt the simple solution would have been a Caesarean section in a sterilised, germ-free maternity hospital theatre. But this was Barton Street, not Great Ormond Street and you had to play the cards as they were dealt.

It's as difficult to imagine the agony Mam went through in labour, as it would be the ecstasy after I was finally delivered (with the aid of a pair of Heath Robinson forceps, which left a facial scar that remains today); albeit lifeless, apparently just another dead-at-birth statistic. But in that chaotic moment, my membership of the human race, was far from the priority. Attending to my mother, drained of blood and completely exhausted into the bargain, became a matter of life and death. It was a hard-fought battle that wasn't won lightly, but thankfully it was won.

It was then, and only then, that the attention of the gathered throng was directed towards the lifeless flotsam dumped elsewhere in the room. And it was Granny Harburn who, according to every well-informed source, gathered the lifeless lump in her hands and uttered the words that surely rank up there among history's immortal declarations, 'There's life in this child!'

Whatever rudimentary persuasion was necessary to speed up the breathing process was taken—a slap on the backside, an impromptu game of pass the parcel—and mother and son made a full recovery. The rest, as they say, is history.

So that was how it all started, a drama that began a lifetime of adventure; meeting, knowing and becoming known by iconic personalities whose acquaintance would be the stuff of any boyhood dream.

Thank God for Granny Harburn? Thank God indeed.

CHAPTER ONE
CLOUGH THE GENIUS

If there is a seriously overused adjective accorded to football people, it is surely 'charismatic'. How many times do you hear footballers beatified with descriptions such as 'great' and 'world-class', especially when spoken by former pros whose knowledge of the game often contrasts in comical circumstances with their lack of basic grammar. It also must be said that there are occasions too when media folk, especially over excited television and radio commentators, reach for even greater ceilings of hyperbole. 'The man's a genius,' they'll scream, searching for the vocabulary to describe a player evading a couple of tackles or stringing a few passes together.

If the dictionary interpretation of 'charisma' is 'a spiritual power given by God', then what of 'genius', 'the special inborn faculty of any individual'? Taken in their strictest context, neither term is appropriate when referring to anybody involved in football. Clever, gifted, talented, even brilliant; but surely not (in their most fundamental meaning anyway) charismatic or genius. And yet, when applied to the man who, for me, stands out as English football's greatest post-war manager, they are entirely justified. When it came to getting the maximum performance out of comparatively minimal resources, the late Brian Howard Clough did indeed have charisma, and he was indeed a genius.

It beats me why, when the fashion in recent years has been to reward many football figures with a knighthood, Cloughie was never invited to bend the knee. The reason certainly has no answer in his lack of achievement. In comparative terms, he stood head and shoulders above any of the other recent football accolades. Sir Alex Ferguson, Sir Bobby Robson, Sir Geoff Hurst, Sir Bobby Charlton and Sir Trevor Brooking may all be knights to remember, mostly fully meriting their recognition—Sir Alex, certainly, having surpassed his predecessor Sir Matt Busby's successes at Manchester United; Sir Bobby Robson too, a true football statesman, dispensed with cruelly and unfeelingly at Newcastle. But, in my submission, had one or all of them not picked up their illustrious prefix, it would not have been the glaring omission that applied to Clough.

Who else could have twice taken over third-rate clubs, struggling in what was the second division, and make them both league champions? Who else could have then guided one of them to four League Cup triumphs? Who else could have projected a bunch of the unlikeliest, least fashionable players in the business to the highest peak of European club football in successive seasons? Kenny Burns, Frank Clark, John McGovern, Ian Bowyer, Larry Lloyd, Garry Birtles et al, were not exactly household names.

Forest's 42 game sequence of unbeaten league matches between November 1977 and December 1978 while in his charge was a stupendous achievement, much more laudable than that of Arsenal in bettering it. In contrast to Clough's homespun heroes, Arsène Wenger's team was packed with players acquired for a fortune from all parts of the globe. When Forest's run was finally ended with a 2-0 defeat by Liverpool at Anfield, there was no haranguing of the referee, no outbursts of criticism of opposition players, no fights in the tunnel, no pizza or soup thrown, no FA investigation; nobody hated to lose more than Cloughie, any one of his players would bear testimony to that. But as brash and big-headed as he undoubtedly was; as rough as badgers' arses as (for the most part) his players were, they could have taught present-day protagonists lessons in dignity and decorum, which, were they heeded, would make English football an altogether more attractive spectacle.

Clough's acquaintance would have enriched any life—it certainly did mine. I first met him in the late sixties after returning to the North-East to join The Journal in Newcastle following a spell in Manchester, first with the now defunct all-horseracing Sporting Chronicle and then as a sports sub on the Daily Mirror. A guy called Alan Sleeman, who had taken over as Journal sports editor after building himself a reputation as a hard-nosed columnist, wanted me to cover both Newcastle and Sunderland, responsibilities which until then had been shared by two long-serving and highly respected journalists, Ken McKenzie and Alf Greenley. Sleeman used me as a catalyst to ease them into less

17

responsible tasks on the sports desk. Selfishly, and in hindsight, without much honour, I co-operated one hundred per cent because of the opportunity to report on a daily basis what was occurring at two high profile First Division clubs.

I leaned towards Sunderland because in those days, myself, Len Hetherington of the Evening Chronicle—whose sons Paul and Clive carry on his reputation as a dignified, knowledgeable journalist—and Bill Butterfield, who wrote under the pseudonym Argus in the Sunderland Echo, travelled to away matches on the team coach, a situation unthinkable today. I was also pleased to meet up again with old acquaintances such as Doug Weatherall and Vince Wilson, journalists whose example I knew I could learn from. Joe Harvey at Newcastle and Ian McColl, who had just taken over at Sunderland, were the principal managerial contacts but Vince helped me to spread my wings further south to Middlesbrough, and Hartlepool.

Five years in Manchester meant only distant admiration of Clough's phenomenal scoring record with his hometown club Middlesbrough. Interest in his shock move to Sunderland was also only peripheral, as was the Boxing Day injury that in effect tragically curtailed his playing career. All that may have been painful history when our paths crossed for the first time, but by then Clough's football life had been blighted by two rejections that were destined to have significant consequences—and my involvement in those situations was far from peripheral.

For a centre-forward whose scoring record was an incomparable 213 goals in 197 appearances for Middlesbrough and 54 in 61 for Sunderland, his international reward was a measly two England caps. He never forgot that, especially when fate robbed him of the opportunity to do something about it after Sunderland was promoted. Then, following a failed attempt to resurrect his career, he was put in charge of the youth team at Roker Park before being summarily shown the door by McColl and effectively thrown on the football scrapheap. He never forgot that either and certainly never forgave the club for it.

Impressions of the man gained at that first meeting never altered much over the years. Outrageous, outspoken, ruthless, at times cringingly embarrassing and ridiculous, but never uncaring and, in my experience, warm and genuine. Once you were involved—and I was hooked from the minute Vince introduced us in tight little manager's office at the Victoria Ground—you were swept along in the fast lane; taken on hair-raising roller-coaster ride with never a dull second.

He had been thrown a dubious life-line at Hartlepool by the chairman Ernest Ord, a short-arsed bully, blessed nevertheless with marvellous judgement and foresight. Clough teamed up with his pal and former Middlesbrough team-mate Peter Taylor, who could spot a potential footballer in a maternity ward, and the trickery he used to get them made David Blaine look like a fairground cardsharp. Vince's Tuesday habit was a trip to Teesside where he would have his lunchtime sessions with Clough and Taylor before moving on to Middlesbrough to talk to their boss Stan Anderson. Whenever it was opportune he was kind enough to take me along.

They were great days, memorable for the laughs and stories as the managerial team at one of England's most impoverished, rock-bottom clubs drove irreverent buses through the loftiest reputations in the game. We all repaired regularly to a local Chinese restaurant where exotically described meals were simplified by an accompanying number and when the pair talked of championships at a club whose fans at that time did a lap of honour when they won a throw-in, you somehow knew it was no flight of fantasy. 'We'll top this league, make no mistake about that,' Taylor once declared between mouthfuls of sweet and sour pork. 'Yes,' I intervened, 'and when we do we'll come here to celebrate by ordering thirty-nine with chips!'

The date was never kept. When Hartlepool did eventually win the Fourth Division title, it was by way of a Clough and Taylor legacy to a gentleman called Gus McLean, a heavy-topped individual whose square jaw gave him the appearance of a hammer-head shark. But he was a genial soul who always made your visit to the Victoria Ground worthwhile. And as if he wasn't enough character, there was plenty of that quality in his side-kick, John Simpson, who had an artificial eye and a permanent twitch, the consequence of which was he just couldn't keep still—a bundle of perpetual bouncing, jerking motion.

The dialogue between the pair was at times so hilarious it was difficult to accept they were deadly serious professionals in charge of a football club. One day in particular stands out when Vince and I got around to discussing strikers. 'There aren't many better than we have here,' declared Gus. 'I wouldn't swap mine for a few in the First Division.' Then he turned to me, looked me straight in the eye and prodded his finger intimidatingly towards my chest. 'Name me one good centre-forward,' he demanded.

As it happened at the time, a chap called Denis Law was doing well at Manchester United, so, meekly, I threw his name into the pot. Gus paused, turned around to glance at Simpson (who, by now was in a frenzy of dervish-like energy, his good eye almost leaping out of its socket) and broke into a loud guffaw. 'Ho, ho, ho,' he chortled. 'Did you hear that, John? He thinks Denis Law can play.' The apparent incredulity of such a notion was altogether too much for Simpson, whose twitching and jerking increased to a level of ferocity that would have defied physical constraint. Magnificent stuff.

By this time of course, Cloughie had moved on to face a new challenge at Derby County, and it was after that I learned, when circumstances dictated, he could be very single-minded—to put it mildly. Our contact, with me looking after the North-East by this time for The Sun, had become remote enough for me to be surprised when I picked up the telephone at home in Durham to hear a familiar voice blasting out. 'Hello, Robert. Remember me? Brian Clough? How are all the shithouses up there in the North-East?'

21

Never one for small talk, he cut quickly to the chase. 'What's the situation with Colin Todd at Sunderland?' I knew enough to be able to tell him that Colin, a local lad from Chester-le-Street who had blossomed into a brilliant defender, was not the happiest of bunnies and was looking to get away. He had been linked with a number of clubs, but Alan Brown, the Sunderland manager, a fearsome character who ruled the club in tyrannical fashion, had repeatedly ruled out any chance of him leaving. 'He wants away but Brownie has told him he'll make him sweat in the reserves rather than let him go.' The information was passed on with some authority. It was then that Clough's curiosity took a decidedly illegal turn. 'I want to sign him and, if I do, you'll get the story,' said the Derby County manager. 'Tell him I want him and that he must not sign for anybody else before he speaks to me. Keep this between you, me and him, but don't worry, I'll look after you.' It was the first of many telephone conversations between us over a period of weeks with Brian desperate for signs that Brown's intransigence would weaken.

Tapping Todd was easy; access to players in those days was part and parcel of your daily routine. You would just turn up at the training ground, watch them finish their workout and catch them before or after they showered. The introduction of football club media officers—for the most part 'jobsworths' who neither know nor care what newspapers are all about—has sanitised the contact which were once sources of genuine football stories. I would even put the majority of them below doctors' receptionists in the league table of co-operation. If it was purely down to the level of information provided by many of the media personnel, supporters would be virtually clueless about what was going on at the clubs they help to subsidise.

And surely another requirement of their role is to advise managers and administrators on likely press reaction to a given situation. Only a handful are capable of that. Remember the furore caused by the pulling of an infamous interview Roy Keane did on MUTV in his latter days at Old Trafford? This was a perfect example of a good 'gagging' story which the papers lapped up. It was naive for whoever decided on the censorship to think it wouldn't get out, and that should have been the advice from the press officers. As it turned out, the attempt to shut the Manchester United skipper up was a much better tale than what he actually said. It ran and ran, but had Keane's apparent criticism been given a public airing it would have been fish and chip paper within days.

Thankfully we could operate without such hindrances; contacts and trusted friendships were made then that were never lost. Football journalists now, sadly, are not afforded the same luxury. Of course, the polarisation of relationships between journos and players has played into the hands of agents who have made fortunes out of doing what we did for nothing more than an exclusive. More fools us I say.

And the players' representatives virtually have it offered to them on a plate. Chairmen, chief executives, managers alike—and I'm talking about many associated with Premier League clubs—make no bones about approaching the agent of a potential target to begin clandestinely the process that leads to multi-million-pound transfers. Sometimes, those involved get careless and get done for illegal approaches, but for every club caught with its trousers down there are fifty with strong braces. Tapping is a way of life in football—'twas ever thus and ever shall be.

Todd was enthusiastic about Brian's interest. With that on his mind it must have been difficult for him to play to his maximum; indeed, it was a mediocre performance in a 4-0 home defeat by Cardiff City in February 1971 which turned out to be the catalyst for his eventual move to Derby. Always, when I passed on the regular sit-reps to Brian, I took my cue from Argus's Monday column. Bill Butterfield tended to toe Brown's party line, even to an extent where, if the manager wanted anything in particular to appear, he would feed it to Bill who would write it as if they were his own thoughts. Nothing wrong with that; in fact, it was a good way of ensuring the paper got first bite on anything Brown wanted published.

I scanned the Argus column on the Monday following the Cardiff match. Sure enough, there was the telling criticism of Todd's performance and a suggestion that perhaps it would be better for all concerned if he moved on. At last the green light, and I wasted no time in contacting Brian. The message was short and simple: 'You'll get him now, don't forget to let me know how you go on.' I was about to write the biggest transfer story of the season; there hadn't been a sniff anywhere about Todd going to Derby and the football world was going to read all about it exclusively under my by-line in The Sun.

Brian promised he would be back if anything started moving. 'You've played a blinder, I owe you one,' he declared. I had deliberately not mentioned anything to the office about the deal. After all, it wasn't certain the transfer would go through and I've learned over the years that giving sports editors too much information can be a dangerous thing. I wanted to wait until it was all done and dusted and then I would deliver it neatly wrapped and tied with a blue ribbon. Silly me.

I didn't really get twitchy when the following day, Clough's secretary, instead of putting me through automatically as she had done in the past weeks, didn't quite know where her boss was. 'Could you tell him I called and ask him to ring me?' I asked. It was the first of several similar calls that day without any response. By evening, instinct told me something was afoot and I felt increasingly frustrated about not being able to nail it down. What made it worse was I was without wheels— my car was off the road after an untimely argument with a rubbish skip. If the deal was going down, the place to be was Roker Park and I had to get there, but how? The idea of a taxi was quickly dismissed—how long would I need it? Where might I need to go?

In the end, I decided that to pursue the tale—if indeed there was one—I might have to share it. The aforementioned Arnold Howe combined his Express job with being mine host at the Grange Inn, a pub ten minutes' walk from my home. I was no regular customer, I didn't care too much for his beer, so he was a little surprised when I walked into the bar. 'Arnold, I think something is happening with Colin Todd,' I told him, dismissing his offer of a pint. 'We need to get to Roker Park and my car is off the road.'

To be fair he didn't mess about and half an hour later we were outside that famous ground, hoping for some sign of tell-tale activity. There was none. In the social club, one of two licensed establishments attached to the ground, I came across the club chairman, Jack Parker, a short, bespectacled old chap with a friendly disposition who was having a quiet drink with a couple of mates. He seemed oblivious to any possibility that the football club (of which he happened to be the principal board member) was involved in major transfer business. 'No, there's nothing going on that I am aware of,' he replied in answer to my inquiry. And I believed him. Silly me again. After apologising to Arnold for getting him out on a wild goose chase, we returned to his pub where I did put up with two or three pints of his ale. I decided to pursue the matter the following day; maybe Cloughie would come out of hiding and tell me what the hell was going on.

It was a 9.30 phone call the following morning that shattered that particular illusion. On the line was my aforementioned Sun colleague, sadly the now late Frank Clough (no relation), who happened to be doing a shift on the desk as sports news editor. 'Here's one you missed,' he declared. 'Colin Todd has signed for Derby County, we'll need you to do a follow-up.' At least I was spared a bollocking.

In the excellent autobiography written by another former Sun mate, the late John Sadler, Clough remembered the Todd signing but somehow forgot the detail: *'Taylor (sic) had left this one to me saying: 'No need for me to look at the lad. You know better than anybody, so if you think he's the one, go and get him.' Sam Longson (the Derby chairman) was on holiday when I did the Todd deal for what was then regarded as a massive fee of £175,000. I told him nothing about it until I sent him a telegram. Rude? Out of order? It may look that way all these years later but then I could do no wrong and, after all I'd just landed the best young defender in England who was about to turn Derby into the best team in the country.'*

And so much for the fairy-tale version of the deal in the acclaimed film version of Clough's brief spell at Leeds, 'The Damned United'. The truth was a lot more dramatic than the fiction.

Angry? Of course, but time heals and Brian's eventual explanation—that Brown had warned him the deal would be off if it appeared in the Sun first—offered some consolation. And he was probably telling the truth. Not much escaped the Sunderland manager and somehow, he had found out about my role in the transfer scenario. Brown was a man you crossed at your peril; compared to him, the so-called hard managers I've dealt with since have been pussy cats.

The upshot of the Todd affair was that I had my press facilities withdrawn; for more than a year I was refused admission to the press box and access to players. Perhaps to vent my spleen at missing out on the tale, I wrote a piece condemning Sunderland, the one-time 'Bank of England club' for becoming reduced to also-rans and needing to sell to ease their financial situation. It was hypocritical and totally inaccurate and it did little to endear me to the manager, who'd clearly made sure I did not profit from my skulduggery.

The following season Derby won the title and I was among a select group of journalists invited to the championship celebration dinner at the Pennine Hotel in Derby. And what a night that turned out to be. The entertainment was provided by the celebrated Geordie comic, Bobby Pattinson, a hilariously funny man whose humour was based on situations familiar to anybody with a North-East background. I'd heard Bobby a few times before and looked forward to another side-splitting evening. In the event, nothing went right for him... in an entertainer's vernacular he died on his arse, mainly because by then the guests were full of drink and were in no mood to appreciate his stories. Bobby accepted the situation and left the stage with total dignity.

But that wasn't the end of it. Like most people, I enjoy telling and listening to jokes, mainly of doubtful genre, which in boozy company are always guaranteed to raise raucous laughter. I had stood up in a local club when Vince had a party to celebrate his leaving the North-East to take the number one football job on the Sunday Mirror in Manchester. It was a sympathetic audience and I had gone down well. The word had got round in the Pennine and somebody shouted: 'Gerrup, Cassie, and tell us a few jokes'—a call that was enjoined by Cloughie, Taylor and a few others.

To my shame I agreed and proceeded with a repertoire that was hardly in the same league as Bobby but suited the purpose of what had degenerated into a less than tasteful evening. Bobby even came over and told me I had done well, adding that he could just as easily have lowered the tone of the entertainment himself but had been under instructions to 'keep the party clean'. But I'm glad he didn't—at least his reputation as a terrific family comedian was spared. We became great friends and often recalled the events of that night in the Pennine. He was a consummate professional who, when he must have felt like slaughtering this abject amateur, was kind and considerate.

CHAPTER TWO
CLOUGH AND COUNTRY

As I said, for the most part I was divorced from Brian Clough's graduation to becoming one of English football's greatest ever managers. We met up socially when his teams visited my patch and he always welcomed me into his office when I ventured into the Midlands to cover matches at Derby County and later Nottingham Forest. He always remained as big a legend—if not bigger—in his native North-East as he was further south and we performed together at a few sporting dinners, either as separate speakers or in enthralling question and answer situations.

But there was one reunion that could hardly have carried greater significance for either of us—an airport meeting and a football trip that triggered off an astonishing sequence of events. I remember the occasions with a mixture of disbelief that they actually happened, and pride that I was bang in the middle of landmark occurrences which I believe had near cataclysmic consequences for English football both on a world and domestic stage.

For reasons that escape me and are now irrelevant anyway, early in October 1978 I was dispatched by the Sun to the Canary Islands to cover an international youth tournament in which the participants were England, Russia and the hosts, Las Palmas. The significance of the trip was it was the first time since their ludicrous appointment as joint managers of the England youth team ten months earlier that Clough and Taylor had managed to escape from their responsibilities at Forest to be involved with the squad. They had been given the job as a sweetener after the FA, in their wisdom, had rejected Clough, as well as Bobby Robson, Jack Charlton, Lawrie McMenemy and Dave Sexton, and handed the England manager's role to Ron Greenwood.

As Taylor remarked at the time, 'It was classic tactics by the Lancaster Gate hierarchy; it is better to have Brian inside the tent pissing out, than outside pissing in. We could hardly criticize the running of England when we ourselves were part of the operation.'

The not so daft FA grandees also had the pair over a barrel inasmuch as if they turned down the youth team invitation, it would be seen as a disloyal act which would clearly put them out of the running if the senior position became available in the future. Their time in charge of England's precocious young starlets would be no more than a test of their patience and willingness to kowtow to the powers that be. Predictably—as anybody, who had the slightest comprehension of Clough's contempt for amateurish authority in general, and the suited fuddy-duddies who ran the game in particular would know—it was a test he would blow big style, and it was me who provided the match that lit the touch paper.

At Heathrow, myself and the other football writers on the trip, Joe Melling (Daily Express), Jeff Farmer (Daily Mail) and Jack Steggles (Daily Mirror) were greeted warmly by the big two—at the very least they were in party mood judging from the champagne that flowed in the departure lounge. In essence, their duties were to observe and to provide support and guidance for Ken Burton, who had been the team's hands-on manager, and who would be responsible for tactics and team selection. Fat chance of that happening with Clough and Taylor around. But all thoughts of that were secondary as the press gang of four boarded the plane and set about planning how to get the most of the best part of a week in the sun. We were well into our second gin and tonic, albeit at the rear end of the aircraft, when Taylor came bouncing down from business class to where I was sitting. 'Cassie, Brian wants to see you; pop up and have a word.' It was more of a command than a request.

Conveniently there was an empty seat between them into which I was ushered to find Clough perusing the back page of the Daily Express. 'What the hell do you think of that?' he demanded, drawing my attention to a lead headline over a story proclaiming Chelsea's interest in appointing former Real Madrid coach Miljan Miljanić as their new manager. To be honest, I couldn't have given a toss one way or another and my nonplussed expression must have registered. 'It's a bloody disgrace,' he stormed. 'These big clubs talk about foreign coaches as if they are the dog's bollocks. They're not as good as us and yet nobody ever bothers to suggest us two could do a job like that.' And on and on and on he went, interrupted only by Taylor utterances such as, 'They couldn't do what we've done... sod 'em... these foreigners couldn't lace our boots.'

It was an amazing rant from two people who, had I not known them better, were demonstrating serious inferiority complexes. Of course, nothing could have been further from the truth. The previous season their Forest team had won the championship by seven points and they hadn't lost a league match for almost a year. The bottom line was they were just peeved that somebody else had been linked with a top job neither would, in truth, have had any intention of taking. I decided to call their bluff, declaring, 'Right you two... the Sunderland job looks like it could become available. What about it?' Clough's response was typically bullish. 'If everything was right, we would be interested, and what's more we'd do a hell of a job.'

Well, we'll get to what happened about that later. First there was the little matter of the youth tournament; under normal circumstances it was a mildly interesting event which might have made a paragraph or two somewhere on the sports pages. Such trips were usually an excuse for little known FA-blazered officials to act like tin Gods and lord it at the FA's expense. But when Messrs, Clough and Taylor were around, normality flew out of the window.

Their brief flirtation with the job is a matter of record. They had jacked it in by the end of the month

33

citing their responsibilities to Forest as the reason. In truth, something happened in Las Palmas which convinced them they had about as much prospect of achieving their ambition to manage England as winning first place in a competition for tact and diplomacy. And, having accepted that inevitability, they decided jointly to deliberately scupper their chances with a series of pre-meditated altercations with several FA staff members on the trip.

The principal FA man on the trip, as he had been on many similar previous England youth team campaigns, was a delightful, inoffensive chap called John Bayliss. John, completely bald when it wasn't the fashion it is today, with a high-pitched cackle of a laugh which reflected his enormous sense of humour, was essentially an easy-going fellow for whom this type of foreign excursion was a bit of a cushy number. He could handle the administration of it in his sleep.

His role was to make sure everything ran smoothly and that the meticulously arranged schedule went according to plan; travel, accommodation, training, dining and matches. He was nursemaid to the elderly FA council members on the trip and handled the exchange of greetings and acquaintances with officials from the opposing countries like the pro he was. But he was also a complete stranger to controversy and that made him woefully ill-equipped to deal with the eruption which, on the Richter Scale, matched anything that Mount Teide, the famous volcano on the neighbouring island of Tenerife, ever had to offer.

At first Clough and Taylor, as had been their remit as 'observers', spent their time relaxing on the beach, seemingly content to leave team selection and tactics for the opening game against Russia to Burton, a dyed in the wool FA man who had been team manager for some time, but who was now forced to share that responsibility with the incoming partnership. It all seemed very cordial, but out there in the mid-Atlantic a storm was brewing and when it hit it left a trail of wreckage that spread from Las Palmas to Lancaster Gate.

The big problem with Brian and Peter was they could hardly camouflage their deep-seated contempt for those in charge of the party, an attitude hardly in keeping with what the blazered brigade expected from paid employees of the FA. The upshot was a unanimous conclusion by the blazers that, when they reported back to the FA hierarchy, they would recommend that Clough and Taylor were kept as far away from the top job as possible. Bayliss said as much as he sat with myself, Joe, Jeff and Jack, discussing the situation over pre-dinner drinks the evening before the Russia match. It was an off the record chat which clearly Bayliss expected would go no further, and in any other circumstances it wouldn't have done, but it left me with a crisis of conscience which eventually precipitated a course of action I accept many, if not the majority, in my profession would deem out of order.

I regarded Clough and (to a lesser extent) Taylor, as personal friends. We had known each other since those early days at Hartlepool; we had enjoyed each other's company at the various sports dinners whenever they took his teams to the North-East. I thought about the many caring things I knew Brian in particular had done, like the unpublicised visits to children's' hospitals; like driving from the Midlands to the North-East on the morning of an important Saturday league match to attend a friend's mother's funeral. I was chuffed he had been so successful and, most of all, I loved the way he spoke from the hip; his hatred of injustice, his total irreverence towards the establishment. And here was a member of football's establishment deriding him as a loudmouth and a bully and declaring he would never aspire to the England manager's job which the FA should have crawled to Nottingham to offer him.

All this may be me trying to justify my decision to 'mark Cloughie's card'—it is certainly no attempt to excuse it. I rang Brian in his room and told him there was something I wanted to discuss with him and maybe Peter should be there as well. Within minutes I was perched on his bed with the pair of them sitting opposite. 'Listen, I want to tell you something because I think you should know. But if I do you must treat it in the strictest confidence and promise it won't go out of this room. Of course, they wanted to know what it was all about. 'How long have you known us? Just tell us what it is and that's as far as it will go,' they said reassuringly.

Convinced enough, after a lengthy preamble, they would keep the conversation between ourselves and with only the slightest self-doubt about what I was going to say, I revealed what Bayliss had said. They looked at each other, muttered something about sticking the

England job 'up their arses', thanked me for putting them in the picture, and promised it would go no further. And that, I thought, would be the end of it. Fat chance.

The balloon went up the following evening as the party were preparing to leave for the Russian match, and if Clough and Taylor were looking for an excuse to make their presence felt, the hapless officials offered it on a velvet cushion. Both, in their respective biographies, are fairly consistent about what happened. According to the Clough version: *'I had seen the England youth players outside the hotel, standing around on a street corner waiting to be taken to the stadium. They must have stood for a quarter of an hour while the team coach went around and round the block because the driver couldn't find enough space to park.*

'Things like that get under my skin—you don't treat any athletes that way. I went berserk. 'What the bloody hell is going on?' I said to the lad in charge. 'Get the police, somebody—anybody to make room for the coach to pick up these lads. They've a job to do, there's a match to win.' I lost my rag at the sight of an England team being made to stand around and wait because of inadequate arrangements.'

And so, it went on. *'When we boarded the coach, the first thing I did was kick off a woman who was already sitting at the front. "You can't put her off," somebody in a blazer told me. "She's the official interpreter." I said: "I don't care who she is, she's got a fag on, get her off my coach." And off she went.'*

Was that the end of it? No way. With all pretensions about being 'observers' now out of the window and

Burton reduced to a bit player in the youth team management pecking order, the pair continued their onslaught on officialdom at half-time. We found out afterwards what happened, but Taylor in his book on Clough, written by Mike Langley, described the astonishing dressing room bust-up at half-time.

'The next bit of discord was caused by the uninvited presence of the team doctor Professor Frank O'Gorman and Mr Bayliss in the dressing room. We hadn't sent for the doctor because no one was injured while the slicing of lemons (or oranges), the self-appointed task of Mr Bayliss, ought to have been done earlier or outside. Brian asked them to leave, explaining, "We never allow outsiders into dressing rooms because that's where we talk privately to players." They went under silent protest and I can't remember the doctor speaking to us throughout the rest of the trip.'

In fact, Clough's recall was more typical. *"I don't know who you are and I don't know who ever gave permission for you to come in here but fuck off."*

Somewhere along the line, whether it came directly from the lips of Clough himself or a more devious route, Bayliss was made aware that I had 'coughed'. Not unnaturally, we didn't speak a lot afterwards but the sad consequence of the whole episode was the status quo was maintained; Clough and Taylor quit and a succession of England managers from that day to this have failed to win anything.

The fact that England beat Russia 1-0 and later Las Palmas as well to take what was euphemistically called The Atlantic Trophy, and at the same time provide

Clough and Taylor with a hundred per cent record in their one hands-on venture into England management, was totally incidental. They used to say Cloughie could walk on water, he could win European Cups, league titles and league cups, but even he couldn't beat the system.

CHAPTER THREE
CLOUGH AND SUNDERLAND

Well, that was England, but what about Sunderland?

There was a well-publicised attempt to get him back to Roker Park soon after he and Taylor quit the England youth set-up, but Keith Collings, the Sunderland chairman, was refused permission to speak to him and with the Forest boss displaying no inclination to push it himself, there ended the matter—apparently. The next time the Clough factor arose it was closely-guarded secret known only to a handful of people.

Two years had gone by during which time Ken Knighton, ably assisted by former Forest full-back Frank Clark, were in charge. They did a good job under difficult circumstances, but not good enough, it seemed, to satisfy the new chairman, the self-made millionaire Tom Cowie. A locally-born man, Cowie, later Sir Tom Cowie, had an abrasive, no-nonsense manner in-keeping with somebody who had made a considerable fortune in the motor trade, starting with a lock-up shop selling second-hand motor bikes and going on to own a chain of car dealerships all over the country. The word failure was just not in his vocabulary.

As with most successful business tycoons, he had an ego that stretched into outer space, but for all that he was an approachable man, and whether or not it was to polish that ego, he genuinely wanted to be the man to waken what for nearly half a century before—and incidentally in the years since as well—had been monotonously described as 'a sleeping giant.' His decision to get rid of Knighton and Clark in 1981 created another window of opportunity to test the validity of the conversation I'd had with Messrs Clough and Taylor on the plane to Las Palmas.

The priority was to get the parties concerned around the table; very difficult and very illegal! But previous dealings with Cloughie taught me that if the whole thing was never going to achieve lift-off, it wouldn't be the fact that he liked to play things by the book that kept it on the ground.

I made the calls, first to the Forest manager. Under the circumstances and bearing in mind his recent record of success, I could understand his singular lack of enthusiasm when I asked him whether he would be interested in the Sunderland job. I'd like to think it was my persuasive tongue that eventually got him round to 'thinking about it'; but it was probably more the mention of Cowie's millions that sparked his interest. Anyway, I had enough encouragement to try and discover what the Sunderland chairman thought of the whole idea, and I have to say at first it wasn't much. 'Wouldn't have him on my mind,' was his initial reaction. 'Don't like the way he works; he doesn't show respect and I couldn't see me having any sort of a working relationship with him.' 'Fair enough,' I said. 'But all I'm saying is if you want to be chairman of the first Sunderland side that wins anything since Pontius was a pilot, he is your best chance of getting you there.'

Bullshit? Certainly, but as I'll explain later, dealing with the gospel according to Joe Melling, the best bullshit is eighty per cent truth. I firmly believed that Clough could have done exactly what I promised Cowie he would do. What's more Cowie believed it too, because he did eventually agreed to discuss the matter with Brian—and, of course, Peter Taylor—at a secret meeting at what was then a well-known roadside restaurant on the A1 at Barnsdale Bar, a few miles north of Doncaster. And having set the whole thing up there was certainly going to be no managerial pow-wow taking place without me being around to find out what happened.

I told two people about the meeting; Joe, who by this time was covering the Midlands for the Express; and in spite of misgivings expressed earlier, my Sun sports editor, the late Frank Nicklin. Joe was enthusiastic, naturally; wanted to know when the meeting was and could he monitor it from somewhere and then we could get together afterwards. No problems there. Frank, a Derby County fan who hadn't much liked it when Cloughie went over to the enemy, thought I had simply gone off my rocker. 'No way is he going anywhere near Sunderland,' he almost chortled, blissfully dismissing my information about the secret get-together as a complete flight of fantasy. Like most of us in the Sun sports department, I enjoyed working for him. He could be cutting, sarcastic, piss-taking, but I measured his fairness to me on one particular day when I got a story spectacularly wrong. (See Big Boobs.)

The meeting was set for a Thursday morning. I was excited because one of the most significant football meetings of the decade was about to go down and, apart from a select seven people—myself, Cowie, his chauffeur, Clough, Taylor, Joe and Nicklin (who didn't believe it anyway)—the world was happy in its ignorance. That seven quickly became eight. I had linked up with Cowie just off the motorway at Durham and tailed him as his chauffeur driven Rolls took him the hundred miles or so to the meeting point. But as soon as I walked into the restaurant I was immediately recognised by a long-distance lorry driver called Tony. I knew him from brief visits to Arnold's pub where he was a regular customer.

'Hi Cassy, what are you doing here?' he inquired cheerily. 'Just popped in for a cup of tea and a sandwich,' I replied, as the glass door behind me swung open again and in came Cowie. 'Sandwich my arse,' scoffed Tony. 'Okay, it's a fair cop; I'm just having a word with Mr Cowie, but do me a favour and keep it to yourself,' I pleaded, hoping and praying that his tachometer would have ticked over a few thousand revolutions before Clough and Taylor came through the door.

But that anxiety was gradually replaced by another, much greater, concern about whether the Forest pair was going to show at all. Time has never ticked by so slowly... minutes... an hour... and not so much as a coo from a carrier pigeon, let alone a phone message. The Sunderland chairman's blood was rapidly reaching boiling point; the expletives were rattling off his tongue like automatic gunfire and I had exhausted every avenue of bullshit known to mankind to try and calm him down. Tony had been long gone down whichever road he was travelling by the time Clough and Taylor did eventually arrive and, if indeed the lorry was homeward bound, Cowie was getting ready to follow him.

Panic? You bet! Then suddenly, relief! The doors flung open western-saloon style and in they came; Cloughie; green-sweater, track-suit bottoms, trainers. Taylor; casual-shirt, trousers. 'Sorry we're late; had things to do.' It was, I suppose, by way of an apology. And after brief introductions: 'Right, where do you want to do this?' After declining Cloughie's invitation to join them at a table in the far corner of what was a sizeable room, deeming my presence slightly counter-productive, I ordered my umpteenth pot of tea and prepared to sit it out in the adjoining lounge. Joe, incidentally, had driven up from the Midlands and was anxiously waiting for a call on a public telephone in a nearby pub (no mobiles in those days, people). A quick call allayed any fears he had about being on a wild goose chase. But he, like me, was prepared to balance anxiety and frustration against what would certainly turn out to be the sports story of the year.

The talks went on for the best part of another hour before the chairs went back; everybody stood up, shook hands and Clough led Taylor in a quick march to the door. Cowie, less briskly, was still some yards behind by the time the other pair reached it. To my astonishment, Clough walked straight past me, offering a cheery wave and a 'see you, Robert' as he headed towards the exit. Fortunately, his sidekick saw the injustice in that. 'Hang on a minute, Brian,' he called after his mate. 'I think we should tell Bob what's gone on.' Cloughie stopped and turned to me. 'Right, we've told him what we want and he's said it's too much. I think he might get as far as Wetherby before he starts to change his mind... ta-rah.' And out they went.

Cowie appeared shell-shocked when he eventually made it through the door, but his attitude quickly evolved into one of almost bemused incredulity. 'The man's fucking mad; he's away with the fairies,' he said, shaking his head. And then he mentioned a figure he said each had asked for, hardly out of place in these days of multi-million-pound managerial contracts, but twenty years ago, it was an absolute fortune. 'Of course, I've told them it's out of the question.' And then he thanked me for my efforts; shook my hand and, by way of a parting gesture, declared, 'Well, you can't say I didn't try.'

In fact, over the next couple of days the Sunderland chairman tried even harder. As Cloughie had rightly predicted, and after consultation with various interested parties, Cowie agreed to meet their demands and that very same evening rang to ask me to pass the message on. I did so in a telephone call to Brian the following morning, only to hear him say, 'Well, you can go back and tell him the price has gone up,' mentioning another astronomical figure. Astonishingly those demands were met too, until, having delivered Cowie's approval of Clough's latest telephone number request to the Forest manager's apparent satisfaction, on the Saturday morning, we reached a point when, with little old me right in the middle of it all, fingers poised over the typewriter keys, I was ready to deliver the big one; the story which would finally convince my ever-doubting sports editor that I hadn't been spending too much time in the bar.

I couldn't wait and neither could Joe, who had greeted my hourly bulletins of every incredible twist and turn with typical Anglo-Saxon expressions of amazement in ever increasing decibels.

Come Saturday evening I was absolutely convinced I would be writing a world football ground-breaking story that Brian Clough and Peter Taylor were about to bring to end an era of unprecedented glory at Nottingham Forest to join Sunderland, the club at which he had suffered the two biggest setbacks of his football career; the injury that finished him as a player and the sack that, to anybody with less resilience and strength of character, could have meant anonymous oblivion.

I'll never forget the phone call that shattered that illusion later that evening. My wife Janet was just about to serve dinner when she picked up the receiver and, with that kind of exasperated expression which wives get when their hope of a restful evening dissipates, shoved it in my direction.

'It's Peter Taylor and he wants to talk to you. He says it's urgent,' she snapped. The dark tone of Taylor's voice told me everything. 'Bob, I have to tell you Brian and I won't be coming to Sunderland. He's decided he doesn't want to leave the Derby area. Thanks for everything you've done. We'll get together sometime.' No word from the man himself but under the circumstances I couldn't hold that against him, and on the many occasions we saw each other after that, no mention was ever made of it.

The inquest, such as it was, came the following day when I had my usual daily chat with Nicklin. After discussing various football topics and story possibilities, I slipped in, by way of an aside you understand, 'By the way, Cloughie won't be going to Sunderland after all.'

'I tried to tell you that four days ago but you wouldn't listen,' he retorted. Maybe I should have done—what, and missed that extra ride on the Clough roller-coaster? Not on your life. Such were the cameos involved in an association with the great man. I knew there would be opportunities for more tales and I was not disappointed.

When I left the Sun to join the Mail on Sunday, I was naturally desperate to signal my arrival with some impact, and who could be a better feature subject than the Forest boss. Appreciating how important it was to me, he readily agreed to be interviewed and we met in a hotel in Yorkshire where Forest were staying before an away match.

'Right,' he said as we sat down in the lounge, 'I've got a good story for you.' That wonderful mischievous grin that lit up his face whenever he was up to something devilish stretched from one corner of the room to the other. 'My lad Nigel was late for the bus and I'm going to fine him two weeks wages,' he announced. 'Will that do you?'

I tried not to be too enthusiastic about Nigel's plight but it needed massive self-control to prevent me throwing my arms around him and shouting, 'You'll absolutely do for me, pal.' But that wasn't the end of it. Brian turned to Ronnie Fenton, the first team trainer, brandishing the envelope containing the punishment letter, 'Right, Ronnie. Which of this set of shithouses would most love to hand this letter to our Nigel,' he gleamed, the chuckle now unabated at the Machiavellian notion that had just entered his brain. 'I've got it,' he declared triumphantly. 'Fetch that Dutch arsehole (Johnny) Metgod in here. He hates our Nigel; he'd love to do it.' Whether Metgod enjoyed the experience is debatable; what isn't is that he couldn't have enjoyed it as much as the Nottingham Forest manager.

The day Brian Clough died, September 20th, 2004, I happened to be attending a family wedding in Nottingham and I was able to join the thousands of Forest and Derby County fans who paid their respects to the great man at the City Ground. I was also privileged to be in Derby's Pride Park a few weeks later for the wonderfully moving service of thanksgiving for his life, and again later when his widow Barbara unveiled that magnificent statue of him in Nottingham city centre.

Everybody who has had even the most incidental dealings with Cloughie will have their own everlasting memories of the man. Mine were encapsulated by the last occasion we met and spoke together. It was the occasion of the League Managers Association annual dinner in Nottingham four months before he passed away. A year earlier, Malcolm Vallerius, my sports editor on the Mail on Sunday, had helped to organise a lunch at Mottram Hall near Wilmslow to mark my retirement from full-time journalism. I'm proud to say the guests included some of football's biggest names and in inviting various people whose company I had enjoyed throughout the years, I wondered about Cloughie before deciding—because he had been in poor health or maybe he might not be bothered—not to include him. Big mistake.

Twelve months on I waited outside the function room at the Moat House Hotel just to have a word as he left the LMA dinner where he had been honoured for his services to football. I was in good company because also waiting, menu card and pen in hand, for his autograph was David Moyes.

'Young man, I've a bone to pick with you,' he said as he came up to me, hand outstretched. 'Where was my invitation to that lunch you had?' Not for the first time in Cloughie's company I was completely blown away, mumbling weakly, 'Brian I didn't think you'd be able to come.' 'Well, I never got the chance, did I?' he called over his shoulder as he headed towards the exit door. 'Ta-rah!'

CHAPTER FOUR
FERGIE TIME

In spite of the odd spat I make no apologies for my high regard for Sir Alex Ferguson. I have always found him fair and honest; one deviation from that which I will also come to later was, I believe, out of a sense of misguided principle and it was condemned more by outsiders who were not involved than it was by me. I have enjoyed his confidence, his confidentiality and his company. Much of what has passed between us will stay under wraps but there were a few experiences that need not stretch the boundaries of discretion, like the day towards the end of April in 1996 when Joe Melling and I arranged to have lunch with Fergie and Roy Evans, then manager of Liverpool, for a feature on the forthcoming FA Cup final meeting between their two sides.

The get-together had been arranged at a restaurant called The Edge in Alderley Edge, which was quite close to Fergie's home. Roy had kindly agreed to attend after a training session. This was an exclusive feature for The Mail on Sunday for which no money changed hands. We received a message from Roy that he had been delayed on club business and would be at least an hour and a half late. It meant putting the lunch back from the one o'clock sit down time but Fergie was quite flexible, agreeing to wait for his Cup final adversary but stipulating he had to leave at five for a reserve team match.

Roy duly arrived all of a fluster, apologising profusely for being late; our problem was to get him relaxed in order for Joe to do the interview after a lunch which was finally served at three. Job done and with a clear afternoon and evening in front of him, Evans was warming up. 'Let's have another bottle of that wine you picked,' he said, nodding towards Ferguson. 'Have as many as you like but I've got to go,' came the reply.

The wine arrived with Evans, now full of running, grasping the bottle and topping up the glasses—all but Fergie's. 'Sod off, Roy. I've got to go,' he protested.

But apparently the momentous evening had not yet ended for Fergie. Back home he was watching the closing stages of a Premier League match between Leeds United and Newcastle United. He himself recalls the occasion in his first highly entertaining autobiography which was written by his pal Hugh McIlvanney: *'As often happens when Cass and Melling are out to play, lunch stretched into the evening and when I arrived home to face (his wife) Cathy's wrath, the game at Elland Road was just finishing so I sat in my favourite seat to watch the closing minutes, hoping that Leeds would snatch an equaliser. After the final whistle, I started to attempt an explanation of why I was so late and was stopped dead in my tracks by Kevin's (Keegan) outburst. God, I felt for him.'*

51

It turned out to be that fateful night when Kevin Keegan's emotional 'I'd love it' tirade against the United manager shocked the nation. It was probably also the night that the then Newcastle manager finally accepted that the Premier League title, which seemed in the bag for the Magpies when they led the table by 13 points at the end of February, had slipped from their grasp. An eventful way to end an eventful day.

Sir Alex's interest in the sport of kings is well known, unhappily from the holes in my pockets, I happen to share it. On occasion, we have been able to enjoy together such great racing spectacles as Cheltenham, Royal Ascot, York, Doncaster; oh yes, and Kuala Lumpur! So far as I can remember I have never come away from any of those courses with my pockets bulging, but if there was one day I seriously believed we were going to hit the jackpot it was when we had a day at the sumptuous track in the capital of Malaysia.

I had the good fortune to be covering Manchester United's pre-season tour in the Far East in July 2001, the significance of the trip being to blood United's two new signings (Ruud Van Nistelrooy and Juan Sebastian Veron, who had both just arrived at Old Trafford at a total cost of a little over £47million) as well as enhance the club's commercial value in countries where they are the number one football club.

We started off in Malaysia followed by matches in Singapore and Bangkok and the mass hysteria that greeted the United players, and especially Beckham, throughout the whole crazy fortnight had to be seen to be believed. But the boss and I managed to escape the mayhem for a day at the races, and with our cards duly marked, there was every indication that fortunes were to be made. Well that's how it started anyway. Our tip in the first event won, pulling the proverbial handcart at a very nice price. Between mouthfuls of magnificent food and all the rest of the trappings of hospitality provided by the course president, I remember remarking as we drew our winnings that the gold Rolls Royce which had brought us from the United hotel might not have a boot big enough to accommodate all the cash we were about to extract from the track's tote pool. Or not!

We lost in the second race; and the next, and the next, with reality setting in very quickly. It didn't help matters when the president and his officials, without the benefit of the kind of inside information we were getting, started landing fancy forecasts which left them with wads of the folding stuff. To cut a short story even shorter, we never backed another winner, a situation that was probably made less painful by the fact that sudden downpour of monsoon proportions flooded the track and caused the abandonment of the final race. Still, we departed as we had arrived; in style, and richer for the experience of being poorer.

There was another day at the races with Sir Alex that I'll never forget—strangely that too did not provide the outcome we had hoped for. Out of the blue one Thursday afternoon he called to see if I fancied going to Doncaster where the Rock of Gibraltar, then part-owned by Sir Alex, was running the following day. My purpose would be then to chauffeur him from the course to Slaley Hall, the hotel in Northumberland where United were staying

53

before playing Newcastle on the Saturday. Fergie was being ferried to the course by Mike Dillon, who had stayed at his house the night before. Dillon, a mad keen United fan, is one of racing's best known personalities in his capacity as PR Director for Ladbrokes the bookmakers.

Few in the sport are as well connected and it was largely through his good offices that the United manager had become involved with the Irish racing fraternity; mega players such as John Magnier, J.P. McManus, Michael Tabor and the rest. The 'Rock' suffered one of his rare defeats but that was the only blemish on a day when I even got to walk a couple of furlongs of the course with Fergie and the horse's legendary Irish trainer, A.P. O'Brien, when he tested the going before racing.

I have to admit there were times when I squeezed every bit of mischief out of knowing Fergie as well as I did. After all, wasn't he the manager of the most famously successful football club in the world? Wasn't his face as recognisable in the back streets of Sao Paulo as it was at Royal Ascot; or walking the lush grassy slopes of Augusta Country Club during Masters week; or, for that matter, leading his Manchester United players out before the final of the European Cup at the Nou Camp Stadium in Barcelona?

When it came to name dropping, hurling Sir Alex Ferguson's moniker into a conversation was guaranteed to silence the most effusive of chatterboxes. 'You know Sir Alex then?' was always a question which prefaced unconditional respect bordering on hero worship.

So, it was on a memorable day's golf in Portugal which featured members of the Press Golfing Society playing against a team entirely made up of Directors and other high-ranking officials representing almost every top golf club on the Algarve. In the grasp of even the least prescient of advantage-takers, this was ammunition beyond one's wildest dreams.

On that sunny day at Quinta do Lago in 2007, new meaning was added to the phrase 'turkey shoot'.

My own particular bullseye came purely by chance in a pleasant, well-mannered conversation between myself, a couple of Portuguese golf officials, one of which was a chap called Luis Matos, the Technical and Golf Director of the Val de Lobo complex, and a bunch of fellow members of the PGS.

Cursory introductions were followed by inquiries about what the English visitors did for a living, myself declaring I covered football at the highest level for the Mail on Sunday.

Clearly, one of the big shots on parade, Sr Matos appeared no more than mildly interested until the subject of Manchester United came up and he declared that Carlos Queiroz, then Fergie's number two at Old Trafford, was a personal friend.

From whence came the inevitable question, 'You know Sir Alex?' 'I do very well,' I answered. Now more than a tad animated, Sr Matos launched into details of his own personal friendship with the United boss. 'Whenever he in Portugal, he always come here for golf and food. He also stays here. I know him very well.'

It was an opportunity too good to miss. Excusing myself for a comfort break, I tapped out Fergie's number on my mobile. 'Hi Alex, its Bob Cass and I've been golfing in Portugal with a friend of yours, Luis Matos.'

To be fair, although declaring the Portuguese to be more of a friend of Querioz than himself, Fergie did acknowledge their association and that was enough! 'Do me a favour and have a word with him.'

Returning to the table I handed Sr Matos my mobile. 'Hi Luis, I've got your pal Sir Alex Ferguson on the phone; he wants to say hello.'

Ten seconds of bluster was followed by something of an awkwardly forced exchange before he returned the phone, allowing Fergie the delight of informing me I was guilty of the worst piece of bullshit he had ever come across.

But it paid off in the grandest of manners. Not only did I enjoy free golf at one of the most spectacular of courses on the Algarve, he also tipped me off about United's interest in two subsequent signings Nani and Anderson.

CHAPTER FIVE
HAIRDRYER TREATMENT

I first met Sir Alex during his amazingly successful time as manager of Aberdeen. I had been asked to cover Dundee United's matches in the UEFA Cup, principally because Jim Black, the Sun's excellent football man in Scotland, had an aversion to flying (a few of us covering grounded North-East clubs at the time might well have shared Jim's phobia but we never got around to finding out!) As well as the trips to the continent, I also reported on the home European matches at Tannadice and it was the habit of Fergie and other Scottish managers and coaches attending the games to meet beforehand and have a drink and a chat with journalists in the bar of the hotel in which I happened to be staying.

The Scots journos were a great bunch and I was on the firm from the word go, largely because, as somebody akin to a Geordie (although my Darlington birthplace hardly qualifies), I was regarded as a Scot with my brains kicked in. I made great lasting relationships on those trips with lads like Glenn Gibbons, Ian Paul, Hughie Keevins, Ray Hepburn, Dick Donnelly and many others. Once Gibbons, then the Scottish Daily Mail's established, knowledgeable and extremely talented operative, endorsed my inclusion in what was as far as one could get from what many biased Sassenachs regarded as a closeted bunch of second-raters it was like demolishing Hadrian's Wall. I was in with the in crowd; friendships with the others followed automatically.

Glenn remained my closest pal. And though, sadly, there was an infrequence in our get-togethers (particularly in retirement), whenever we did meet there was always warmth, humour, reminiscences and an awful lot of piss-taking. In his role as Deputy Chief Press Officer for the European Golf Tour, his son Michael not only demonstrates how much he has inherited his dad's charm and bonhomie, he was also able to convey mutual good wishes between Gibbons senior and myself.

I was devastated to hear of Glenn's passing on October 20th, 2014. He had been abstemious for thirty years, always wearing his badge of sobriety with pride and, it must be said, a kind of aloofness when surrounded by artists such as yours truly. And, if he did prove he really didn't need a Bacardi and coke to feature prominently in any company or conversation, there was no doubt, nobody enjoyed a bevvy more than he did. Because back in those days covering football north of the border, the basic requirement for qualification for membership of that particular circle of friends was regular inebriation and in such states, we did laugh a lot!

Like on a trip to Belgium in 1982 when Dundee United were drawn away in the first leg of their third-round tie against Winterslag. For a reason that now escapes me I found myself billeted with Gibbons and the rest in an establishment called the Pits Hotel. The place was far nicer than it sounded—it was so called because of its situation next to the motor racing circuit at Zolder.

As it happened, and I don't know why or how with it being out of season, the proprietress, a very attractive lady named Magda, opened the hotel just to accommodate half a dozen press men. We were the only guests for three days and nights and virtually had the run of the place. My everlasting memory of the bar was of a magnificent old style juke box that was packed with great records from the sixties and seventies. The snag was it operated by playing only one number (E11 as I recall), but we got around that little problem when Magda took the back off enabling us to switch any of the 45s to the appropriate available slot.

Being miles away from anywhere, we ventured out only for pre-match press conferences, and anyway it absolutely bucketed down from the minute we arrived, so much so that the match was in serious danger of being postponed. The pitch was in such a waterlogged state the powers that be called for an afternoon pitch inspection before the scheduled evening kick-off. With the surface resembling a paddy field we were all convinced the game would be postponed—at least for 24 hours.

Everybody—that is everybody save Gibbons who we left sublimely dishevelled in his room—journeyed to Winterslag for the inspection. On that trip Glenn made it to the bar, the restaurant and the toilet, but no further. 'Just stay there and we'll keep you in the picture,' we told him, and off we went.

To cut a long story short, and much to the wrath of United's fiercely competitive manager Jim McLean, the referee—who, since he came from France was probably accustomed to surviving in boggy conditions—inexplicably declared the pitch playable. I was designated to disturb the leisurely relaxation of Gibbons back in his room at the Pits and inform him the game was on and that he'd better get his backside over quickly. He was incandescent with fury. 'It's a fucking disgrace,' he yelled. 'How can they think about playing football on a pitch like that? The game will be nothing more than a lottery.' An amazingly shrewd observation, especially coming from somebody who had never even taken a breath of fresh air since he arrived in Belgium.

His demeanour concurred with that of McLean, whose deepening outrage exploded in a volcanic blast against the match official, UEFA, Paris, the Eiffel Tower, the Arc de Triomphe, and just about everything Gallic. And it got worse.

Although the pitch was given the green light, the players had been told they would not be allowed to encroach on to the playing area to do their pre-match warm-up. Imagine McLean's apoplexy when—in the process of angrily sounding off to a bunch of us—we suddenly heard a loud fanfare from a chorus of kazoos, followed by drums banging and a general cacophony of ear-piercing attempts at musical sounds. McLean's jaw dropping was simultaneous with his eyes leaping out of their sockets as he and the rest of the gathered throng watched in amazement as about fifty uniformed kids, their leader twirling and throwing aloft the baton, began to tramp proudly—and almost up to their knees in mud—from one of the goalmouths towards the centre of the pitch leaving a trail of black footprints in their wake. McLean almost choked, spewing forth a succession of expletives which would have crossed any language barrier.

Fortunately, the result (a goalless draw which, followed by a resounding 5-0 victory in the second leg) meant all was well that ended well. But there was no soothing McLean whose verbal onslaught, which continued long after the final whistle in Winterslag, reached the outer limits of comedy in a conversation about the game he had with a local paper reporter. 'What about that fucking band?' screamed Jim, to which the scribe, and I kid you not he was deadly serious, opined mildly, 'I know, Jim; they were seriously out of tune weren't they.'

On the subsequent quarter-final trip to Yugoslavia to play Radnicki Nis, our return charter flight coincided with Gold Cup day at the Cheltenham racing festival. A few of the press lads, and some of the players as well for that matter, liked a bet so we had a sweep on the race. The pilot agreed to get the result on his radio, and having got his permission and that of McLean, I concocted a fictitious commentary on the race over the plane's PA system.

Knowing only the final placings, off I went, mentioning as many horses as possible to keep everybody's interest until we came to the last fence. At this point, well aware it hadn't been placed, I had Ian Paul's horse well in front. Of course, the horse had to take a crashing fall, prompting Ian to leap out of his seat, cursing his luck and bawling, 'That's just typical—that horse never could fucking jump!'

Sadly, I didn't bring Dundee United much luck—I saw them lose successive UEFA Cup quarter finals in Nis and the following year against Bohemians in Prague. I do remember recommending a young Darlington player called David Speedie to McLean and his then coach and later Everton and Rangers manager, Walter Smith. Speedie went on to have a great career with Chelsea and Liverpool and both told me since how much they regretted not taking the hint.

My tartan trips petered out when I left the Sun to join The Mail on Sunday. The 'currant' had changed a lot since those early exciting days when we all did our bit in helping to make it the UK's bestselling daily. I didn't go along with the paper's preoccupation with what players did off the field more than what they did on it. Discretion has won me many more contacts and consequently more stories than snitching on any football personality who might have strayed from the straight and narrow. Nowadays all the papers are at it from the red tops upwards, and the crazy thing is, footballers, having acquired wealth bordering on the obscene, too often make themselves easy targets.

I can recall a conversation about players' salaries I once had with Rick Parry, the significance of which has become so devastatingly ironic it is almost laughable. It was in the days when he did a magnificent job as the first chief executive of the Premier League, helping to spearhead the negotiations in what became the forerunner of subsequent multi-million and ultimately billion-pound television deals. It was his premise then that football clubs would use their new-found wealth to develop the game from grass roots level upwards. 'We must make sure it doesn't go straight into the pockets of footballers,' he told me. I wonder whether he remembers that when, as the chief administrator of Liverpool Football Club, he agreed players' contracts which make a lottery jackpot seem like petty cash.

And, if footballers have their noses dipped permanently in the financial trough, they don't have to look far for company. Agents—many jacks of all trades in previous lives, car and vacuum cleaner salesmen, window cleaners, bus drivers, solicitors, accountants—are coining it in. And the game abounds with lurid speculation about some managers and so-called directors of football also grabbing a slice of the action.

But there are more transparent and strictly above board instances of high-rolling shareholders making huge profits out of selling their interest in clubs. For example, should anyone really have been surprised when Messrs Magnier and McManus advanced the cause of the Glazer family at Manchester United with financial dealings which netted them a profit of around £92 million?

But I digress back to those early days in Scotland. Having reported on Dundee United achieving a smattering of good fortune, I was then switched to Aberdeen just in time for the first leg of their semi-final in Porto. I remember I had a rather special chauffeur from the airport to my hotel; Fergie himself. As it turned out, it did him no good, the team's one-goal defeat in Portugal was compounded by a similar result in the home leg but I couldn't be blamed for that—I wasn't even at that match. Needless to say, that having left The Sun, I was nowhere near when Aberdeen recorded their magnificent success in the European Cup Winner's Cup in 1983.

In fact, the next time I saw Fergie was in the Four Seasons Hotel near Wilmslow one Friday evening towards the end of November 1986 after he had taken over from Ron Atkinson as manager of Manchester United and had been in the job for three largely inconspicuous weeks. As it happened, the following day United were playing Queens Park Rangers and the team along with their manager, Jim Smith, were staying overnight at the Four Seasons. Jim, like Ron, is a mate from way back and we had all arranged to meet before Ron flew out that night for a break in the Canaries. Sniffing a more than convivial evening with two of the game's great characters, I checked in as well and soon discovered my anticipation of the get-together was absolutely spot on.

Ron was still choked about losing his job at United but nobody in the Bald Eagle's company can be miserable for long and soon the chat, the stories, jokes and laughter were blasting around the room. Which was all very well until we noticed Fergie standing some distance away. Loyalty overcame pragmatism and, with Ron and Jim barely acknowledging the new boss's presence, I stayed where I was until his Old Trafford predecessor departed for Manchester Airport and Jim moved away to accept one of several telephone calls he received that night from his chairman, Jim Gregory. I was on the point of calling it a night myself when Fergie came across and spoke. 'Look, Bob, I know you've had a great relationship with Ron while he has been at United, I hope it will be the same with me.' I'll never forget that.

And, in the 27 years he ruled the roost, I'd like to think we did have. Of course, it hasn't been without its ups and downs—amusing and otherwise, there are times when you have to stand your corner with Fergie or he'll verbally batter you into submission. There was one altercation over an interview with David Beckham which I will refer to in a later chapter, but a recent bust-up between us resulted in a much longer ban and—not for the first time—the fault lay fairly and squarely with my newspaper. It happened on another United pre-season tour, this time in the United States in 2011. And it spoiled what was otherwise a great trip visiting cities such as Seattle, Chicago, New York and finally a mouth-watering friendly against Barcelona in Washington DC. I also managed to slip in a quick stopover in Vancouver for a Manchester City game against the Whitecaps.

Everything was hunky-dory; a couple of top-class United tales, and on a personal level, useful card-marks from the United boss which produced some decent exclusives; and then it all went suddenly and dramatically pear-shaped. During a chat with Fergie I wanted to establish whether he was serious about having a go for Inter's extremely talented Wesley Sneijder. The interest was certainly there but only if the Dutch midfielder dropped his wage demands from around £250,000 a week. Fergie okayed a tale quoting a United source saying a Sneijder deal would only happen if he agreed to a cut in wages. It was a superb exclusive and a great way to end a terrific trip.

That was until an on-line sub-editor felt the need to drop the 'United source' and make it a direct quote from the manager. Of course, I thought the other journos were taking the piss when they told me Fergie had been quoted in the online story until Mark Ogden of the Daily Telegraph demonstrated that it was no leg-pull by calling the tale up on his laptop. Any chance it might have gone unnoticed by the manager had been blown apart when he was questioned about it in the after-match media conference. To put it mildly, he was incandescent; and standing in the mixed zone, I caught the full blast of the blowtorch in a finger-pointing, expletive-laced confrontation which was captured and posted on YouTube by television cameras from all over the world. I tried to protest it was none of my doing but to no avail. I was back in his sin bin.

In the event, Fergie's fury was matched by my own. I felt he should have realised I would never have jeopardised our long-standing relationship by breaching such a confidence. But, obviously believing the story was not just online but would also appear in the Mail on Sunday, my main anger was directed at the crassly incompetent sub responsible for dropping me in it. Fortunately, the newspaper version was as I sent it but it didn't stop me becoming something of a YouTube celebrity, even if for a long time afterwards it felt like I was perched in the stocks getting pelted by a barrage of rotten tomatoes. And again, our split barely lasted a month until our paths crossed at the York races August meeting, and we sorted it out.

CHAPTER SIX
OOH AAH CANTONA

I was in at the very start of Eric Cantona's magnificent four-and-a-half-year reign as 'King' of Manchester United. I was also involved on the night he attained the pinnacle of that reign when, as chairman of the Football Writers' Association, I had the honour and privilege of presenting him with the Footballer of the Year statuette at our annual dinner at The Royal Lancaster Hotel, London.

I could have been celebrating the scoop of the year after Cantona decided to pack his bags and quit Manchester United and football when—if not at the peak of his career—then certainly at a time when he still had an enormous contribution to make to the game. But, for reasons I came to understand and appreciate, Fergie elected to steer me away from writing the story. The real facts of what happened on that FA Cup final weekend in May 1997 have been embellished by many people, some sympathetic and well-meaning; others, I suspect, more to get at Fergie than out of any sense of injustice done to a fellow journalist.

But let's go back to the beginning with Monsieur Cantona. In December 1992, Melling and I had arranged to have lunch with Fergie and Peter Reid, who was then manager of Manchester City, to write a preview of the forthcoming Manchester derby match. We met in the Portland Thistle Hotel in Piccadilly. The craic was good—it normally is when Reidy gets in full flow—but on this occasion, as is typical whenever a decent session beckons, we had also been joined by the late and much missed Keith Pinner, whose company, Arena International, had expertly handled the sponsorship of the Premier League and latterly the League and FA Cups.

Keith was a great character and just the best ever company. He was a great pal who knew everybody there was to know in the game but he was particularly close to Joe. There was never a dull moment when Keith was around and on this occasion Fergie was in high spirits, even behaving mischievously.

There was clearly a good reason why he should have been full of the joys of the approaching festive season— we were to discover what it was that afternoon. Without warning, the United boss announced he had business to attend to; he made his apologies and left the company. Of course, nobody suspected anything untoward and his departure only mildly interrupted the copious red flow.

The mood of conviviality was being maintained with ever increasing decibels of noise when suddenly Joe noticed his recording machine was missing. Naturally, I was the immediate suspect. 'Have you got my recorder?' It was more of an accusation than a question. 'I haven't touched your recorder,' I replied firmly and quite truthfully. With some justification because he is always liable to pull a daft stunt like that, the finger of suspicion switched to Reidy, who also protested his innocence. And so did Keith, with Joe becoming increasingly irate and not a little panic-stricken. Of course, we looked high and low; emptied our pockets, revisited the toilets. Not a sign of the recorder. And then Pinner's mobile rang. It was Fergie's secretary, Lyn Laffin, wondering on the boss's behalf whether we were still there. 'Of course, and likely to be for some time yet,' he declared.

Fifteen minutes later the United manager reappeared, this time accompanied by club chairman Martin Edwards. Fergie's expression was one of smug satisfaction as he sat down and poured himself another sizeable glass of red. 'Gentlemen,' he announced triumphantly. 'I've just done the deal of the season. I've paid a million pounds for Eric Cantona.' To be honest Reidy thought he was taking the piss. 'Bollocks,' he exclaimed, and then, realising Fergie was deadly serious and he was sounding less than enthusiastic about the transfer swoop, quickly added: 'Tremendous, pal. You've bought yourself a player there.'

Whereupon Fergie reached into his pocket and, grinning broadly, produced the missing recorder. 'Sorry, Joe. I must have picked this up by mistake!' I thought Joe's shirt buttons were about to pop; he didn't see the funny side of it at all in spite of the revelation about Cantona's signing, but after a few token recriminations, good humour was restored. It was left to Edwards to provide the punchline to the afternoon after his manager finally left. 'I'm a bit worried about this chap we've bought. Do you think he is any good?' History demonstrated just how good—good enough to be chosen as Footballer of the Year in 1996. And who could have guessed as he celebrated the game's top honour and apparently in his prime, that exactly a year later Cantona would, by his own volition, be an ex-footballer.

There have been many occasions throughout my time as a journalist which for one reason or another will never be forgotten. Talking to contacts close to United in the early part of that crucial week, I had sensed something might be afoot with Cantona. The feeling was strong enough for me to pick up the phone and make check calls here and there before being assured everything was normal.

Suspicions put to bed, the matter of Cantona's future had gone completely out of my mind when suddenly and dramatically it reared its head on the morning of the FA Cup final. I was in my room at The Royal Lancaster where I had been staying for the FWA dinner and before the match between Chelsea and Middlesbrough that afternoon, when I took a call from The Mail on Sunday sports editor, Roger Kelly. 'We've heard that Eric Cantona is quitting Manchester United,' said Roger. 'Could you give Ferguson a call to check it out?'

Unusually, the information came from within the office. I say unusually because I can count on the fingers of one hand the number of times I've been tipped off from High Street Kensington about genuine blockbuster stories. Worse still, this one emanated from the executive floor; a card-mark from director level to the assistant editor Roderick Gilchrist. And I have to say, after the vibes I had picked up earlier in the week, it rang bells.

I called Fergie and repeated the question I'd asked earlier in the week. 'Look I'm sorry to keep harping on about Cantona but I've had this tip from someone in the office that he's going to quit. Is there any truth in it?' The reply in the negative was clear enough for me to call the sports editor back to tell him I had checked it out and to forget it. I was comfortable with that, and covering Chelsea's 2-0 victory over Middlesbrough took precedence over a non-story about Cantona.

Sir Alex was the last person I expected a call from around 9.30 the following Sunday morning. 'Bob,' said the voice on the other end of the line as mild surprise suddenly became a gut-churning sense of dark foreboding which swiftly and literally developed into an uncontrollable movement of the bowels. As realisation began to dawn, I remember spluttering out something like, 'I hope you're not going to tell me what I think you're going to tell me'. 'Look, Bob, I couldn't mark your card yesterday because I had an agreement with Cantona that nothing would be announced until he left the country,' he said. 'He flew out last night and there will be a press conference announcing his retirement later today. I hope you understand I couldn't break my word.'

It seems there had been the added complication that Peter Fitton, a former colleague on The Sun and later The Mail on Sunday, had asked about Cantona on the Friday and had received a similar response. It was out of a sense of loyalty to Peter that the United manager felt he could hardly tell him one thing and me the other. It crossed my mind that it would have saved me a lot of aggravation had he given the tale to Peter. But, misguided though Fergie's reasons were after all, giving me the story would not have broken his pledge to Cantona who would have been long gone by the time The Mail on Sunday appeared; I saw where he was coming from. I couldn't give a toss about how other people regarded it; I recognised and accepted without reservation his motives. It mattered a lot that he thought enough about my situation to pick up the phone and give me a personal explanation of what had happened.

But it didn't get me off the hook. Apart from thanking Fergie for the call there wasn't a lot I could say; and, speaking of explanations, I knew there were a few I had to come up with myself. Number one on the list was Roger. It would be fair to say that we didn't have the best of working relationships; call it a clash of personalities more than anything. For some reason, I don't think I was his favourite person and the feeling was mutual. But on this particular Sunday morning when my backside was hanging out of my trousers, he could not have been more supportive and understanding. He played a blinder in attempting to justify my actions with the powers that be and, save for a letter from Roddy rapping my knuckles, the situation was never as bad as others made out. Sometimes you win; sometimes you lose.

The fact is, if I could have turned the clock back 24 hours to the Saturday morning, I would have acted in exactly the same way. You get a tip and you check it out; I'm glad I know enough people to be able to do that. There's always another tale, and what happened over Cantona did nothing to alter my regard for Sir Alex.

CHAPTER SEVEN
THE LOONY TOON

The massive investment in football clubs such as Chelsea and the two Manchester clubs, United and City, together with the outstanding way Arsene Wenger has continued to manage Arsenal over the years has maintained the polarisation of football's top division when it comes to challenging for the title.

Latterly there has been the breath-taking rise of Leicester City and the resurgence of Liverpool and Tottenham.

Still, and not discounting these exceptions, it would be a brave man who would put his money any of the others fulfilling a role other than merely filling up the dates in the fixtures schedule. The tendency for different clubs at different times to threaten near invincibility is nothing new in the game. Even the likes of Everton, Leeds United, Aston Villa, and Blackburn Rovers have flourished enough to win the title in the previous three decades.

Sadly, from a committed North-East football follower's point of view, the notable odd men out are the area's so-called big three; Newcastle, not since 1927; or

Sunderland - 1936; or Middlesbrough—not ever. And yet for a spell in the nineties even the Magpies had aspirations, not only to rub shoulders with but also to whip the crème de la crème of the game. The man who without any doubt was the catalyst for that improvement was Sir John Hall, a property developer whose first breath was a mixture of fresh air and coal dust having been born in the shadow of the Ashington Colliery pit head.

It was his entrepreneurial skills combined with a swashbuckling sense of adventure that provided the launching pad for everything good that happened at the club during that all too brief period of success. Kevin Keegan, Alan Shearer, Sir Bobby Robson, yes, even Michael Owen. And Sir John, for reasons that will be explained later, has never wasted an opportunity to hand me the credit for persuading him to get involved in the first place.

But let's go back to my beginning with Newcastle. It was no fun working in Manchester in the sixties, having star-studded United constantly shoved down one's throat by the locals. As a sub-editor on the late Sporting Chronicle and then The Daily Mirror, I didn't watch much live big-time football. For a spell, I covered mostly Second Division matches on a Saturday before giving that up to do better paid shifts, firstly on The People and then The News of the World. Being a Darlington supporter—and Hartlepool hater—with slight leanings towards Middlesbrough, I had no particular affinity to Newcastle, or Sunderland for that matter, but tribal instinct came to the fore on the rare occasions any of the

North-East teams (except Hartlepool) did anything remotely spectacular. These celebrations were tolerated condescendingly by Mancunians, comfortable in the certain knowledge they would be brief and worthy of no more than passing interest.

When I eventually returned to the North-East to cover Newcastle and Sunderland for the Journal, it was usually to record their defeats, especially when the star formations came to town. Soon, you were gripped with the same sense of resignation and acceptance of one's lot that had engulfed both sets of supporters for years. Championships and Cups—save for the fading memories of United's Wembley victories in the fifties; their success in landing the forerunner of the Europa League, the Inter Cities Fairs Cup in 1969 and, of course, Sunderland's fantastic FA Cup triumph in 1973—were won by the other teams and not a lot has changed.

One of the reasons offered for Newcastle's more recent inconsistencies has been the lack of continuity in the manager's office. It could hardly have been the situation back then. Joe Harvey bossed the team for 13 years from 1962; the club has had 30 plus in the 50 odd years since, and though Joe did well with limited resources, the closest he came to emulating the FA Cup successes he enjoyed as team captain in 1951 and 1952 was when he led the team out at Wembley before their comprehensive 3-0 defeat by Liverpool in 1974.

I didn't know Harvey as a player but we had a good manager-reporter relationship. On the occasions he didn't like what I had written, he'd deliver the bollocking and then it was quickly forgotten. The highlight of his reign as manager had to be when the team crowned their European debut by lifting the Fairs Cup in. Typically for a club that ridiculed conformity, their triumph was as clear-cut as their qualification stretched credulity. Their entry was not so much by way of the back door, more like through the keyhole.

Newcastle made it as the result of a convoluted interpretation of the rules. They had finished tenth in First Division the previous season, but because the regulations then stipulated that entry was restricted to one club per city and competitions such as the European and Cup-winners Cups took precedence, teams like Everton, Tottenham and Arsenal, in spite of finishing higher in the table, were ineligible. But, as blue-chip European rivals such as Chelsea, Liverpool and Leeds United all fell by the wayside, astonishingly, Harvey's boys qualified for a two-legged final against Leeds' quarter-final conquerors, Ujpest Dozsa, from Hungary.

While all that was going on, I had to deal with a personal issue which quite frankly had diminished any appreciation of the black and whites' European exploits. Having covered United through thick and mainly thin, I had been eagerly anticipating a trip or two either across the North Sea or the English Channel. Unfortunately, the Journal sports editor Alan Sleeman had other ideas. For reasons best known to himself he decided to jock me off the away games in Europe and, in my place, send Ivor Broadis, the former professional footballer, whose main job on the paper was to report on Carlisle United. Of course, I wasn't best pleased to the extent that I was desperate for the chance to tell Sleeman to stick his job where the sun doesn't shine. But to go where, and when? I had a wife, two daughters and a mortgage. Initiative was never my greatest asset but I dug some up from somewhere.

The Sunday Sun, the Journal's sister paper, was edited by a chap called Norman Batey, an odd, unconventional character who had always struck me as being slightly off his trolley. But he skippered a good ship which was manned mainly by casuals whose main jobs were with the two dailies, The Journal and Evening Chronicle. In fact, at the time there was not one single full-time sports employee on the staff—a situation which, with a little friendly persuasion, I hoped Mr Batey would remedy by appointing me. And bless him, that's exactly what he did, although I was absolutely convinced his decision to give me a job was influenced by a Machiavellian delight in being able to put one over on Sleeman.

Suddenly, everything in the garden was rosy. I was earning a few more quid and my departure from The Journal coincided with Newcastle's march to the Fairs Cup final. They had already obtained a huge advantage from the first leg with a 3-0 victory over Ujpest, but nevertheless, the Hungarians had shown enough to indicate the Cup was far from won.

However, my concern was not so much whether the Magpies could hang on but whether I would be in Budapest to see the showdown. Getting to Hungary was never going to be the problem; getting in to see the match was. The deadline for press ticket applications had long passed and I couldn't buy an ordinary brief at any price. That said, having been stranded at home when earlier rounds were played in Holland, Portugal and Spain, I was determined to be in the city on the Danube for what might be Newcastle's finest European hour.

Persuading Batey to let me go required bullshit of the highest order, 'Trust me, I've got friends in high places,' I lied. Fine words which had something of a hollow ring when I arrived at the Nep Stadium to face expressionless Magyar ground staff on whose ears even platinum bullshit failed to register a flicker of understanding. I was left standing outside the main entrance, alone, forlorn, desperate and totally bereft of any hope of getting in to the stadium. My colleagues, of course, condescendingly sympathising with my plight, had long gone. Their eager anticipation of the pre-match hospitality had diminished any thoughts of how I would cope. They had a job to do; my problem was my problem. I thought, 'Bollocks, I'll go back to the hotel; watch it on TV and beg the quotes of the lads.'

That's when salvation appeared in the shape of the Newcastle team bus. Harvey was first off. 'Joe,' I pleaded, 'any chance of a ticket. I'm absolutely desperate.' Harvey stopped, shook his head, threw me a 'useless bugger' expression and muttered something about more important things on his plate. He said he would see what he could do and then disappeared through the players' entrance door.

Enough minutes had gone by for despair to set in when, God bless him, Harvey suddenly came to the entrance and beckoned to me to follow him. Waving aside all the uniformed jobsworths, he ushered me through the door and down the corridor before propping me against the wall outside the Newcastle dressing room with another instruction to 'stand there until I come back out.' I waited, avoiding any threatening glances from the polizei, until skipper, Bobby Moncur, led his players clip-clopping past me, down the tunnel and on to the pitch—no pre-match warm-ups in those days. Joe followed, pursued by his number two, Dave Smith, the rest of the back-room staff and the sub, Alan Foggon. 'Come on then, what are you waiting for?' he barked, gesturing towards the opening on to a pitch bathed in light.

I could feel around twenty pairs of incredulous Newcastle-leaning journalists' eyes bulging from their sockets high in the press box at the sight of yours truly dutifully following Harvey and the rest out of the tunnel and along the touchline to the dugout where the manager, pointing a finger at a vacant space on the bench, ordered, 'You sit next to me.' And I did. And it was from precisely that priceless vantage point that I had the best possible view of United's magnificent Fairs Cup victory. Of course, it was a heaven sent opportunity to re-enact every nuance of what was an emotion-packed evening and I tried to grab it the best way I could, recording how Harvey (and I at the time) chain-smoked our way through the match.

Joe's football rhetoric was never conceived in a coaching manual—his long-time number two Jimmy Greenhalgh's favoured pre-match instruction was 'don't let the opposition panic you into playing football'—and if his words had little to do with 'areas' or 'final thirds' or 'bodies', they surely reflected his passion and commitment; qualities he passed on in abundance to his players.

Beginning with, 'Right, c'mon lads; let's give it everything we've got,' and in between toenail-curling pulls on his cigarettes, he kept up a torrent of dialogue ranging from fierce abuse to canny cajoling depending on whether he thought the Swiss referee had erred— 'Ref, why don't you stick that whistle up yer arse'—or one of his defenders had won the ball with a fearsome tackle. 'That's it Ollie (Burton), let's see how fast he can limp.' Only twice was he stunned into temporary silence; when Ujpest pulled one and then two goals back before the whistle ended the first half.

Left alone on the bench, I wouldn't have given a forint for Joe's half-time pep talk altering the flow of the Hungarians' pressure and, judging from the mood of the salivating home fans baying their throats hoarse behind me, I don't think they did either.

I'd been wrong before and have been since. And I was magnificently way off the mark then. Within minutes of the restart skipper, Moncur, two-goal hero of the first match, restored United's two-goal advantage with a cracker, prompting Joe to leap to his feet, hugging me and anybody within touching distance and yelling: 'That's five the bastards have to get now to beat us—no way they're going to do that.' But even he could not have imagined the way the Hungarians simply disintegrated. Danish international, Benny Arentoft, made it 2-2 on the night, triggering more jumping up and down on the touchline. And then, unexpected drama.

Smith went on the pitch to treat a Jackie Sinclair injury and returned with the message: 'Scotty's (Jimmy Scott) got cramp again; he's buggered.'

Joe turned to Foggon, straining at the leash like a greyhound at Altcar, and uttered one unforgettable sentence: 'Right Foggon, get on that pitch and run your bollocks off.' It was a timely, if hardly tactical, substitution. Foggon was soon in action, picking up the ball and heading straight for goal with Harvey's deafening encouragement bursting my left ear drum, 'Go on, son; you've got him, son; hit it, son.' And then, 'He's scored; the young bugger has scored, that's bloody seven they'll need now.'

I remember Joe being strangely subdued in the moment of victory. Grinding his last smoke into the cinder track, his voice broken by the fags and the bawling, he turned to me and beamed: 'How about that then; that's something to write about isn't it?' He was not wrong. Batey was more than happy with my first-hand account of what it was like to sit on the bench and give the inside track on a Newcastle football triumph that was up there with that magnificent FA Cup treble of the early fifties. I was also grateful he didn't ask how I'd got there—or what I would have done if Joe hadn't come to my rescue.

The party afterwards was something to be remembered; press and players together without a hint of the demarcation that exists today. But first there was the trophy presentation on the pitch when I happened to be standing close enough to Moncur as he received silver cup for the United skipper to remark later he thought the

UEFA official was going to hand it to me instead of him. As it happened, I did get my hands on the trophy; in fact, the Fairs Cup took pride of place on my dining room table for the whole of the Christmas holiday in 1969. I asked Harvey if I could borrow it for an evening in the pub. 'Take it but make sure you bring it back after Christmas,' he said. As one famous columnist might say; you couldn't make it up.

Harvey's mood in Budapest contrasted sharply with another unforgettable football occasion in Newcastle's history. The day they were dumped out of the FA Cup by non-league Hereford United may even yet appeal as a fairy-tale to non-committed romanticists, but every coin has two sides. The gut-wrenching heartbreak felt by the United boss after the worst ever defeat in his years in charge was no fairy-tale. A home draw against the Southern League outfit appeared to hand the Magpies with a bye into the fourth round and even a shock 2-2 draw at St James's Park was dismissed as a hiccup that would be put right in the replay at Edgar Street.

Along with the rest of the North-Eastern press gang, I headed west into rural Herefordshire to a city famous for its beautiful cathedral and age-old traditions—but not its football team; that is not until February 5th, 1972. The game had been postponed several times due to the pitch being waterlogged. Because the rearrangement was always within a couple of days, we all stayed in Hereford and became pretty friendly with the locals, enjoying the wonderful hospitality of the club; it's manager Colin Addison (who has since become a great mate), and the officials.

The replay finally went ahead on a quagmire of a pitch and the rest, as they say, is history. I just happened to be commiserating with the Hereford supporters around me after Malcolm Macdonald had given Newcastle the lead ten minutes from the end, when Ronnie Radford swung his boot to bury a 30-yard equaliser past Willie McFaul. There was only one team going through after that, and I was already in the bar drowning my sorrows when Ricky George banged in the winner.

But my emotions were inconsequential compared to the depths of Harvey's misery. I've known many managers since; I've seen how they react to defeat. Some bawl and shout and kick buckets, some shrug their shoulders, some roll up their sleeves. But I have never seen anybody so totally drained of emotion as Harvey was on that day. Before the game and because of return travel complications, he had kindly agreed to allow Doug Weatherall and myself to travel back on the team bus. Had the result changed everything I wondered. Doug's advice was a snappy, 'Just get on the bus; sit down and say nowt.' And we did.

How many times do you hear someone in the game say he was 'sick' after a result? In Harvey's case, it was the truth. In fact, the driver had to stop the bus on the motorway several times while the manager of Newcastle United threw his insides up. I ask you to tell me any manager today who would be hurt by defeat as much as that.

CHAPTER EIGHT
ARISE SIR JOHN

Unscripted it may have been, but the Hereford result was still the kind of failure that anyone who had anything to do with Newcastle over the years seemed prepared to accept. It was as if they knew their place in the grand scheme of things and just got on with it. There never seemed any great ambition in a nepotistic boardroom; nice people (by and large); pillars of the community, but immersed in the self-importance which came with running a famous football club. It was the quintessential protection racket. There may have been people who could have done better but they never got the chance. Nobody but the people in charge were going to play with their toy—their football yo-yo—and that remained the situation throughout the seventies and eighties, apart from the all too brief flirtation with greatness when Kevin Keegan chose Tyneside for the swansong to his magnificent playing career.

It wasn't that Newcastle didn't produce great players; Paul Gascoigne, Chris Waddle, Peter Beardsley, Alan Kennedy to name a few, who, in order to fulfil their potential, sought their fortunes elsewhere because

Newcastle just weren't big enough to keep them. The generations of supporters may have changed but today's sons and daughters have, for the most part, inherited the frustrations of their forebears. It remains to be seen whether Rafa Benitez is the man to buck that trend and, until very recently, it has been a case of lifting and dusting off headlines like 'CRISIS' or 'REVOLT' or 'RESIGN' or 'WHAT'S GONE WRONG AT NEWCASTLE' which, by the way, was the headline on a series of articles I wrote for the Sun in February 1978.

In those days, the chairman of the Toon Army wanted to get rid of was Bob Rutherford. Before him it was Lord Westwood and after him Gordon McKeag. I wrote then of the board, 'Such is the power of the men in the upper room at St James' Park that the situation will probably remain unchanged.'

But I was wrong—again! Because for an all too brief but memorable five-year period it did change and little old me played a major role in helping it to do so. The Newcastle-based Evening Chronicle, led by the paper's number one football man, my old mate John Gibson, had instigated a campaign for a boardroom revolution by backing the Magpie Group, a rebel consortium which had as one of its leading lights Malcolm Dix, a well-meaning local businessman who had been a thorn in the sides of the Newcastle board for years but had been simply banging his head against a brick wall. The campaign was solid, but as had happened too often in the past and in spite of everybody's best efforts, it seemed to be foundering. It seemed the apparently impregnable

United boardroom was living up to its reputation as a fortress that defied even the strongest siege.

I believed what was needed was fresh impetus to breathe new life into the campaign. John Hall—a lifelong United supporter and a pitman's son who used to travel from Ashington as a kid to watch the team play, was well known as the man behind the construction of the Metro Centre, then Europe's biggest shopping mall—had flirted with the idea of getting involved, giving the Magpie Group his verbal blessing. But that seemed to be as far as he wanted to go, happy enough to remain very much on the fringe of the whole issue. I was convinced, if the so-called revolution had any chance at all, the powerful multi-millionaire property developer had to be persuaded to stick his head above the parapet a little further.

And so, in early April 1988, I found himself being ushered into a rather plush Portakabin in a restricted area close to where the then plain Mr Hall's company, Cameron Hall Developments, was nearing completion of the shopping behemoth on the banks of the Tyne. I had never met the man before and instantly found him brusque, impatient and, although he was interested enough in the subject of Newcastle United FC to grant me half an hour of his precious time, I got the distinct impression that the second he detected I was less than useful, I would be heading for the exit.

Fortunately for me and Newcastle United that did not happen. Sir John himself has since recounted in many interviews on television, radio and in newspapers, how, following initial exchanges during which we both established what the other was all about, he reached into his drinks cabinet, got out a bottle of malt and two glasses and said, 'Let's talk about what can be done.' He is also on record several times as saying, 'It was that bugger Cass who got me started with Newcastle in the first place.'

Does that make me feel proud? You bet it does.

I am no pioneer—far from it. My first priority may have been to affect a change for the better in the United boardroom with Sir John looking a likely candidate to help bring that about, but I also wanted an exclusive in which I could reveal to the Tyneside public that he was going to be their knight in shining armour. As it happened, I managed to do both. Under a banner headline 'RESCUE ACT', with a sub-head which read 'Hall bids for Newcastle', the article appeared in The Mail on Sunday on April 10th, 1988—by any standards a red-letter day in the history of Newcastle United FC.

Sir John's original intention was to promote a peaceful transition in which the current directors would open the doors to new ideas and finance for the mutual benefit of everybody concerned, not the least of whom were the supporters. He called for a restructuring of the club's shareholding, proposing a rights issue of half a million £10 shares or any other necessary amount. 'The present directors and shareholders would have the opportunity to get involved like anybody else,' he said. Then, sensing what was an inevitable cold shoulder, he declared, 'I'd like an orderly transition without any bloodletting. But if the people running things at the moment are not prepared to do that, many of us on the outside would be then forced to consider whether we went for a full battle which would not be in the short term interests of the club.'

Once he warmed to the theme, Sir John went into top gear with rhetoric most of Tyneside was waiting to hear. I was excited both by what was his declaration of intent and the fact that it was yours truly who had been the catalyst for what was then the dawn of the wind of change. He told me, 'I don't want to be disparaging towards the present board. Stan Seymour, the chairman, and his colleagues have their hearts in the club but the time has come when, in fairness to the supporters, they must consider their position.

'We have been denied success for too long now. In any other line of business, the directors would have been forced out. They know that being businessmen themselves. But, because they have been able to manipulate their control they have remained in power. If I wanted to buy shares, the application would have to go before the board and they would block it. We supporters have been taken for granted for too long. It's easy to follow a winning team but, by God, it's hard to keep yourself motivated fortnight after fortnight to watch the rubbish served up season after season.'

Surely it would have been better for all concerned had the then club chairman, Stan Seymour and his eventual successor Gordon McKeag, at least got Sir John and his associates around a table to hear what they had to say. I had no axe to grind with either of them, nor their boardroom colleagues for that matter. I have no doubt they wanted the club to be successful as much as the next man—they just did not want it badly enough to jeopardise their authority at the club. Predictably they reacted to my article by manning the St James's Park barricades. Within days they launched a vicious attack on Sir John, issuing a statement in which they accused him of 'having a driving ambition to gain personal control.'

Looking back, their words revealed their utter stupidity and total lack of foresight. The statement went on: 'The recent history of football is littered with millionaires with no experience of football or an understanding its management complexities who buy up league clubs in the belief that their money (or their company's money) is bound to bring success. A glance at the record of such clubs shows that it is not so. We do not need a Robert Maxwell here.'

And it looked very much like John Hall and his motley crew wouldn't have got over the doormat at Newcastle either—such arrogance. Was it any wonder Newcastle had been stranded in a football no-man's land for nearly a century?

The fact is, having swatted away all previous attempts, mainly led in more recent years by Dix and a few frustrated friends, the directors were absolutely convinced the boardroom was impregnable. And it really was difficult to visualise how the so-called Magpie Group were going to break their stranglehold. As I wrote at the time: 'Hall is the man who built a shopping mountain on a soggy coal ash wilderness by the banks of the River Tyne. In six years he turned a bleak, black wasteland into the largest shopping and leisure complex in Europe. But, having achieved the unlikely, the 54-year-old miner's son from Ashington—the Northumberland colliery town that produced Jackie Milburn as well as the Charlton brothers—is attempting what even he fears could be the impossible to disturb the dynastic regime which has ruled St James's Park for decades.'

So why should it be different this time? Could the Hall bandwagon pick enough momentum to crash through those barricades? The first salvoes in what developed into an intense, bitterly-fought battle for power that lasted two long years were fired the following week when both sides launched a massive search for key dormant shareholders who had the potential to tilt the balance of that power. Significantly, Seymour wrote letters to all known shareholders appealing for their support at the same time conducting a fierce personal attack on Hall as well as claiming the club had been subjected to a 'vendetta' by sections of the media. And he pointed an unequivocal finger in my direction when he declared, 'Mr John Hall has made no secret over the past two or three years of his ambition to take control at St. James's Park. After a period of quiescence, he chose last Sunday and The Mail On Sunday to launch his latest campaign.' It was the first little ripple of boardroom panic. They were nervous and, as events proved, they had every right to be.

Having said that, there is no doubt it was the establishment who had the better of the early exchanges in what soon developed into a bitter, acrimonious battle for power. The rebels' opening gambit was an offer of

£500 for originally priced 50p shares with a guaranteed £50 per share if they failed to obtain control. But, in an attempt to gain the key 60-share hoard of one particularly family, they subsequently increased their offer to a straight £1000—a share with no strings attached, an astonishing bid but not good enough. There was clearly no limit to the extent of the United board's determination to cling on to their positions. They snapped up the shares by going even higher; in effect, in poker parlance, it was a case of 'Okay, there's their 'grand' and there's a few quid more.' It was enough for the new chairman Gordon McKeag to claim in October 1988 that he and his fellow directors had acquired more than 51% of the shareholding.

McKeag, whose father William had preceded him as chairman, was entitled to his moment of glory. Unwittingly, I felt he put his finger on what was wrong at the club when he observed in an interview with me, 'We have been very sad we have been forced into a situation where family ties which have lasted for years have been broken. We have prided ourselves on the fact there has been this family involvement which has been handed down from generation to generation.' Gordon was an honest, strongly-principled man who genuinely felt Newcastle's best chance of a brighter future was with the club's status quo, but he just could not see the wood for the family trees. Hall and Co believed the old guard had had their day; so did I, and judging from the mood of the hundreds of supporters who turned up at the many Magpie group's sports forums all over the area, so did they. As it turned out, it may have been round one to the board, but the fight was just getting started.

Predictably and justifiably, Hall pounced on the reference to the 'families' in another interview with me when he made it clear he was not going to take this first major setback lying down. 'When he (McKeag) talks about families, I presume he doesn't include the supporters,' he told me. 'Their money is acceptable through the turnstiles on match days but not when it comes to allowing them to buy a stake in the club. He accuses me (Hall) of trying to buy the family silver but whose family silver is it anyway? I believe Newcastle should not be owned by small families. It should be for the people. I'm confident enough we will acquire enough to democratise Newcastle—that is the biggest difference between the views of the club chairman and myself.'

It was evident before the turn of the year that McKeag was fighting a losing battle. One by one his supporters—and eventually his boardroom colleagues—caved in, coaxed more by the ridiculous offers for shares which hit a ceiling of around 12,000 times their original 50p value than more public spirited motives such as a genuine belief that Hall could keep his promise of success for the fans. More than two years had passed since the day of The Mail On Sunday's 'RESCUE ACT' headline when he marked his arrival in the United boardroom with another exclusive interview—appropriately in the paper on May 27 1990—my birthday.

'In that first interview in The Mail On Sunday I made it clear personal power was not my ambition,' he recalled. 'My aim was to act as a catalyst for change; to spearhead an end to the dynastic stranglehold which certain families have had on this great club through decades of failure. If anything, I would be proud only to be remembered as the person who helped give United back to its loyal, rank and file supporters. It has taken me this long to get my foot in the door but my plans haven't changed one iota—democratisation is still the target.'

Well, it has to be said, things didn't work out quite like that either. If sharing the club with the fans really was John Hall's dream, it was only a pipe dream. When he precipitated the launch of a rights issue in December 1990, there were very few takers—the so-called Toon Army just did not want to know. It meant absolute control of the club was virtually forced on him to save it going under completely and so, three and a half years of ferocious financial street-fighting finally ended in almost meek surrender when in November 1991, Hall, by now Sir John, his son Douglas and a later chairman, Freddie Shepherd, ousted McKeag and his cohorts from the club's decision-making body. The reality—not to mention the deliciously rich irony—was the ownership of the club had merely switched to another family, the Hall family. What price Sir John's statement, 'I believe the club should not be owned by small families. It should be for the people,' when he became the top banana?

But what the hell, at least he managed to stir the sleeping giant into fluttering its eyelids. The Kevin Keegan era was marvellous until it all went pear-shaped; Kenny Dalglish took the team into the Champions League for the first time but ultimately failed; Ruud

Gullit flopped; Sir Bobby Robson got it going again briefly until he was summarily and unfairly dismissed; Graeme Souness flopped and so did Glenn Roeder.

At the time, the list of possible successors, candidates who were genuinely chasing the job, was impressive, underlining just what a massive product Newcastle United Football Club is in world football. It needed someone massive in the manager's office. I thought, of all those in the frame at the time, that Shepherd had targeted Sam Allardyce, a man I believed then and now was absolutely right for the job; someone who was tailor-made for Tyneside; bags of managerial experience at every level. If he had taken charge, then I doubt very much whether the team would have found themselves in the predicament they were in in the middle of November, separated from the Premier League's bottom spot by the difference of a goal. Instead, albeit persuaded by the team's surge up the league table during Roeder's reign as caretaker boss, the chairman chose instead a convenient option that satisfied the short-sighted aspirations of supporters and the local media. Sadly, it didn't take long for the promise of prosperous years under the new management team to be revealed as mere fools' gold.

I do not doubt Shepherd had Newcastle at heart; cut him and he'll bleed black and white. As I wrote in my report after Newcastle's 1-0 defeat by Sheffield United in November, the chairman hardly deserved to bear the brunt of the supporters' after-match abuse; he had, after all, appointed the manager they clamoured for. On the other hand, if he didn't deserve it he surely brought it on himself. Sadly for Newcastle, I believe Shepherd got it right in the end. His appointment of Allardyce may have been his legacy to the Toon Army but big Sam was never given the time and opportunity to become the success I am convinced he would have been.

Newcastle supporters have been lauded as among the most passionately committed in football. No argument with that, but over the years their voice in crucially pivotal situations has carried too many decibels. They blasted Shepherd, they praised Roeder and they ridiculed Allardyce for what they felt was 'not the style of football they wanted to see from a team in black and white stripes'. Such audacity. And big Sam surely made them pay for their misguidedly lofty ideals when he steered Blackburn Rovers from almost a position of no hope to Premier League safety while United staggered blindly into the Championship at the end of the season.

As for Sir John Hall, if he is accorded with the credit of piloting United through their most successful period in over seventy years, he has few friends among the Toon Army after selling his interest in the club to billionaire sports goods entrepreneur Mike Ashley.

Whether Ashley's heart is really in the club is questionable. If his intention when he took it on was to sell it at a profit at some future date, he sure as hell went about it in a strange way, firstly by sacking Allardyce and then surrounding himself with cohorts who, had they even the will, certainly did not have the way to succeed; bowing to the clamour to bring back Keegan—a mistake he knew he had made almost within days—appointing Joe Kinnear as an interim, then astonishingly, permanent manager (he was never up to the job), and finally giving Alan Shearer just eight games to resuscitate a club whose heart had already stopped beating.

We will never know whether that great local hero would have cut the mustard as Newcastle manager. Maybe one day if another managerial opportunity knocks, he will vacate his role as a Match of the Day pundit and return to the dugout. It is a worrying truism that power breeds sycophancy. The impression that Ashley goes walkies with a bunch of nodding dogs fit only for the rear windows of cars is inescapable. He treated Chris Hughton abominably, but if the price of the former manager's silence was a lot more than the pittance he was paid while he was in charge, good luck to him. His employer was always looking for an excuse to get rid of him. In the end, he did it anyway when he did not have one, as his subsequent achievements with Birmingham, Norwich and Brighton have shown. Alan Pardew knew enough of Ashley to be able to form a judgement about what he would be like to work for. And anyway, one would think taking over a team in the top half of the Premier League, even if it meant working for a dictatorial demi-god, was better than being on the dole. Well, it is, isn't it?

Under the circumstances, his record in his four years in charge was highly commendable; a double manager of the year award was a fitting reward for someone who was tethered to the owner's financial restraints.

No wonder when Crystal Palace offered to double their former playing idol's paltry wages, he grabbed the opportunity to jump ship. A relegation battle at an inferior club was, he decided, an infinitely better option than coping with the distorted great expectations of fans hoping in vain to resuscitate a dormant football giant.

Caretaker boss John Carver went on to save Newcastle, tenth when Pardew departed, from relegation by the skin of their teeth before Steve McClaren (more of him later) arrived under a cloud given his messy divorce with Derby.

McClaren's ill-fated reign lasted just nine months, Ashley going on to pull off the crowd pleasing coup of appointing Benitez, even though the Spaniard was ultimately unable to prevent Newcastle sliding into the second tier once more.

I'm reminded of Gordon McKeag's statement about football club ownership when Hall was marauding around boardroom door. It is worth repeating: 'The recent history of football is littered with millionaires with no experience of football or understanding of its management complexities who buy up league clubs in the belief that their money (or their company's money) is bound to bring success. A glance at the record of such clubs shows that it is not so. We do not need a Robert Maxwell here.'

By persuading a manager of Benitez's pedigree to remain at the helm and lead the club to yet another promotion, albeit by the promise of healthy bonuses and finally equipping his manager with necessary level of autonomy to do the job properly, Ashley's stock has never been so high with the Toon Army.

But there remains an awful long way to go if the Newcastle's much maligned owner is to win over the club's long-suffering supporters once and for all.

If his ambitions for Newcastle do, at last, match the thickness of his skin, then Toon fans could soon be basking in the glory of a miraculous rise like that enjoyed by Leicester in their remarkable championship winning campaign.

If not, even with a manager of Bentiez's pedigree at the helm, Newcastle United are, at best, destined for another lifetime as mid-table makeweights.

CHAPTER NINE
STEVE'S JOB

When Steve McClaren was sacked as England's head coach, he lost the only one of the top three appointments he had secured in the previous eight years that were not down to me. I was directly responsible for Steve becoming Sir Alex Ferguson's number two at Manchester United and later, when he took over at Middlesbrough, I got him that job too. But I would never have put him in for England—he just was not ready for it.

That is absolutely no reflection on his talents as a coach and a manager; his record at Old Trafford and Middlesbrough is ample evidence of that. No, I just felt his five-year association with Sven Goran Eriksson—a man regarded as something of a busted flush by my colleagues in the media—made McClaren a sitting target for those same critics. And so, it proved. He didn't have a lot going for him with injuries to key players and goalkeepers responsible for schoolboy howlers in vital matches, but his team did not qualify for the European Championship finals out of a not too difficult group—

end of story. He will ever be remembered as the 'Wally With the Brolly', whatever he achieves subsequently.

But surely the supposedly more enlightened will realise there is something fundamentally wrong with our international set-up that will not be remedied merely by a change of coach. In fairness Greg Dyke, the latest to jettison the job of FA chairman, did so after warming to the theme, but when the Premier League continues to stunt the development of English talent by importing high-priced foreigners, so-called five-year plans to breed home-grown stars, whether players or coaches, will only be mere lip service.

Sir Bobby Robson took us to the threshold in 1990 and I am almost tempted to excuse the failings of McClaren's successor Fabio Capello who, at times, looked simply bewildered as well as clueless while our World Cup hopes disintegrated in South Africa in 2010. Sod those who disagree, I'm prepared to give him the benefit of the doubt about what might have happened had Frank Lampard's 'goal' stood against Germany.

But back to the beginning of the McClaren story. I was happy and proud of my role in his rise and rise; I would have been a lot happier if I had been able to write the stories which corresponded to it. After all, when it comes down to it, that's all we hacks are in it for—certainly not the fortunes made by others who knew sod all about how it all came about and only got involved when it came down to dotting the 'i's' and crossing the 't's'. And it's not much of a consolation either to occupy the central role in a situation full of secrecy and intrigue when the tales later drop into the laptops of rivals.

For instance, few people knew what went on behind the scenes when Howard Kendall was appointed Everton manager for the second time early in November 1990. There's a saying in football that a manager should never go back to a club he has worked at previously. Whether, in hindsight, Kendall would subscribe to that having twice returned to Goodison Park is debatable. But I have vivid memories of the circumstances behind his first attempt to rekindle those halcyon days in the eighties when he proved himself to be one of England's greatest post-war managers by steering Everton to two league championships in three years.

Less than three years later Howard was boss at Manchester City having stunned Everton supporters by quitting after the second title success. His reasons were apparently political but also, in no small way, as a result of his frustration at not being allowed to take his team into Europe because of the UEFA ban on English teams which followed the Heysel disaster. Sadly, the European grass he discovered at Spanish club Atletico Bilbao was certainly no greener than that on Merseyside and when the opportunity arose to return to England with City he grasped it eagerly.

Kendall did well at a club, which at the time lacked the sort of talent he had nurtured at Everton. That's why he believed, with some justification, criticism he received (more from the local media than City supporters) was undeserved, especially when the team were in a healthy fifth position in the table. It was in complete contrast to the hero worship he had been used to 25 miles down the East Lancs road and it was getting under his skin. When City were beaten at home 2-1 by George Graham's Arsenal in a third round Rumbelows (League) Cup-tie at the end of October, he could sense the hatchet men would be sharpening their weapons and his situation was the subject of some discussion when he, his midfielder and number two Peter Reid and myself met up in the Copthorne Hotel in Salford Quays after the match.

It turned out to be a marathon session from which at one point in the early hours I attempted to escape only to be hauled back from my room by the indestructible Kendall. We were still going strong at dawn and beyond when word came through that Colin Harvey, Howard's close friend, former assistant and then successor at Everton, had been sacked. The previous evening had not been a good one for Harvey either, with his team losing their Rumbelows Cup match at Sheffield United. The pair exchanged telephone calls and shared mutual sympathies before Kendall shook his head reflectively. It was clearly the thought that he had probably made the wrong decision to leave Goodison which was behind his sudden exclamation, 'I wouldn't mind going back there if I got the chance.'

Reidy responded immediately by telling his boss that he was off his rocker. 'Forget it,' he snapped. 'It wouldn't be the same for you, and anyway we're doing all right where we are.' But Kendall, thoughts gathering pace, would not be swayed. Sure, we'd had a drink or three but his mind-set was as clear and precise as if he had been stone cold sober. 'I really do fancy it, come with me and we could sort it out between us,' he urged

Reidy who, it must be said, was clearly not for persuading. He turned to me, 'Is there anything you can do on the QT?'

It was a difficult one; Kendall was becoming more certain with every second that he wanted the job; Reidy, equally, was increasingly convinced he should stay where he was. 'Okay, Howard,' I told him. 'If you want me to make a call, I will.' Eventually we agreed if he felt the same when we arranged to meet again at lunchtime, I would make a call. As it turned out, after three or four hours kip he was even more convinced he wanted a crack at it.

We went back to my room where I picked up the phone and called Everton's long-serving club secretary, Jim Greenwood, who was a terrific bloke and a good contact of mine. 'What can I do for you, young man?' Greenwood's voice was warm and friendly. 'Sad about Colin,' I offered, adding, 'Look, Jim, if you've got somebody lined up for the job, I won't waste your time any further. But, if you haven't, I could suggest a name you may want to consider.' After assuring me there was no immediate replacement in the frame, he asked, 'Who did you have in mind?'

'What about Howard Kendall?' I wondered, looking straight at a very anxious Howard Kendall as he perched on the edge of my bed. 'He's doing too well at City. He wouldn't come back here, would he?' Greenwood's reply was slightly dismissive, but at the same time, hopefully curious. 'Well he might be doing all right but judging from what he told me last night, he's not really happy. He really thinks he made a mistake leaving Everton.'

I was putting Howard's case as persuasively as I could while he nodded vigorously in agreement. Jim had had an excellent working relationship with Howard at Goodison and he knew the two of them could always have a discreet conversation—that's all we were after. 'I might have a word,' he said. 'Do you know where he is?'

We were in business. 'Well he was staying at the Copthorne Hotel last night so you could try him there. I've got the number here,' I replied. The conversation ended with me wishing him the best of luck and then ordering Kendall to scarper to his room as soon as possible because he was about to get a call.

And there was where it ended, with Kendall promising to keep me up to speed with any developments. True to his word he telephoned me around nine o'clock that evening. 'I've spoken to the Everton people and I think I've got a good chance of the job,' he announced. 'There are just one or two things which need tidying up.' Unable to contain myself I rang my mate, Joe Melling, who happened to be at a sportsman's dinner in London sharing a table with a number of personalities including Gary Lineker. 'Joe, guess who's got the Everton job?' I spluttered. 'Howard Kendall!' And then I went on to explain the events of the day.

Joe was as pleased as I was, and although we needed to keep the lid on it until I intended breaking the story on the following Sunday. He did mention it in confidence to

Lineker, who had spent a season playing for Kendall at Goodison Park before departing for Barcelona. 'Bollocks, he'll never go back,' observed the disbelieving, later to become Match of the Day anchorman. Joe did tell me afterwards when, four days later, came the announcement of Kendall's appointment at Everton, he took a call from Lineker who told him, 'Joe Melling, I'll never doubt another word you tell me!'

But my priority now was the tale, and my chances of getting it improved greatly when circumstances delivered Kendall into my hands, gift-wrapped and tied neatly with an Everton- blue (as opposed to a City-light-blue) ribbon! As luck would have it, City were playing at Sunderland the following Saturday and were staying on the previous night just down the road from my home in Durham at the Royal County Hotel in the city centre. Not so fortunate was the fact that, before he left for the North-East, Kendall had to give an assessment of the City playing situation and its future prospects at the club's annual meeting. Like the man said, it's all about timing!

Blissfully unaware of anything that could possibly spoil what was going to be a wonderful weekend, I took a taxi to the County for a pre-arranged meeting with Kendall. 'No problems?' I ventured. 'Is it all still on and how far can I go with it on Sunday?' My man's expression told me everything, 'Yes, it's all done, but sorry pal, you won't be able to use it.' My enthusiasm drained away like bathwater down the plughole. 'It was never on to tell the City people today with the annual meeting and then coming up here. I won't be doing that until Monday, so I'm afraid we're going have to leave it.'

My mild attempts at protest were pointless; of course, I could see where he was coming from and there wasn't a lot I could do about it. But he did promise to do a first person article for the paper the following weekend; a promise he kept in spite of being offered a lot of money by a couple of red top Sundays.

Now back to McClaren. Steve and I first got acquainted when I had the pleasure of writing the biography of Jim Smith who, at that time, was manager of Derby County. Listening to the Bald Eagle's colourful football stories and then putting them down on paper was a labour of love which necessitated the pair of us getting together on numerous occasions, many of them before and after matches at Pride Park. Jim always invited me into his office for a glass or two of red, and usually it was dispensed by his assistant, Steve McClaren. Smithy had been made aware of this bright, up-and-coming young coach by Maurice Evans, who during his third stint as manager at Oxford United, employed McClaren to look after the reserve team.

Smith, not for the first time demonstrating uncanny foresight, made McClaren his assistant manager and first-team coach. His largely insignificant playing career at places like Hull City, Derby County, Bristol City and finally Oxford, had ended prematurely because of a back injury. Obviously, my close relationship with the 'Eagle'—a diamond of a bloke, albeit at times slightly uncut—contributed, but McClaren and I got on from the word go. Under his wily, vastly knowledgeable and experienced mentor, the young coach blossomed, and together they devised and adopted tactical, mental and physical innovations that have since been copied by every top club in the country.

The results—Derby's comfortable promotion to the Premier League with meagre financial resources—reflected the value of their partnership and Smith felt a great sense of pride knowing he had picked a winner. He also knew that his number two was ambitious and didn't blame him for it. It was no reflection on Derby's status to suggest McClaren was destined for bigger things; indeed Smith harboured intentions of recommending his protégé to succeed him at Pride Park when he felt his time was over.

Up at Old Trafford, Sir Alex Ferguson had been on the lookout for a number two following Brian Kidd's decision to try his luck in management at Blackburn Rovers. Various people had been linked with the job, particularly David Moyes who was doing a great job in charge at Preston North End. In conversations with the Manchester United boss, I knew he rated Moyes, but there was no imminent appointment.

I thought about McClaren; might he be the solution to Fergie's problem? One thing was certain, I could never drop his name in without first clearing it with Jim, and so on one of my visits to Derby, I decided to give it a try. 'Jim. You know Fergie is looking for a number two; would it bother you if I mentioned Steve's name to him?' I ventured. I have to say that your man was not exactly bowled over by the idea, but he didn't knock it either. And I sensed an element of satisfaction in that his 'discovery' could be linked with such a prestigious situation. 'It's up to you. I don't want to lose him but I wouldn't want to stand in his way either,' he said.

A few days later I called Sir Alex who told me he'd had one or two ideas about his number two but it had gone no further than that. 'What about Jim Smith's man at Derby, Steve McClaren,' I wondered. 'Jim thinks he's the business.'

A week or so later I was driving back from covering Newcastle's 2-1 home victory over Aston Villa when Fergie called me on my mobile. 'Cassy, just to let you know I'm going to offer Steve the job.' To say I was ecstatic would be a serious understatement. 'Brilliant,' I bellowed. 'Thanks for telling me. Is it okay to do the tale for tomorrow?' I should have known better. 'No, you'll have to keep it quiet because he doesn't know yet and I'm not going to tell him until next week.'

It was a familiar situation that I knew I would have to go along with. 'But I'll do my best to keep it for you.' His was a well-meaning gesture that was only going to cause me days of mental anguish, hoping and praying that such a headline-making story could lay dormant for seven whole days; the fact that it almost did only made the whole thing worse.

Sunday came and went without a peep. Monday too, and Tuesday. I was twitching like a fried egg but so far so good. However, I just couldn't see the story lasting past Wednesday or, if it did, it would certainly break by Thursday because Derby County were at Old Trafford for a league game on the Wednesday evening, by which time the approach would have been made and the wheels set in motion. In situations like that, football clubs usually have more leaks than a tattered trilby, and with McClaren making what turned out to be his last appearance in the Derby dugout, I couldn't see somebody not getting a sniff.

But Thursday dawned; nothing. Now, I was really starting to believe in miracles. Somehow, I got through the day; making calls, taking calls, always expecting the next one was going to be the one that blew the gaff. It didn't come, and Friday's newspapers were the usual collection of everything that was happening in football— apart from Steve McClaren being appointed number two at Manchester United. Just one more day—that's all I needed; that's how close I was.

The call from the office early in the afternoon was the kick in the guts I'd been expecting all week. There are times when all of us—myself, those who believe they are (in journalistic terms) the greatest thing since lunar travel, and believe me there are many—need to be brought back to earth. This was one of them. Of course, the tale got out; it was bound to. Even if it hadn't, the sight of McClaren supervising the United players in their pre-match warm-up at Nottingham Forest's City Ground on the Saturday afternoon was a bit of a give-away.

I read the stories in the Saturday papers on how McClaren's head was 'spinning' at the prospect of him becoming Ferguson's number two. 'Everything has happened so quickly, I'm in a bit of a whirl and can hardly think straight.' I salvaged a piece for Sunday... how Fergie had made the contact with Jim after the Wednesday game; how the whole thing had been settled at a meeting with the United boss the following day. 'We agreed the package in two minutes and talked football for two hours.' Nice words but in newspaper terms, that's all they were: just words.

By the time they appeared, the real story was history. Ironically, the Forest manager that Saturday was none other than Fergie's United predecessor, Ron Atkinson, who by the final whistle that afternoon had cause to remember McClaren's United debut more than the man himself—his team were demolished 8-1! And, if that wasn't enough of a dream start, it was at the end of that season that United achieved their magnificent European Cup, league title and FA Cup treble, and McClaren was being hailed as one of the best young coaches in the world.

Not that all that was much use to Moyes at the time, but as we all know, he was to have his day at Old Trafford as Ferguson's chosen successor, albeit after a tremendous eleven years in charge at Everton. And, even though his time at Old Trafford soon turned sour, I thought (and still think) he was the right man for the job—if only because it stopped him moaning to me about how I'd cost him the chance to join one of the biggest clubs in the world.

To me there was a surreal irony about Moyes' appointment; it was almost as if United was his destiny. And perhaps for that reason alone, I am convinced that, given time, he would have been successful. As it turned out, applying the principle of sliding doors, Moyes may have been better served by being passed over when McClaren was appointed. Fate was certainly dealing from a stacked deck when United's number two was left high and dry by the events which followed Ferguson's dramatic announcement in May 2001 that he would be quitting at the end of the following season, only to have an about turn some months later.

Certainly, the manager's unforeseen declaration plunged Manchester United into a state of confusion and disarray. 'The decision has been taken that I am going to leave the club. I will have no further involvement. I was offered something I didn't like. I'm off at the end of next season,' he said in a statement on the club's television channel.

At the heart of the turmoil was a personality clash in the corridors of power at Old Trafford, which Ferguson felt was undermining his position. The brinkmanship did not last and common sense kicked in when both sides realised they couldn't do without each other.

CHAPTER TEN
THE BORO BOY

Sir Alex Ferguson's stated intention to stay for just one more season forced Steve McClaren to consider his options, and one of those was abruptly removed by the United hierarchy when they made it clear he would not be considered as the Scot's successor. The probability that whoever did come in would recruit his own back-room staff meant the coach had little choice but to look for another job.

Fortunately, West Ham United made him their number one target to take over from the recently sacked Harry Redknapp, who added weight to what was popular speculation by announcing that McClaren would indeed be switching to Upton Park. 'Steve has been speaking to the club all week and it's obvious he fancies the job,' said Harry at the time. Believing this to be the situation, especially with back page headlines suggesting McClaren was on the brink of being named The Hammers' new boss, I had no reason to contact him save for wishing him the best of luck when it did happen.

I was more occupied with the managerial situation at Middlesbrough which more than matched the Casey's court that was occurring at Old Trafford. Confused? We certainly were. Bryan Robson's relationship with the supporters had deteriorated in spite of the manager's excellent record in his seven years in charge. Robbo had shown great courage in bringing in Terry Venables as first team coach to successfully retrieve what had seemed like a lost cause when the team escaped relegation but, with all the indications pointing to Venables reverting to his regular role as a television pundit, the big question was where did that leave the manager.

Robbo wanted to return to the pre-Venables position when he was in sole control, but my inside information was that the club's owner and benefactor, Steve Gibson, had no intention of allowing that to happen. Without question Gibson's desire at the time was to persuade Venables to take over as manager, with Robbo occupying a lesser role—and he tried his utmost to make it happen. On May 20[th,] I wrote a story revealing that the former England manager had had a dramatic change of mind about leaving the club, just hours after informing Gibson he was on his way out. He told me, 'Steve put something to me and asked what I felt about it. I said I would have to think about it but we're still talking.'

With the McClaren for West Ham story all over the papers the following day, it seemed Venables only had to say 'yes' to get back into full-time football management. Well not quite, because 24 hours later, as far as El Tel was concerned, all bets were off.

I had been a guest at the League Managers' Association annual dinner in Nottingham on the Monday evening; as always it was a cracking do with anybody who's anybody in attendance. I've always had a good relationship with the LMA in general and with their then Chief Executive John Barnwell, and I was desperately sorry when Barny retired after ten years expertly running the show. Of course, such an occasion couldn't be better for contacts; old and new and it was good to see, talk to and have a drink with many friends. But one of the conversations turned out to be far more significant than the rest.

In one of the bars I spied Billy McEwan, a Scot with whom I had an allegiance because of his brief spell as Darlington manager in the early nineties. We became re-acquainted at Derby County where he was a member of Jim Smith's back-room staff, and it was good to chat with him again. 'What's happening at Middlesbrough?' he wondered. I told him what I knew, which wasn't a lot; Venables could have the job if he wanted it but Robbo seemed to be struggling to stay in there.

'What about Stevie Mac? Why hasn't he had a mention about the job?' I reminded Billy about that morning's back pages. 'Well he's off to West Ham, isn't he?' I said. 'I don't know about that, but I'd bet he'd fancy the Middlesbrough job more if he got the chance.' Billy, switched on as usual, had a point! It was getting late and I promised him I would make a few calls the next day and let him know the score.

The more I contemplated it, the more it began to ring bells. My last thought before sleep was the same as my first when I woke up in my room at the Moat House Hotel, Nottingham. The next morning I needed to ring

Steve Gibson. I've always believed he was someone I could have an off-the-record conversation with; a card mark. If he was going to tell me the manager was going to be Venables—or even Robson for that matter—that would have been where the conversation ended without any mention of McClaren. I had no intention of back-stabbing anybody.

The drama that was to change the lives of Steve McClaren, Steve Gibson, a handful of coaches and back-room staff, thousands of Middlesbrough supporters (but sadly not mine—not by much anyway) began a little after eight o'clock that morning when I made the first of several phone calls, starting with Gibson. After the primary niceties such as apologising for ringing so early, I cut to the chase. 'Steve, I might have something of interest to pass on but first are you able to tell me off the record what is the situation regarding the manager.'

We fenced around for a few minutes before I established that both Venables and Robson were not in the frame. It was then, and only then, that I introduced McClaren into the conversation. 'Would you be interested in talking to him?' I wondered. He reacted instantly; in fact, he almost came down the phone line. 'I would, very much. Can you arrange it?' he said. I told him I would get back as soon as possible before contemplating my next move which, as it happened, was to discover whether McClaren was as keen about moving to Teesside as Gibson was in getting him there. As far as I knew, he had never even thought about taking over at Middlesbrough; it was all my idea with a bit of help from Billy McEwan of course.

The next call was to McClaren's mobile. I caught him as he was preparing to leave for a meeting with representatives of West Ham that would clinch the deal. 'If it's not too late, Steve Gibson wants to talk to you about Middlesbrough. Would you be interested or not?' I asked him. There was no immediate response this time, just questions about Boro. What was happening to the people already there and so on. In fact, I spent the next hour making several calls alternately to the two Steves, eliciting and passing on information and requests, and finally the demands which would be conditional to any direct personal contact between the pair.

McClaren clearly wavered to the extent that—in our penultimate conversation that morning—he told me to thank Gibson for his interest but he was going ahead with the West Ham meeting. But he did agree to allow me to pass on his number to the Middlesbrough chairman. 'At least talk to him before you decide what to do; what have you got to lose?' I urged, setting a great store by Gibson's gift of the gab.

Few chairmen have a greater devotion to their clubs than the former ICI office boy who had not only (almost single-handedly) built up a multi-million-pound business bulk-hauling chemicals all over Europe, but also dragged his home-town football club back from the brink of extinction and established it in the Premier League—and all before he was forty. I knew if they got together, Gibson's enterprise and enthusiasm would rub off. And I was right.

I was on the M1 heading back to the North-East when McClaren called to say the two of them would be meeting that afternoon. Game, set and match to Middlesbrough! At least this time I was spared the suspense of wondering whether the story would keep until the weekend; Boro's hijacking of McClaren was big news the following day, although the suggestion in some papers that he was going as first-team coach to Venables's director of football was a long way from the truth. I spoke of McClaren's conditions; two of those were that neither he nor Robson would be involved— McClaren was adamant about bringing in his own men.

Once again, I was left to pick up the pieces which I managed to do by speaking to the new Boro boss in Florida, where he and his family had escaped for a holiday. I obtained an exclusive interview, and he didn't pull any punches, declaring he had left what he had regarded as his dream job as assistant boss at Manchester United after it became clear he would not be promoted to the manager's office when Ferguson quit at the end of the following season.

He also revealed that he had been cold-shouldered by the Old Trafford hierarchy in spite of his former boss recommending to them that he should become his successor. 'I realised I was well down the pecking order,' he told me. 'Sir Alex thought I was good enough to take over from him—there can be no higher praise than that. At Middlesbrough, I hope to prove he was right. McClaren also disclosed just how close he was to going to West Ham—and Southampton for that matter— before I intervened. 'I was impressed with what I heard when speaking to their chairmen. They represented tremendous opportunities for someone like me attempting to bridge the gap between coaching and management.

'But, as soon as I spoke to Steve Gibson, I knew it was the club for me. I am ambitious but I don't think I've come across anybody who combines Gibson's ambition with such enthusiasm, optimism and drive. People say that nobody in their right mind would leave Manchester United and ninety-nine times out of a hundred that would be true, but I had reached the stage where I needed to take a change in direction and the chance to manage a terrific club like Middlesbrough provided it.'

I feel proud about my part in McClaren's elevation from Derby first team coach to England team manager. Granted he would never have made it had he not proved himself, first at Man U where he was part of the back-room staff which helped the team win the European Cup, an FA Cup and three successive Premier League titles, and then at Middlesbrough, where in his five years he guided them to their first European competition, the final of the UEFA Cup where they lost to Sevilla, their highest Premier League finish, and last but certainly not least, the first major trophy in their 128-year history, the 2004 League Cup.

And there was nobody in the whole of Cardiff leaping higher on the Leap Year day than Steve Gibson, who even ran on to the pitch with the rest of the punters and was carried shoulder high by the players. 'We needed a trophy,' he said later. 'It may not mean much to Arsenal, Manchester United or Chelsea, but it's so important for us.'

Would it all have happened if McClaren had gone to West Ham five years earlier? For that matter, would it have happened had he not gone to United when, as seemed likely, his first managerial job would have been succeeding Jim Smith at Derby County? We'll never know. As it turned out, McClaren need never have left Old Trafford. Sir Alex—having set the wheels in motion to take up an ambassadorial role when he quit at the end of the 2001-2 season—decided the day after his 60th birthday, the previous New Year's Eve, that he would be better spreading the United gospel by staying on as manager.

He later told me what happened in the dressing room at the club's Carrington training quarters when he told the players he'd changed his mind. 'Lads, I have something important I want to tell you. I have decided to stay on as your manager.' He remembered the pause was long enough for him to start believing he might not have done the right thing, and then: spontaneous applause. 'They just clapped, every one of them. It was embarrassing.' It's neither here nor there that he also told me the contract he had signed until 2005 would be his last. Well, we all know what happened to that well-intentioned declaration!

'The way things have worked out I am sure Steve would have stayed. I'll be speaking to him because I owe him that,' he told me. And he did, and McClaren wavered before deciding to stay at Middlesbrough.

If fate shaped Moyes' path to Old Trafford, it was no less active in orchestrating McClaren's managerial career.

Of course, the whole England thing went belly up. Dignity and reputation were restored after he followed Sir Bobby Robson's example by achieving success in Holland, albeit with a much less fashionable club.

Winning the Dutch Eredivisie title with Twente Enschede in his first venture since leaving England was the equivalent of Wigan Athletic landing the Premier League title.

CHAPTER ELEVEN
'WE'RE IN HEAVEN...

...we've got Kevin'. All right, the couplet was a colourful attempt by Newcastle United's popular chief executive Russell Cushing to triumphantly reveal a secret that, at the very least, was going to revolutionise life as we knew it. There was just one slight problem. As revelations go, this was just about on a par with the non-existence of fairies at the bottom of your garden.

Two years earlier, Lawrie McMenemy, Southampton's Geordie-born manager, had stopped the football world in its tracks with his magnificent, totally unexpected swoop for Kevin Keegan. The former Liverpool star's arrival at The Dell from SV Hamburg may have caught the Southern press with their pants down but if there was to be a surprise this time it could only have been the fact that United officials entertained notions of doing the same on Tyneside.

Above all, they should have realised who they were dealing with. This was the North-East; the hotbed of soccer, where dogs bark the best kept secrets and the internet comes a poor second to the pigeons. We were on to Keegan even before his alarm clock woke him up that morning. We were waiting at St James' Park when he arrived, we trailed him to and from his medical at the club doctor's surgery in Sedgefield, forty miles away; and we were in place at the hotel alongside Newcastle racecourse almost before it was declared to be the venue for a 'significant' press conference.

But hey, what the hell. It was a great occasion and I was completely engulfed in the sheer spectacle of it all in spite of a typically wonderful element of farce when the great man entered stage left and Cushing, after delivering his rhyme, gestured to the opposite wing. Laugh? I'll say. In fact, the 'stunned' media in the Gosforth Park Hotel on the evening of Thursday, August 19th, 1982 were falling off their seats with uncontrollable mirth.

I couldn't resist having my tanner's worth. 'It's a good job you didn't sign Ritchie Pitt!' I shouted to even more side-splitting hysterics.

So, all right we weren't 'stunned' by the time Keegan emerged I doubt whether his arrival on Tyneside would have surprised a sleepy septuagenarian in a care home in Craster. After all, for most of the previous twelve hours or so hadn't he been pursued all over the North-East by a crazy convoy of journalists' cars that made 'Wacky Races' look like the London to Brighton vintage car rally.

Surprise, surprise; it wasn't.

If the occasion was the beginning of a magnificent obsession, Newcastle supporters enjoyed with somebody who ranks alongside immortals such as Jackie Milburn, Joe Harvey, Hughie Gallagher and Alan Shearer in the

Toon Army's affections, it was also the start of a personal relationship which had more ups and downs than the biggest big dipper. Mostly, beginning with his time at United, first as a player and then manager, Keegan and I got on pretty well. I was privileged to work closely with him and to become acquainted with his immediate family.

We broke great stories, accompanied each other on trips all over Europe, enjoyed social occasions, played golf, had days at the races, and even fall afoul of the law together! Professionally in all my dealings with players, managers, officials, whether it be football or any other sport for that matter, I have never come across anybody (with the possible exception of Brian Clough) who was better to deal with inasmuch as he knew exactly what newspapers wanted in terms of a story. He talked in headline type; he was a football journo's Godsend.

But let's go back to the beginning and that night in Newcastle. I had never met Keegan before and my brief from The Sun's sports editor, Peter Boyer, was not only to cover the Press conference but also to get him signed up to do a series for the paper for which he would obviously be handsomely paid. I took advice from Vince Wilson who had 'ghosted' Keegan for many years on the Sunday Mirror, 'He's great to deal with, as long as you stay on the right side of him,' Vince told me. It was a veiled warning that I was determined to heed; after all, Keegan was the epitome of every schoolboy's football idol; he was one of the game's great icons and I was thrilled to have the opportunity of working closely with him.

I was relieved when he gave his tacit approval to the arrangement; the nuts and bolts of the deal were sorted out with his agent, the indomitable Harry Swales, and within a couple of days we were in business. Keegan was signed up to do a series of first person articles for The Sun and yours truly was entrusted with the not insignificant role of interviewing him and writing them. It was an exciting assignment, as important as I've ever had.

During the course of our association I became the first journalist to hear him come out with some of the best football stories of the decade. But always I was conscious of having to watch my p's and q's. Keegan had (and probably still has) the kind of precious personality that required kid glove treatment. His demeanour could change in a heartbeat. At one of our first meetings, he made it clear that everything would be done on his terms. 'If you ever let me down, there will be no way back,' he warned.

If, regrettably, our relationship did turn sour, it was more because of circumstances rather than me letting him down. He would not accept that. I suppose when you afford yourself the luxury of an outlook which is totally without compromise; where there is only black and white, it was inevitable that he should play for and later manage Newcastle United.

But all that came later. On Saturday August 28th, 1982, I hitched a ride on Kevin Keegan's bandwagon and over the next two years wrote some of the best stories The Sun's cash could buy. I didn't know what it cost the paper; what's more I didn't care. All I did know was that if there is a price to pay for impact, it was money well spent.

Sure, I was proud to commit his words to paper and I certainly got a kick out of the blockbuster headlines and the 'herograms' from the gaffer, but in truth, give or take a tickle here or a comma there, it took no writing at all. It was a complete doddle.

Let's start with day one; a screaming white on black that almost filled the back page: 'KEEGAN'S KINGDOM'. It sat above a piece in which our hero proclaimed that his new role as Newcastle captain would be equal to anything he had done before, and this was a man who had played in European Cup finals, FA Cup finals, league championship victories—even for England during the World Cup!

Inevitably when it came to showing Newcastle fans what he was made of, he made the headlines, scoring the only goal on his debut against Queen's Park Rangers. Equally inevitable was the blanket coverage in the Saturday sports editions and the Sunday papers. Much to my alarm, Keegan, ever the showman on AND off the field, haemorrhaged quotes to voracious colleagues like someone celebrating a recently bestowed gift of speech.

I was worried; as far as I was concerned Saturday's Sun was fish and chip paper; now it was all about Monday. My rivals went away with bulging notebooks and white hot recording machines but my arse was against the wall. How the hell was Keegan going to come up with something different for his follow-up piece for us?

Should I have been concerned? Of course not. He may have sung like a canary to the others but he kept quiet about the little nugget that produced another eyeball clutching back page headline. 'MY SECRET AGONY' bellowed the block heading in 144 points with Keegan dramatically revealing how it had been touch and go whether he made his dream debut. Obligingly he had aggravated a nagging heel injury in training and the extent of the problem had been the best-kept secret of the week. The United skipper had even risked further serious injury by declining a pain-killing injection before the game. 'After all, what was a bit of a twinge on a day I'll always remember.' Like I said, pure theatre!

Almost in passing, he made reference at the end of the piece to the fact that the newly appointed England manager Bobby Robson had been at the game. 'I hope he liked what he saw. I still want to be involved with the international team.' The significance of those words were to hit home a few weeks later when Keegan called me to deliver another sensational exclusive; the day he blasted Robson for ending his England career.

In a scenario that was mirrored by Steve McClaren's apparent rejection of David Beckham almost 25 years later, Robson had shaken the soccer world to its foundations with his decision to omit the then England skipper from his first international squad for a match against Denmark. The big difference, in Keegan's book anyway, was the way the news was imparted to him; McClaren informed Beckham privately before announcing his line-up for a friendly against Greece— Keegan, clearly devastated as well as hopping mad, learned it from the United manager Arthur Cox who had heard it on the radio. And, unlike Beckham, he was not about to go quietly.

It wasn't long before he was on the phone telling me he wanted to see me. I drove up to meet him at Matfen Hall, north of Newcastle, where he and his team-mates had been playing golf. He didn't mess about, launching into a furious attack on Robson.

The intro to yet another back page stormer was a taste of what followed: 'I'm finished with England. I'll never kick a ball for my country again.' And he went on to charge the England boss with shocking man management as well as judgement—no personal contact with a player who had won 60 caps in ten years, just an announcement to the media. 'In my opinion, the way he has handled the selection of his first squad is disgraceful,' he ranted. It might have been England's loss, but it was certainly The Sun's gain. The powers that be were delighted.

Later after he broke thousands of Geordie hearts by hanging up his boots, Keegan elaborated on his beef with Robson in a week-long series of articles that put thousands on the circulation. But there was to be plenty of water to flow under the famous Tyne Bridge before that. Whenever there was an issue worthy of his attention and comment, out came my cassette recorder to register more gems for posterity; like when he threatened to quit Newcastle because he felt the club was selling the fans short in the transfer market. That did the trick all right! And particularly when he chose the occasion of his 33rd birthday, February 14th, 1984, to announce to a shocked football world in general and a devastated Toon Army in particular that he was in his last season as a player, ironically observing in the same article, 'I have absolutely no interest in management. It's just not me.'

Peter Boyer, well pleased with everything that had gone before, had allowed the momentum of Keegan's apparent farewell to football subside before handing me another special assignment. Without question the series of articles that followed were the biggest and best he's done for the paper—before or since. 'I want the definitive Kevin Keegan story from his days as a kid in Doncaster when he washed cars for pocket money to the end of his playing career, and I want you to write it,' said Boyer.

Arranging the time and place of the interviews was hardly the most onerous task I had ever undertaken. 'Look, it's up to you,' Keegan offered. 'You can either come and see me at my place in Hampshire or wait for a few days when I'll be taking the family to our villa in Spain. If you want to tell your office that's where I want to do the stuff it's okay by me.' Well it was okay by me too, and it wasn't long before I was on my way to Marbella and the beautiful Los Monteros Hotel close to where the Keegan family were staying in their villa on the edge of the seventh green at the fabulous Rio Real golf course.

'Right, when do you want to start?' asked Keegan as we chatted over a morning coffee, soaking up the late August sunshine in an idyllic setting by the hotel pool. 'We could have daily sessions around this time or I could come this afternoon and we do the lot in one hit.

That way you he can relax for the rest of the week; get some rays, play a bit of golf and take your time over writing the articles.'

Not unnaturally I plumped for the latter and his hospitality knew no limits, from a couple of friendly four-balls to dinners with himself and his family. And, as always, the stuff just leapt off the keyboard, starting with the real reasons for his shock decision to leave Liverpool at his peak to join Hamburg, which was all to do with his disenchantment following Bill Shankly's resignation and Bob Paisley's appointment. As he put it: 'Liverpool died for me when Shankly left. Without him the club was never the same.'

That was followed the next day by revelations about why he quit Southampton and an even stronger blast at Lawrie McMenemy. As the paper claimed a 'Sun Sport world scoop' under the gigantic one-word headline 'CHEAT', Keegan pulled no punches. 'The transfer that shocked football—my move to Southampton from Hamburg—all started because Lawrie McMenemy wanted me to get him a lamp. But when I left the Saints two years later my feelings towards him weren't worth a light! All my respect and regard for the Southampton manager died the day he called me a cheat.' He went on to claim that McMenemy accused him of cheating in a match against Aston Villa. 'The minute he said that he'd lost me. I just told him, "that's it, finished," and I walked out.'

And as comedian Jimmy Cricket would say: there was more, a lot more. Day three was a disclosure about how his Newcastle contract was based on a share of the gate, netting him around £3,000 a week over the two years—chicken feed now but a small fortune two decades ago. In day four he told of his struggle for recognition at Hamburg before (in the fifth and final article) the sledgehammer came out again with another pummelling for Bobby Robson, citing him for hastening the end of his 16-year playing career. 'Had I still been in the England team I would still be playing league football. It's as simple as that.'

Having listened to him not only sound off about some of the game's luminaries but also give the green light to his somewhat controversial views being published, it was interesting to note how time and circumstances had changed his perception of people when it came to his autobiography some twelve years later. His views on Paisley were similar but carried none of the emotional rhetoric of the Sun article and his reference to his final days and reasons for leaving Southampton were considerably milder. McMenemy got off lightly in comparison.

Maybe the kind of uncharacteristic diplomacy I witnessed since he returned as manager of Newcastle had kicked in but, no matter, when he was in full flow that decade or so earlier Keegan was a red top's dream as he delivered every withering word, hardly sparing some of the game's most precious reputations. Ghosting his articles may have been hard work under a lot of pressure but it was fun too. There were many pleasant diversions, especially when it came to our mutual interest in horse racing. He instigated what for me became something of an obsession with my favourite racehorse ever, Desert Orchid, by telling me to watch out for it when it had barely seen a racecourse.

And there was an afternoon at Sedgefield races that is etched forever in my memory. It was a freezing, wet day in late autumn, but I, Keegan and a gang of Newcastle players including Terry McDermott and Glenn Roeder braved the elements. As well as fancying a couple at Sedgefield, they had good information about another horse—the name of which escapes me, but let's call it 'Blunderbuss'—running at Newmarket at what looked like being a big price. After lumping a small fortune on the animal at 16-1 we stood huddled together against the grandstand wall listening to the race commentary on the blower (no SIS in warm betting offices in those days).

Understandably the lads had been hoping to be relatively invisible, wanting to enjoy the races without being pestered too much by punters. That would probably have happened too had the horse craved similar anonymity! 'They're running at Newmarket,' rasped the female voice over the blower before going on to mention almost every horse apart from ours in what was a relatively short race. Muttered recriminations had already begun, 'Where did you get that from'—I think the accusing finger was pointing at Roeder—and then suddenly, dramatically, as the field entered the last furlong, 'And finishing best of all is Blunderbuss'. The change of mood was instant as half a dozen would-be incognito football stars started dancing up and down like deranged dervishes. 'Go on my son! C'mon Blunderbuss, get in you beauty.' All right, so they had to sign a few autographs after it was called the winner, but it was worth it.

On another occasion Keegan informed me he was returning to Germany to play in a testimonial match and invited me along for the trip. He made sure I wasn't left out of anything; directors' box for the match, VIP treatment at the official reception, introduction to some of Germany's greatest international players. Ludicrously he blotted his copybook once when he and I went for dinner with that great midfielder, Gunther Netzer. The pair chatted happily in German, making me feel like something that was spare at a wedding. And then, incredibly, they started whispering in German! 'Excuse me, Kev. Why are you whispering?' I said. 'Talk as loud as you like in German. I can't understand a word of it.' We had a great laugh about that.

So where did it all go wrong? At best, it was a misunderstanding that mushroomed into something much more serious; at worse it was either Keegan chickening out on a statement he'd made, or a grave error of judgement on my part. Either way the pair of us was done no favours by my colleagues on the paper. Our arrangement throughout our association was he would either see the articles before they went into print or I read them out to him. My understanding was, during our interviews, everything was on the record unless stipulated otherwise by him or my experience told me it would be better if certain statements were toned down. It was never a problem and his willing corroboration meant the paper could trailer the following day's article in terms such as 'Tomorrow Keegan reveals so and so.'

It was during another series of articles, which again necessitated a few days in sunny Spain, that he took exception to one such trailer. 'I don't want that in; it was off the record,' he insisted to my surprise. My protests that 'off the record' was never mentioned (he certainly never said it on tape) were angrily waved aside. 'Look, it is not going in and that's an end to it.' Fair enough. I told him I would contact my sports desk and get the offending article pulled, simple as that—or so I thought. The message from a chap called John Roberts who was in charge that day was, 'No chance, the pages are already made up and it's too late to change.' And none of my begging and pleading could alter the situation. The article went in and as far as Keegan was concerned, I went out!

Roll the calendar on eight years or so, during which time I had moved from The Sun to work alongside Joe Melling at The Mail on Sunday. Keegan had always been cool and unresponsive when we met, usually when he was doing promotional work in the North-East or when he became part of the media circus covering England. But our paths crossed most unexpectedly when, following the John Hall-sparked boardroom metamorphosis at Newcastle United, Keegan underwent what was for him a seismographic change of direction when he was appointed manager. So much for his earlier pronouncements that management was not his style or that he was never coming back to football full-time. Even the reasons for his return; 'Managing Newcastle was the only job I would come back to football for,' had (in hindsight) a hollow ring when he later took the jobs with Fulham, England and Manchester City.

CHAPTER TWELVE
KEV'S HAPPY RETURN

Keegan's second coming to Tyneside in 1992 was a master stroke, orchestrated solely by the United Chief Executive, the late and sadly missed Freddie Fletcher. Freddie was a brilliant administrator who achieved as much off the field in those glory years as the manager did on it. Stand on me, although several have attempted to take the credit for the appointment, it was a blinding flash of inspiration on Fletcher's part that not only set the wheels in motion but also made sure the train arrived at its destination.

Shrewdly, he engineered the initial approach through Alistair Wilson, a wonderful man as well as being the big cheese at Scottish and Newcastle Breweries. If any persuasion was needed, Alistair—a close friend and confidante of Keegan's since the company sponsored his soccer days when he was a player at United—was just the man to apply it. Once Keegan had given Alistair the green light, Fletcher, with only minor acknowledgment from his superiors, ruthlessly dispensed with the previous managerial incumbent, Ossie Ardiles, along with a couple of hopeful successors, ironically including future manager, Glenn Roeder.

From a professional as well as personal point of view, most of the time Keegan was a dream to work with. Notwithstanding the fact he was always liable to regurgitate our previous problem, gradually we went some of the way towards resuming our earlier relationship. I accept there was none of the intimacy we enjoyed when I was ghosting his stuff (incidentally any argument he had with The Sun did not deter him from later resuming a highly remunerative association with the paper). Guiding Newcastle on that march that took them from the bowels of what was the equivalent of today's Championship to the top of the Premier League earned him universal veneration from supporters as well as the media.

In those days, Newcastle United were everybody's second team. It was open house at the training ground in Durham; unlimited access to players, daily press conferences—we didn't know we were born. And, if the opportunity presented itself, he was always generous with his time even when the circumstances made it seem unlikely.

My eldest daughter Alison is now head at a school in Corby, Northamptonshire, but she was running the English department when the then headmaster wondered if Keegan would be prepared to open a new wing at the school. It seemed a dead liberty to even ask him and, in fairness, he did wonder how he could fit such a journey into his hectic schedule. But he didn't rule it out and unbelievably, he eventually agreed to do it on a Friday evening before Newcastle played at Aston Villa the following day. It meant a four-hour round trip from the team's hotel in Birmingham on one of the busiest traffic nights of the week but, accompanied by the aforementioned Freddie Fletcher, and after battling through the huge crowd that had gathered outside the school, he performed the ceremony in his own inimitable style, meeting and greeting everybody, posing for countless cameras, acceding to every autograph request.

The remarkable thing was that Princess Margaret was attending an official function in the area that night and special police arrangements had been made to control the large number of sightseers that had been expected. As it turned out, most of the police were diverted to the school where the turnout was twenty times more. The special plaque on the wall of Lodge Park School—September 30th, 1994—bears testimony to Keegan's visit, and he was never offered nor asked for a penny. In fact, doing me a favour cost him money!

Unfortunately for the pair of us, not all of the Northamptonshire Constabulary were concerned with Keegan or Princess Margaret. In a lay-by on the A14 lurked a copper with a camera, and he was snap-happy. I had made the trip myself, albeit in my own car, and on the dash back to Birmingham, the vigilant bobby nicked us both in quick succession for speeding. Keegan picked up a fine and three points on his driving licence for his trouble. Fortunately, he managed another three points the following day when Newcastle gained a superb 2-0 victory at Villa.

As Keegan reflected in his autobiography, his love affair with Newcastle United began to wane after he lost out to Manchester United in the title race in 1996. It is a crying shame that for all he achieved while in charge at St James's Park, he will be forever remembered for his emotionally charged 'I'd love it' televised rant at Sir Alex Ferguson. I've already mentioned how the Man United boss regarded that particular occasion, but ill-advised though it might have been, it nevertheless reflected the way Keegan wore his heart on his sleeve. Rarely from a manager do you see such unreserved passion and commitment on public display. It also showed how much he hated to lose.

But really, it was the beginning of the end of his time on Tyneside. After the crushing disappointment of throwing away an 11-point Premier League lead at the end of February, it was only a matter of time before he quit. In fact, he threatened to do just that on several occasions, one of which was the catalyst for our second major fall-out.

Myself and—to an even greater degree—Joe Melling, always enjoyed a close relationship with Sir John Hall to the extent that Joe had his card marked by the United chairman on any number of important club issues. One of which led Joe to tip me off that Keegan had cried wolf once too often—he was going to resign after the last game of that season against Tottenham Hotspur.

It was a sensational story that was the perfect Sunday morning scoop on the day of the match, but there was a complication. Joe wanted me to write it because he was concerned people at Newcastle knew of his association with the chairman and would guess the source of the story if his name appeared on it. I agreed on the proviso that I could make my own checks. I rang Fletcher and asked if the story was correct. He replied, 'No, you are a week too late. It has all been sorted out and he is staying.'

I subsequently learned that Keegan had indeed informed the chief executive that the Spurs game would be his last, so much so that Fletcher had contacted a number of managers including Roy Hodgson who was with Blackburn Rovers at the time, John Toshack who was coaching in Spain, and Sir Bobby Robson who was gathering trophies like apples in an orchard in Portugal. But then Keegan apparently had second thoughts to the extent that he asked his assistant Terry McDermott to call the chief executive and tell him he had changed his mind. Unfortunately, Fletcher was at a wedding and could not be reached, so McDermott rang Sir John Hall's son Douglas, who was also a director, instead. By the time Fletcher could be contacted the matter had been resolved, hence his explanation when I called him.

I wanted to kill the story, but under sufferance agreed to a toned-down version under the headline 'Keegan on the Brink'. The first sentence read, 'Kevin Keegan will decide in the next 48 hours whether to stay as manager of Newcastle,' but I was more pleased with the quote from Fletcher later in the piece which assured fans he would be manager on the opening day of the following season—which he was. Of course, I knew Keegan would not be happy but I was too upset about writing something I knew to be inaccurate to give a toss. And he was gone within nine months anyway.

I didn't see much of him when he was manager of Fulham and our contact when he was in charge of England—and to a lesser extent during his time at Manchester City—was strictly professional. It was a pity he came back to Newcastle after allowing himself to be drawn into the three-ringed managerial circus at Newcastle instigated by Mike Ashley and his cronies, even if his brief involvement highlighted the ham-fisted manner in which the club was run.

If our association did not exactly end in tears, I would have preferred a more convivial conclusion. Because, in spite of the disagreements, had our paths never crossed, my career as a football journalist would have been considerably less fulfilled.

CHAPTER THIRTEEN
HILLSBOROUGH

The evening of Friday April 14, 1989 passed like most pre-match evenings when Joe Melling and I got together; hotel, a nice dinner preceded by the obligatory g and t's, a couple of bottles of decent red, maybe a brandy or three and an agreement to hit the sack only when we'd chewed the fat until our jaws ached, hurling a few smart-arsed reputations into the waste-bin in the process.

On this particular evening, it took us even longer to reach Slumberland. That was because Melling decided the attraction of a neon-lit snooker hall sign was one which just could not be ignored. I agreed under protest: a) because I was nowhere near as good on the green baize as he was when I was sober; b) because being more than a touch myopic it was difficult to co-ordinate proper cue action from one end of the table to the other; and c) because in my inebriated condition I could see twice as many balls on the table than there should have been.

So much for how professional journalists should prepare for a big game and this was indeed a big one: Brian Clough's Nottingham Forest against Kenny

Dalglish's Liverpool in the semi-final of the FA Cup at Hillsborough, the home of Sheffield Wednesday. It was a repeat of the previous season's semi when Liverpool won 2-1 at the same venue and the place was beginning to throb with excitement.

But not quite as much as my head on that Saturday morning, and it was only mild consolation to discover Melling in a similar state. After the usual fry-up breakfast, we both decided fresh air would be the best remedy for our fragile condition, so off we trudged on a pretty long walk to Hillsborough.

Fortunately, we arrived some time before the buses and trains ferried in the fans. There were a few familiar faces in the guest room, including Lawrie McMenemy and we swapped a few opinions about the likely outcome of the match and football in general, so much so that by the time I climbed the stairs and found my seat in the press box, a couple of paracetamols had perked me up no end.

The instructions were what they always were when the pair of us covered a match together; Joe would write the report and I was responsible for the quotes story. We had the use of a normal telephone landline but Joe was also carrying one of the new-fangled mobiles, which was about the size of a building brick.

The first hint of a problem came before the players came out of the tunnel, when a young-looking male was lifted over the fence at the Leppings Lane end, clearly in an unconscious state. The medics took immediate action, giving him mouth-to-mouth and other methods of resuscitation while the crowd watched silent and spellbound. There was even a spontaneous cheer when it seemed the chap had regained consciousness before being stretchered from the pitch.

From where we were watching this looked like an isolated incident. We had no idea of the tragedy developing to our left—and neither it seemed did the match referee, Ray Lewis, or his fellow officials. Nor the players, managers and bench personnel—when the game kicked off on time.

Initially, the first trickle of fans, either climbing or being lifted over the fence at the Leppings Lane end, indicated a possible pitch invasion. There were a few chants of 'hooligans' aimed at the Liverpool end from Forest supporters on the opposite terraces and I certainly witnessed some police attempts to prevent people getting on to the pitch by pushing them back into the enclosure.

But when the trickle became an overwhelming torrent, with fans littering the area around the goalmouth after reaching the safety of the playing area, it was clear this was no pitch invasion. Slowly the realisation dawned on everybody watching the catastrophic scene, that this was much, much worse than that.

Referee Lewis had no option but to stop the game six minutes after he started it and order the players back to their dressing rooms. Inevitably the press box landlines were hot with calls from bosses desperate to be put in the picture. Television stations covering the game live were able to depict the whole sorry debacle, but there was no indication about its cause or the scale of the horror occurring before their cameras.

Joe took yet another call from the boss before turning to me to say, 'Right. They want you to find out what's happening. Try to find someone who will give you an official comment.' He handed me the 'building brick' and added, 'Write down our number and call me when you've got something.'

Along with a bunch of other journos, I dashed down the stairs and out into the perimeter of the ground. But, while the others turned left towards the main entrance, I headed in the opposite direction and the chaos of Leppings Lane.

In the utter confusion of the situation there was no need to appear inconspicuous. Police, ambulance crews and other medical people, stewards and supporters were rushing to and fro, assisting the walking wounded and carrying out prostrate bodies on any makeshift apparatus. A couple of nurses came up to me, told me where they were from and asked if they could help. I pointed towards a shirt-sleeved guy bending over a stretched out body and advised them to go and talk to him.

And then I saw something which stopped me in my tracks; a sight that will live forever in my memory. Lined up in a row alongside the fence which separated the path from the River Don there must have been twenty or thirty lifeless figures, most of them lying on blankets or advertising boards doubling as makeshift stretchers. The image of the first—a heavy, dark-haired guy with his white tee shirt stretched over his stomach—is still an indelible one.

I approached a young St Johns Ambulance uniformed female and asked, 'Have they fainted?' 'Sadly no,' she replied. 'I'm afraid these poor people have died.'

It was a stomach-churning moment and I quickly realised this was no longer a safe place to be. I had to leave, and quickly; both out of respect for the victims and because I was in danger of being accosted by anyone of a number of police personnel desperately trying to bring order to the situation.

I raced back to the press box, calling Joe on the way to inform him about what I'd seen. By the time we got together again, having passed the news on to the office, he grabbed me and demanded, 'Pal, are you sure about the number of dead? All the BBC is saying is that they believe there have been serious casualties.'

My shaking condition plus a few expletives about useless Mail On Sunday staff sitting on their arses in front of television screens convinced him what I had seen was genuine. But for me the trauma of that afternoon was far from over.

The landline rang again. Joe picked it up, told the caller 'He's standing next to me' and passed it over. 'It's the editor. He wants to speak to you.' I recognised the voice of Stewart Steven. 'Bob, it's Stewart. Look we've had a report that the police are saying Liverpool fans smashed the gates down. I need you to go and look at them to check whether it's true'.

There could be no discussion; no dissent. This was a crucial factor which was eventually going to expose and then condemn the police's handling of the situation. I had to go back to Leppings Lane.

This time I did not hang about. Keeping my head down and disregarding anything en route I walked quickly towards the end of the ground and looked up at the exit gates. Quite plainly they had been rolled back on their runners and were standing open. In any event they must have been three or four inches thick and would have needed a bulldozer to break them down.

As before, I passed on my findings to Joe on the way back. Relieved, but still shaking, I sought the sanctuary of the stairs and the press box where my colleague was waiting, wearing an expression which swiftly turned relief into more anxiety. 'Look, Bob, the editor says it's vital we have to be one hundred and ten per cent sure about the gates,' he said. 'You have to go back, just to look at them again and make certain.'

So, I did and drew the same conclusion. And that was my last foray into that scene of indescribable devastation.

Joe wrote the story, for which he won an award, under the front-page banner headline: 'THE GATES OF HELL'. Probably just as well because by this time, I was a hyperactive mess, struggling to erase the images of that afternoon from my mind. I still can't.

But, after contributing to the story by complying with every demand, I flatly refused the final one when Joe passed on another instruction that I was required to write a piece describing everything I had seen. 'Joe, I just can't do it, I feel wiped out,' I told him. 'Look,' he said, 'you don't have to write anything. I've got a copy-taker on the line, just talk to her.'

I took the phone, apologised to the lady on the other end of line for my stuttering state and ad-libbed my story, starting with: 'I witnessed the hell of the Leppings Lane end at Hillsborough yesterday and couldn't believe what I saw.

'They brought out the bodies one after another and laid them in rows alongside the fence which borders the stream which runs next to the ground.

'I watched with horror and disbelief, giving a helping hand where I could as doctors and police fought to bring life to seemingly lifeless bodies. Feverishly they applied mouth-to-mouth resuscitation. Fiercely they pummelled chests.

'Any sign of life in the prostrate figures was met with an army of medical people tearing away clothes and pounding on chests.

'It was horrific. Stunned relatives and friends stood helpless when it became obvious that supporters were dead. Their faces were covered with coats, jumpers and other clothing.

'The pitiful line of bodies grew. I just couldn't believe what I saw.

'I came to enjoy what promised to be a football spectacle on a beautiful spring afternoon in Sheffield. I ended by counting dead bodies. I'll never forget it as long as I live.'

Joe and I remained at the ground long into the evening, adding information as we got it. Stewart Steven refused to allow any news reporters to assist us, declaring, 'I've already got two men up there and they are doing well enough. They don't need any help.' We checked into another hotel but sleep was hard to come by that night.

There was ample evidence that Hillsborough was a disaster waiting to happen. Chosen as the venue for the 1981 semi-final between Tottenham Hotspur and Wolverhampton Wanderers, hundreds of fans were permitted to enter an area where there was not enough space and 38 people received injuries such as broken ribs, legs and arms. The general view was it could have been a lot worse. Hillsborough was removed from the Football Association's rota for six years.

There were overcrowding problems at the quarter and semi-finals in 1987 when normal service was resumed. There were even reports of crushing at the Leppings Lane end in 1988 which prompted Liverpool to complain to the FA before the fateful return a year later.

Such was the backdrop to tragedy, the scale of which was due to a combination of unforeseen circumstances, mostly logistical, which prompted the catastrophic, panic-stricken decision to order the opening of an exit gate. The tragic consequence was 96 Liverpool supporters losing their lives.

For me the images of that day have not gone away. They never will. If my vivid recollections of the devastation are constantly revived by each passing anniversary, there has also been the determined battle for justice for the bereaved families, culminating finally in the definitive lengthy inquest and the shockingly belated admission of deceit by the man in charge of policing the event, Chief Superintendent David Duckenfield.

It took him 26 years to admit what my own eyes had witnessed on that terrible afternoon and what was published in The Mail on Sunday the following day.

Bill Shankly once said: 'Some people believe football is a matter of life and death. I am very disappointed with that attitude. I can assure you it's much, much more important than that.'

For once the late, great former Liverpool manager got it wrong.

CHAPTER FOURTEEN
YOU'RE HIRED, CHRISTIAN

Of all the managerial appointments, I have been involved in—even reported—the arrival of Christian Gross at Tottenham Hotspur in November 1997 has to be light years ahead of the rest, not only because it came as a complete shock to anybody who was not as close to it as I was, but also for the sheer surrealism of the way it went down.

But before describing the circumstances behind the Swiss-born coach's pantomimic arrival at White Hart Lane, I suppose it would be appropriate to divulge just how I happened to be in the thick of everything that went on. Unfortunately, that would mean having to expose just about my best contact (and no—it's not Fergie!) which is something I am not prepared to do.

It's enough to say that I might have had a better grasp of what was going on at Tottenham if I had bugged the boardroom but only just!

For personal reasons, I was happy to put one over on multi-millionaire Alan Sugar, then the owner of the North London outfit. He may rejoice in his image and reputation as a hard-nosed businessman on The

Apprentice, but in my experience, you could also add arrogant, ignorant, ill-mannered, and foul-mouthed— pretty much anything which sums up a not very nice person.

It must be quite easy for him to portray himself as a bit of a bully on television because in the one short and not very sweet meeting I had with him, that's exactly how he came across.

Sometime before the Gross episode the office had arranged for me to do a one-on-one interview with Sugar at his home in Chigwell. I journeyed down from the North-East and made my way by tube and taxi to the front door of his mansion where I was met (eventually) by his associate, the now equally well known Nick Hewer, who had been (apparently) instrumental in arranging the interview.

Hewer seemed the kind of nice chap he comes across as on television. Mentioning that Sugar would be with me shortly, he bade me sit down in the lounge, provided coffee and biscuits and engaged in some friendly small talk while we waited for his boss. And then Sugar arrived, clad in tennis gear and carrying a racquet, apparently just having come off the court.

Without even a glance in my direction he said to Hewer, 'Who's he?' 'It's the journalist from The Mail on Sunday,' answered Hewer. 'He's here to interview you as arranged.' Still without acknowledging my presence, Sugar snapped, 'Well I'm not doing any interviews; just tell him to fuck off.'

And with that he walked out, leaving an embarrassed Hewer to apologise profusely for getting me there on a complete wild goose chase. 'I'm really sorry to have wasted your time,' he said, shaking my hand. The many well documented bust-ups Sugar has had with different people give some indication of what kind of bloke he is. It was really well worth the trip to discover it for myself.

Gross was one of seven managers employed during Sugar's time as chairman at White Hart Lane. On reflection, the Swiss gentleman may have just survived the trauma of an entrance which apparently had the Spurs owner spluttering through a range of emotions from exasperation to furious apoplexy had his managerial capabilities matched the sum of the talents of Sir Alex Ferguson, Jose Mourinho and Pep Guardiola, but sadly they fell some way short of that.

But what about that introduction and that infamous tube ride? A week or so earlier I had been tipped off that Gerry Francis was on his way out and that Gross—a huge success as coach of his hometown club Grasshopper Zurich, where he had won two Swiss titles and the Swiss Cup, but little known outside the scenic splendour of that tax haven—was lined up as his replacement.

Not only that, my information suggested there was the added bonus for Spurs fans of Jurgen Klinsmann returning to White Hart Lane as well. Although I was sworn to secrecy about the identity of Francis's successor, I was able to reveal exclusively on November 16th that the current manager would be gone by the end of the month and that the new man would be a continental coach and that the German international striker was on his way back.

Francis duly quit three days later at the same time as it was announced that Gross would be taking over. To say that followers of the Lilywhites were underwhelmed would be no exaggeration. Over in Zurich where I was ensconced with Gross's entourage of representatives, family and friends, one could almost hear the pin which dropped in N17. But in the ensuing furore there were many critics eager to stand up and be counted.

In fairness, Sugar lambasted Alan Mullery for the former Spurs and England midfielder's fiercely couched condemnation of the appointment in which he said he was not impressed with Gross's credentials as a leading Swiss coach. 'We could all do what he has done in Switzerland,' he declared. To which the owner countered, 'I am truly disgusted with Mullery's irresponsible outburst in response to the appointment of my new coach, particularly as the man has not put one foot in this country yet.'

Which was precisely what Gross was about to do. And I was with him all the way!

I had met him at the Letzigrund (the home of Grasshopper) the previous evening before he sent out his team for his final home game in charge against Etoile Carouge. He may have become something of a football pariah in England but on that chilly night in Zurich there was no doubting his hometown popularity. His impending departure reduced many fans to tears. Good luck messages were draped around the ground as he was given a hero's send-off. And the players responded in the grandest of manners, spanking Etoile 6-0.

Over dinner later with Gross and his fitness coach Fritz Schmid, the discussion turned to the most spectacular way Gross could announce his arrival as a Premier League manager the following day and somebody hit on the idea of him demonstrating a unique affinity with the fans by scorning a chauffeur-driven limousine and travelling to White Hart Lane as THEY would—by way of the underground!

The guy was so hyper he would have agreed to have been dropped in by parachute, but the more mundane form of travel was decided on. While the nation's sporting media circus was gathering for Gross's introductory press conference, he would arrive—briefed almost to the word about what he would say—courtesy of London transport.

There was not a flicker of recognition from fellow travellers when we arrived at Heathrow. We passed completely unrecognised through passport control and customs clearance before walking to the tube platform. Even when—together with one of the paper's photographers who had met us at arrivals—we boarded a crowded Piccadilly Line train grasping our all-day travel cards, nobody noticed us.

I mention the travel cards because Gross brandished the ticket at the press conference, uttering at the same time, 'This is the ticket to my dreams. This is the ticket which has taken me from Heathrow to White Hart Lane this morning so I can use the same route as Tottenham fans will on Monday when we play Crystal Palace. I wanted to see how they would come and show that I am one of them.'

And yet in his report the following day one national daily journo analysed the logistics of a possible tube journey from the airport complete with timetable and likely changes and claimed, because the exit machine would have retained his ticket anyway, it was more or less total bollocks.

I was more than happy to prove him wrong in The Mail On Sunday two days later with an exclusive station by station report, complete with pictures, of Gross's underground journey, an abbreviated version of which started:

'Somewhere between South Kensington and Knightsbridge, Christian Gross glanced across the Tube carriage, took in the message of the back-page banner headlines and realised the enormity of the task ahead.

'They are saying Christian who? Well, soon they will know,' said the man charged with reviving the ailing giant of N17.

Gross may have chosen the Underground route to his new job but he does not intend being known as the man who finally took Tottenham down the tube.

'I know I will be competing against some of the best coaches in the world.

'I will be calling them all on Tuesday to introduce myself; it is a good neighbourly thing to do. But I fear nobody. I sense I am going to do well.'

Our journey had started in Zurich with talk of discipline, commitment and statistical analysis. But by the time we got to Covent Garden, Gross was ready to take his new charges out on the town.

As our Piccadilly Line shuttle from Heathrow rattled along, he treated commuters and early Christmas shoppers to his views on the need for team-bonding. 'I will be taking them on trips to West End shows and rock concerts. We will do lots of things together,' he said.

And, in case all the talk of concerts and nights out gave anybody the wrong idea, Gross was quickly back on a familiar track. By Russell Square, he was promising to stiffen team discipline by adopting the Continental approach of isolating his players in hotels the night before matches—even those at home and to abandon the routine of players getting a day off after a game.

'I do not tolerate bad behaviour off the field. The players have to respect there are certain limits,' he said. 'I know in England it is customary to have a few beers after the game. I would prefer them to drink water and eat potatoes or pasta.

'Everybody will come in the day after a game to be checked over by the physio and start the right therapy as quickly as possible. It is very important to cut down on all those injuries which have tortured Tottenham this season.'

The mood lightened, though, when we pulled into Arsenal station. The dour disciplinarian gave way again as a grin of delight spread across his face and Gross looked forward to clashes with Tottenham's old rivals.

'Ah, yes. I know about the rivalry between the two teams. They are having the best of it at the moment, but all I can ask the Tottenham supporters to do is to have faith. One day it will be our turn to be on top. '

I felt it best to leave out of the article the Keystone Cops-like antics of us trying to get the new Spurs manager to the press conference for half past eleven, the appointed starting time. The aforementioned hack had observed in his report how he would have relished a comment from Sugar like, 'I am sorry that we will have to delay Christian's press conference because he is stuck in a tube train at Earls Court.' He didn't know how close to the truth he was.

As the train rumbled on, we were subjected to a number of delays which made us realise we were going to be nowhere near White Hart Lane when we were supposed to be. The plan, to get as far as Finsbury Park and then grab a couple of cabs, sounded good in its conception; in its execution, it was one problem after another. Arriving at Finsbury Park well after eleven o'clock was bad enough but then we seemed to have chosen a day when the taxis were avoiding the area like the plague.

It must have taken ten minutes before we stopped one which Gross and his representatives scrambled into. By the time another had conveyed the snapper and myself to the ground, the press conference was in full swing.

I didn't see much of him during his brief spell at Spurs when he found it difficult to reproduce the success he had at Grasshopper, and indeed later when he surpassed those achievements after switching to Basel. I did meet him again though when Manchester United went to Switzerland for a Champions League game when his disappointment over what happened in England still burned deep.

At least, with the help of Klinsmann who, as I had predicted, returned on loan from Sampdoria until the end of the season before hanging up his boots, Gross managed to keep Spurs in the Premier League. But I think I can safely say he never travelled on the underground again.

A day at the races with Sir Alex Ferguson

Brendan Foster setting the pace

Eric Cantona receives his FWA Player of the Year award

Everton legend, Howard Kendall

Happy times with Peter Taylor (left) and Brian Clough (right)

In action for Newcastle against Ivor Broadis (left) and Keith Burkinshaw (right)

Keeping Sir Alex Ferguson, Peter Reid and Sam Allardyce entertained

Lester Pigott and friend

Life's a beach with Kevin Keegan

Liverpool legend, Bob Paisley

National Service (far left front row)

Newcastle boss, Joe Harvey

Newcastle's saviour, Sir John Hall

Brian Clough on the mic

Sunderland's FA Cup winning boss, Bob Stokoe

*Sir Alex Ferguson attends my failed attempt at a
retirement do*

CHAPTER FIFTEEN
SLIM JIM

It is ironic and a little hypocritical for some Premier League managers to bleat about being personally disappointed and gutted for the fans when they get knocked out of either of the domestic cup competitions, especially after turning out less than full strength sides. Left to them there would be about as much magic in the cups as there was in Tommy Cooper's stage act.

Teams reach the final almost by default, getting there because their fringe players were better than that of the opposition. There was a time when clubs were fined for not fielding their strongest line-ups but that law was abused so much it was done away with. Sure, there could be tinges of regret when the team bosses witness the pleasure supporters of the final participants derive from their day at Wembley, but it is minor and soon passes. For them, successfully frying bigger fish is what will keep them in their jobs.

The financial gluttony of the Premier League together with European competition has been at the expense of football tradition. The cups are now a distant second behind the Champions and Europa Leagues.

161

That certainly was not the situation back in 1973 when Sunderland's shock victory over star-studded Leeds United and everything associated with it gave me some of the happiest memories of my reporting career. Of that side only goalkeeper Jimmy Montgomery and, to a lesser extent, youth team players such as Billy Hughes, Dennis Tueart and Bobby Kerr, were around when I first started covering the team for North-East local paper The Journal.

The manager then was Ian McColl, a dour Scot who had not only been a massive crowd hero in his 15 years as a player and then captain with Rangers, he was also an accomplished Scotland team manager—the second most successful in their history—having led the side to successive British Home Championships in the early sixties.

If he had a major fault at Sunderland, it was the way he blatantly indulged his fellow countryman and former Rangers team-mate, the mercurial Jim Baxter who had moved to Sunderland from Ibrox. Team camaraderie was not at a premium in that dressing room with Baxter and his clique of Scottish players in one corner and Charlie Hurley heading a faction of more established players in the other.

Any hope I would be able to take a neutral stance in order to keep my professional options open was completely shattered when I covered one of Sunderland's early away games; a mid-week trip to Leeds. As I have already mentioned, local paper scribes were permitted to travel on the team coach and I was quite excited by being in close proximity to stellar names such as Baxter and Hurley.

Being early September, it was quite a warm evening, but a hint of precipitation in the air persuaded me to take a raincoat. The previous weekend had seen Sunderland record a notable home 4-0 win over Blackpool with Neil Martin scoring a hat-trick and I had got on really well with the Scottish striker when I interviewed him for Monday's paper.

But it was still a surprise when, soon after we started the return journey from Leeds where the team had lost 2-1, Martin came up from the back of the coach and plonked himself down in the empty seat next to me. 'You haven't really met Jim yet, have you?' he said. Having decided not to rush things with the famous midfielder beyond a cursory nod, I agreed.

'He wants you to do him a favour,' continued Martin. 'The coach will make a refreshment stop at Wetherby and he wants you to buy a couple of bottles of Bacardi and bring them on for him. Will you do it? Here's the cash. I'll leave it with you,' and off he went.

I don't know which I felt more, the pounding heart or the churning bowels. But while agonising over what to do, what I did realise was that if I refused, that was me and Baxter as good as done. As they say now, it was a no-brainer, which left me with the problem of getting the Bacardi on the coach without anybody noticing.

In spite of it being a lovely sunny evening with no sign of the predicted rain, in spite of the fact the players were all wearing casual shirts as well as tracksuit bottoms, and in spite of others dispensing with jackets and walking into the restaurant in shirt sleeve order, the only way I could do this was by carrying a bottle in each of two my deep raincoat pockets and then making sure I was first back on the coach.

Bob, the bus driver, was hysterical when he let me in, sweating my cobs off. 'I'm glad we didn't get the weather you were expecting,' he chortled. I didn't care. I was back in my seat with the Bacardi lying next to me. And I've never felt so relieved than when I slipped the contraband to Martin as he passed me on the way to the back seat.

But my anguish was far from over. Having already been legitimately given bottles of coke and glasses, the Scottish contingent got stuck in and the sounds of jollity and raucous laughter increased by decibels on the way back to Wearside. I just shrank into my seat halfway up the coach; shrinking even further when, horrified, I heard and then saw an empty Bacardi bottle rolling down the aisle from the back towards the front. How the hell there wasn't an inquest into it all I'll never know—but there was none.

Needless to say, Baxter and I got on like a house on fire after that and there were many fun occasions in his company. One in particular was a rail journey back from London after Sunderland played at Fulham. The train had barely pulled out of King's Cross when Slim Jim, as he was known, and a few others including his cousin George Kinnell, a midfield player who had joined the club from Oldham Athletic, got up and headed for the bar. The nudge I received from one of them was the signal for me to follow. It was not yet noon but it made little difference—the bar was where we spent the rest of the journey.

Three things I remember vividly from that trip. One was when Kinnell did his party piece of taking his teeth out and doing a rubber-mouthed impersonation of Freddie 'Parrot-face' Davies. Using a trilby which he had manage to borrow from one of the directors, he had just started his routine when Baxter snatched the hat from his head, opened a window and cast the titfer to the winds, leaving his cousin stunned into open-gobbed silence.

The second was a favourite Baxter number. Taking a half-crown, he dropped it and caught it on his left shoe which he held a couple of inches off the ground in spite of the rocking carriage. He then flicked it on to his other foot, lifted it over his head on to the back of his neck before nudging into his shirt pocket.

The third was a decision by McColl that—with a bunch of supporters very probably waiting to greet the players at Durham Station where they were catching a bus to take them back to Roker Park—Baxter was in no condition to get off with them. It was hastily arranged for him, suitably chaperoned, to stay on to Newcastle where a car would be waiting.

The legendary Baxter's finest days may have been behind him when he joined Sunderland but he was still an artist on the ball with passing skills you do not often see in present day football. When he stopped playing, myself and a few of his former team-mates joined him in Glasgow when he opened a pub. His way of despatching the punters at closing time was a friendly 'Right lads, let's see your arses tonight and your faces tomorrow', albeit with a wink in our direction which said, 'that doesn't mean you.'

Two liver transplants before he died of pancreatic cancer at the age of 61 told the story of a life in the fast lane. Being a passenger for a couple of years was an unforgettably happy if somewhat decidedly unhealthy experience.

Sunderland's record when Alan Brown returned for a second spell in charge after McColl was sacked was uneventful until 'The Bomber', as Brownie was known, was also shown the door at the end of November 1972 with the team fourth bottom of what was then the equivalent of the Championship.

Enter a rugged Northumbrian who had spent ten years as a player at Newcastle and four at Bury before an inconspicuous club boss roll-call which began at Gigg Lane and took in places like Charlton Athletic, Carlisle United (three spells) and Blackpool. Enter Bob Stokoe, a managerial wizard who cast a dressing room spell which transformed a team of dead beats into one which six months later became the most celebrated football team in the land. The FA Cup certainly had magic by the truckload then.

Stokoe signed just three players before and during their run: defenders Ron Guthrie and David Young before the third round and striker Vic Halom before the fifth. Of equal significance was when Arthur Cox was enlisted as assistant manager before a fourth-round replay at Reading.

If there was a dearth of genuine team spirit in McColl's time at the club, under Stokoe it simmered, bubbled and then boiled over as victims—albeit after replays in rounds three, four and five—were cast adrift. And we hacks, were with the team all the way, hitching a ride on that mad, magical journey.

There were memorable personal cameos, like when I made up a golf four-ball partnering Stokoe against Cox and the great Jackie Milburn, then writing for the

News of the World, when the team were in Buxton, preparing for the semi-final against Arsenal. The weather was atrocious, heavy rain and a gale-force wind. Much to the manager's fury we lost on the 17th green when the opposition refused to concede me an 18-inch putt which I missed. Stokoe's mood was hardly sweetened when he discovered he'd left his putter on the 16th and the last the three of us saw of him that day was when he stormed off into the murk after angrily refusing Cox's offer to retrieve it.

Being involved in the whole final experience is just an awesome memory for lots of reasons, starting with the media joining the team at their Selsdon Park Hotel headquarters near Croydon from the Monday onwards. Traditionally on the Thursday evening before the final, the Football Writers' Association enjoy our annual dinner at the Lancaster Hotel in London. It was also a tradition (sadly no longer) that the two Wembley managers attended as special guests.

On this occasion, present were not only Stokoe and his Leeds counterpart Don Revie, but also the whole of the Sunderland squad, officials and back-room staff. It had never happened before and it has certainly not happened since.

And the cavalier-like all for one and one for all scenario did not end there either. The Sunderland chairman Keith Collings made sure the wives, partners, girlfriends of every journalist who regularly wrote about the club joined the official party at Wembley. They were transported by coach, allocated accommodation in London for two nights and tickets for the game. Afterwards, win or lose, we were invited to attend the official banquet in the Grosvenor Hotel. Lose after such hospitality? It was never an option.

Times had not changed for the better when it came to the 2014 Capital One Cup final, the media were not even given the opportunity to buy a ticket for Sunderland's match against Manchester City.

The drama and spectacle of Sunderland's historic victory over Leeds is captured in posterity and forever in the hearts and memories of every red and white fan; the Ian Porterfield goal, the Jimmy Montgomery save et al. But what is glossed over and is certainly evident in the several times I have seen a re-run of the game is that the result was far from a fluke. Stokoe's team were magnificent on the day.

Afterwards it was open house in the Sunderland dressing room—champagne, singing, back-slapping, laughter, tears. It was all there. I think it was during the raucous rendition of Cliff Richard's Congratulations, glass of bubbly in hand by the side of the bath, when I was given a friendly shove from Tueart and in I went, new brown suit and all. And just to add to the hilarity, there were a few duckings from the lads already in the bath as well. As I wrote in The Sun the following Monday, I swear that had I not been wearing huge platform heels, I might have drowned— that was a deep bath! Fortunately, Vic Halom lent me his tracksuit to wear on the bus back to the hotel.

The return to Wearside the following week was via Cardiff, where Sunderland had to fulfil a league fixture commitment. And then it was the long eventful journey home with selected members of the fourth estate, Cass and Melling included naturally, on the team coach. We were to get to Scotch Corner where an open-topped bus was waiting to take the team—and us (naturally)—on the triumphant parade back to Roker Park. Only I nearly didn't make that part of the trip.

Whether it was the food, the drink or maybe just the happy ambience of the journey, I suddenly had severe wind pains followed by bouts of uncontrollable flatulence, the ensuing fall-out of which resembled pure hydrogen sulphide. It must have contaminated the coach from where I was at the rear to the front because suddenly the victorious FA Cup final manager Bob Stokoe stormed down to where I was sitting, stuck his finger up my nose and bellowed, 'Right! One more fart and you're off!'

But we did make the open-topped bus, even if we scribes stayed below, deferring to the manager and his players above as they held the silver pot aloft before what was estimated at crowds of up to well over a million standing up to twenty deep on either side of the road on that memorable victory parade.

And we managed to stretch the celebration to a week in Majorca, paid for by a 'Mickey Mouse' match against Cannes which meant a quick chartered hop over to the south of France and back. My boss at the Sun was happy for me to enjoy the trip; 'I'll only hear from you if anything unexpected happens,' was his message. And not much did in the way of a story until I took a call in the hotel lobby in Magaluf and the office voice at the other end declared, 'Cassy, you're gonna have to work today. We're struggling for a back-page lead in the first edition.' I mentioned something about getting on it and then started wondering where I was going to get one from.

169

Melling and I were sharing a room so I went up to ask if he had any ideas only to find him snoring his head off and lying on the bedside table next to him a hand-written cock and bull story about Vic Halom being in line for a shock Hungarian cap, a contrived suggestion because of flimsy Magyar connections in his ancestry. Of course, it would not have been good manners to disturb his slumber so I just picked up the phone, dialled The Sun's number and asked for a copy taker.

I was almost done when my room-mate opened his eyes, uttered some expletive about what was I doing and went ballistic. The upshot was he had to rewrite the tale which got about four pars in The Express while The Sun's back page headline screamed something about Halom's Hungarian call-up. Once he calmed down and guzzled the champagne peace-offering, all was well again—in fact, he never wasted an opportunity to tell the others about it, sharing in the fun of it.

Another highlight was a rib-tickling gem involving Sunderland's goal hero, Porterfield. The itinerary for one particular evening was the usual dinner followed by a visit to a cabaret and piano bar, which we were assured would provide excellent entertainment. A dozen or so of us duly formed an orderly queue at the entrance ready to fork out the admission charge which a few had already done, when Porterfield stormed past us to the reception area and promptly told whoever was in charge that we should be allowed in for nothing.

There followed a hilarious conversation between the Scot and the Spanish receptionist which sounded like a cross between West Highland and Apache. 'We Sunderlando,' began Porterfield with a sweeping arm which embraced the rest of us. 'We win cup.' And prodding his thumb against his chest, he said, 'Me GOL-DEN boot. We no pay. You say we pay I take my friends away.' And he was still debating the issue with the receptionist as we all filed past him, placing our pesetas on the counter. He may have been big in Britain, but the lad was just another failed freeloader in the Balearics.

They say good times don't last forever and sadly neither did this Sunderland fairy story. A number of unforeseen circumstances came together the following season to hasten the break-up of that wonderful team, but basically the club became a victim of its own success. A government wage freeze prevented the club handing the players the contracts they deserved, but more significantly Second Division football did not match the ambitions of the likes of Tueart and Dave Watson who, along with Micky Horswill, were sold to Manchester City where the former pair had tremendous careers at club and international level with England.

With the romance gone and Sunderland narrowly missing out on promotion the following two seasons, the media relationship with Stokoe also deteriorated. The frustration of not being able to build on the Cup success and losing his star players made him grumpy and uncooperative. Love him as we did, he could still be a right miserable sod.

There was one particular confrontation which Melling constantly dined out on afterwards. I have always found American politics fascinating and one day I picked up a copy of All The President's Men, the Carl Bernstein—Bob Woodward's story of Watergate and their roles in the humiliation of Richard Nixon. I was gripped by the whole incredible story from start to finish.

It was just the incentive I needed to tackle Stokoe at a time when we were going through a particularly rough spell with the Sunderland manager. Without telling him why, I called Melling and told him we were going to the training ground—then, ironically, at Washington, County Durham—to have it out with the manager.

After pleading with us not to upset his boss, Tommy the groundsman showed us into Stokoe's office with my pal still totally unaware of what I had in mind. Ten minutes later the manager arrived wearing his red track suit and a red and white bobble woolly perched on his head. Leaning back against the radiator, he demanded: 'Right, you pair, what's on your mind?'

'Bob,' I said. 'I've just read a book called All The President's Men. It's a story about how two journalists brought down the President of the United States. So, my advice to you is that you'd better watch yourself in future.' And, beckoning to Melling, the meeting was over. I said, 'Right, Joe. We're out of here.' Neither he nor Bob said another word, although outside my pal mumbled something about the whole thing being a waste of a journey.

But there was always a great deal of mutual respect between Bob Stokoe and myself. After he quit football we had a few games of golf together and shared top tables at sports dinners. And the football world will never forget him shedding that brown trilby as he raced on to the Wembley pitch to lift up his pint-sized captain, Bobby Kerr.

That historic gallop is replicated in a statue erected at the Stadium of Light, just about as far from the official entrance as it could be. They might as well have stuck on nearby Seaburn Beach. You could visit the ground a thousand times and not even notice it. The great man deserves better.

CHAPTER SIXTEEN
BECKHAM CALL

I am an enormous fan of David Beckham both as a player and a bloke. Football is a game of opinions; mine is that pundits, be they journalists or former professionals, who questioned his enormous contribution to world football, deriding him as little more than a show pony, are quite simply wrong.

Even worse were those who seek to minimize his intelligence; pontificating writers who, without any particular evidence to justify their opinion save to jump on a popular bandwagon, allude sarcastically to the suggestion that Beckham may not have been at the front of the queue when brains were handed out.

Beats me how someone with an apparent IQ lower than that of a dung beetle ever rose to be one of the world's greatest sporting icons, creating for himself a vast commercial and financial empire. Blessed with even a nanogram of grey matter, he would surely have ruled the world! But that's Beckham; a player and a person who can elicit praise from some media commentators and poison from others. I am biased; for me he was a top footballer—he IS a top bloke— friendly, engaging, ever accommodating, and he's done me a few favours which I'll always be grateful for.

I first interviewed him as a 16-year-old when he was part of the England youth team which took part in the annual international tournament in Toulon, but I have a vivid recollection of an article I wrote in October 1997 when he was beginning to establish himself in the Manchester United side, because the repercussions in terms of raising the hackles of his manager and mentor were memorable and something I now literally dine out on, even when sharing a top table with the former boss.

I had pestered Sir Alex Ferguson into allowing me to do a one-on-one with Beckham, who was fast emerging as a force on the world football stage. Coupled with that, his well-publicised relationship with Spice Girl, Victoria Adams, meant then, as now, his name was as much in the gossip columns as it was on the sports pages. As it was something of a scoop, I was happy to let Fergie dictate the terms of the interview. 'Make it football only,' he warned.

The interview was fixed for a Friday when United were staying in a hotel in Derbyshire before an away match against the Rams, and I spoke to Beckham in his room the evening before the game. The chat was all about football; how he loved being a United player, how much he admired Paul Gascoigne and how much he had set his heart on emulating Gazza by playing a central midfield role for England. 'I enjoy being more involved in the middle of the park because there you see more of the ball and engage in more of the play,' he said.

Clearly, football was his life. 'Forget the money, the cars, the limelight. It's football that counts and I am enjoying it just as much as I did when I played in the Sunday leagues as a kid,' he said. And so, it went on with me adhering strictly to Fergie's template. I merely ventured to inquire how Becks was coping with being increasingly in the media spotlight. 'Victoria helps a lot,' he volunteered. 'She is used to the fame and all the adulation. We talk about it a lot. Football has become like show business which is something everybody in the game will have to contend with.' Prophetic words, which I foolishly attempted to submerge under his Gascoigne assertions; what his football ambitions were; role models such as Bryan Robson, Glenn Hoddle and Alan Shearer etc.

Unfortunately, what I composed had little to do with what appeared as a double page spread in The Mail on Sunday under the headline 'Beckham: How My Posh Spice Helps Me Cope With Pressure'. I hardly needed to be told in newspaper terms that this was the obvious angle, but it was far removed from the parameters agreed with his manager. My instant reaction was, although Beckham himself would be perfectly happy with the piece, Fergie might be a different kettle of fish. I didn't have to wait too long to find out.

The following day I was due to fly from Manchester to Dublin to cover the first leg of Ireland's two-match World Cup play-off against Belgium. As it happened, en route from the North-East, as a favour to Fergie's then number two, Brian Kidd, I had called in at a hotel in north Yorkshire where the team had stayed before a match at Middlesbrough to collect 24 jars of marmalade. Kiddo had developed a taste for the stuff made specially by the hotel chef. The intention was to drop the marmalade off at The Cliff (then the club's training quarters) on the way to the airport.

I thought it wise to let Fergie know I was coming so I called him on his private number. Despite a 7-0 thrashing of Barnsley the previous day, his disposition had been darkened by another Sunday paper story about one of his player's being involved in a nightclub bust-up and he didn't beat about the bush. 'That article was supposed to be about football. I don't want to see or speak to you for a month.' Down went the phone. Vainly I called back to try and reason with him but my opening words were greeted with the receiver slamming down again. So that was that he had a point and I was resigned to accepting the consequences.

But there was another major problem: how was I to get 24 jars of marmalade to Kiddo when I had no access to The Cliff. I called Brian in the coach's room. 'I've got your marmalade but I don't know how to get it to you because I'm banned,' I told him. 'You're banned from driving? How bad is that pal,' he answered. After explaining the ban was only from the training ground the marmalade was duly handed over at a secret meeting outside the gates.

That wasn't the end of it; not by a long chalk. The following Saturday I had the doubtful pleasure of covering United's home game against Sheffield Wednesday. I had been warned to expect some icy treatment from Fergie so I decided to keep a low profile in the after-match press conference and let my colleagues ask the questions. It was another terrific United performance, a 6-1 victory that consolidated their position at the top of the Premier League. At least that should have kept the boss happy. You hardly thought so had you caught his glare in my direction as I stood against the wall in the interview theatre.

I listened and made notes as the boys did their stuff until I decided enough was enough. Why should I have to rely on others to get my story? 'I thought Gary Pallister had a particularly good game today, Alex,' I offered. 'Yes,' he snapped, without even so much as a glance in my direction. I decided to venture further with calamitous folly. 'Pally has done well for you because he was one of your first buys, wasn't he?' Suddenly, I had Fergie's undivided attention while my colleagues either had a sharp intake or hid their mirth behind their programmes. 'One of my first buys? One of my first buys…' sneered the United manager. 'Get your facts right. I was here nearly three years when I bought him.' The cackles went around the theatre with my fellow scribes now revelling in my total discomfort. I thought, sod it in for a penny in for a pound. 'Well, he was one of your first good ones then.' I detected half a smile at my brassed neck cheek as he stood up and strode out of the room, shouting over his shoulder, 'Don't forget you're banned for a month.' The ban, such as it was, lasted a couple of weeks.

Sadly, a few years later, similar reconciliation was not to be the order of the day as far as manager and player were concerned—the flying boot episode just one of a few well publicised spats between the pair which inevitably led to the parting of the ways.

Such a situation would have been unthinkable during the celebrations which followed United's sensational European Cup triumph over Bayern

Munich in Barcelona's Nou Camp Stadium on May 26, 1999—in fact, Beckham said as much when we spoke after the game on the United team coach.

While the daily newspapermen were milking quotes in the mixed zone like there was no tomorrow, Sunday scribes like myself needed something different, and the United midfielder could not have supplied it any better, albeit after a few terrifying moments when it seemed we were going to get precisely nothing. By the time they got as far as where my Sunday colleagues and I were standing, the players were talked out—even Beckham, who smiled and shook his head as he paraded past, clasping the famous trophy by one of its handles. To say we were struggling was massively understating our plight.

I'd given up when I saw Sky's former football anchorman Richard Keys walking past with an armful of match programmes. At least if I had a few of those in response to the requests I'd had from friends and family it would be some consolation. Keysie told me he had happened on a box full of them behind a hut a few yards away, so off I went, found the box and helped myself to half a dozen. That was when fortune smiled on me from the greatest height. Glancing around in case I was caught in my larcenous act, I noticed the United team coach parked about fifty yards away in splendid isolation, and standing at the door, chatting to a group of family members (and still clutching the European Cup) was Beckham himself.

Notwithstanding my angina problem which, incidentally, necessitated a quadruple heart by-pass operation two months later, I dashed across and caught him just as he was about to put foot on the coach steps.

'Any chance of a quick two minutes?' I pleaded. 'Well, we'll have to do it on the bus because we're leaving in five minutes.' And that's how, with his team-mates filing past, ribbing him with good humour about being a glory hunter, I came to be on that famous bus, topping off that historic evening with a superb interview which began 'David Beckham, the most coveted of Manchester United's array of stars, refuses to contemplate life beyond Old Trafford.'

He went on to say, 'I have always wanted to be a Manchester United player. When you achieve what we have achieved this season, why would you want anything else? Why go anywhere else? It couldn't get better wherever you went.'

And he spoke warmly of the contribution of team-mates such as the Neville brothers (Gary and Phil), Paul Scholes and Nicky Butt, pals since they were starry-eyed kids together. 'It's been particularly brilliant for myself and the rest of the lads who have come through, first as schoolboys and then from the youth team upwards. We all wanted to be successful but this is unbelievable.

'You can tell there is a great spirit, friendship and feeling of togetherness between us. For a group of young lads to grow up and win titles, FA Cups and now the European Cup is a dream come true. Amazing!'

It is such a treasured memory, especially when I made the night for the rest of the Sunday boys by passing on Beckham's quotes. In a later interview, he hinted his departure from Old Trafford was not totally of his making when he told me, 'I always said, if I had my choice, I would never have left Manchester United because that was where I always wanted to start my career and finish it.'

After his transfer to Real Madrid, covering England meant our paths crossed regularly, although not as often as they did between him and my son, Simon, after he joined The Daily Mail sports reporting team. Simon's arrival at the paper almost coincided with Beckham's move to Spain and his sports editor, Colin Gibson, mindful of the fact that Cass Junior can speak Spanish like a native having lived for some years in places such as Pamplona and Seville, dispatched him to Madrid to cover his arrival, ostensibly for a limited six-month period. I thought a little word with Beckham would not go amiss so it was after an England game I mentioned he would probably be seeing a lot of Simon in Madrid and would he make his life as comfortable as possible. And he did; and that six months stay lasted for three years!

I interviewed him three times in Los Angeles after his surprise decision to join MLS side LA Galaxy: in July 2007 at his star spangled welcome to the Home Depot Centre, in October 2009 when I revealed exclusively that he was to rejoin AC Milan on loan the following year, and in December 2012 before and after his emotional farewell to the Galaxy. There was no exclusive to be had at the welcoming bun fight but, at the second meeting arranged with the help of his personal manager Simon Oliveira, he spoke passionately about his desire to be involved in the England squad for the World Cup in 2010.

I brook little argument in paying tribute to the professional dedication which made such a prospect even viable, especially after he was ditched by Steve

McClaren when Sven Goran Eriksson's former two was given the top job following the team's exit from the 2006 World Cup in Germany. Perhaps Beckham had seen the writing on the wall when he announced he was giving up the captaincy at a press gathering at the team's training quarters in Baden-Baden the day after England lost a penalty shoot-out to Portugal. My personal memory of that was getting bollocked by the TV cameramen when I obscured their view of the proceedings as I attempted to get him to autograph a team shirt. 'Get out of the fucking way you idiot,' they bawled, much to my embarrassment.

Then, a few weeks later in August 2006, McClaren put what seemed to be the final nail in the player's international coffin when he left him out of his first squad, declaring, 'It's a clean sheet of paper. That's why I've decided not to pick Beckham. He was a fantastic captain for England. He was a great player and still is a great player. He's got pride and was disappointed but he said he understood and wanted to fight for his place. He's got to do what he said he would do; perform the best he can for Real Madrid and hope the door is still open.'

The door was closed for just nine months. That's when I revealed (again exclusively in The Mail on Sunday) that McClaren was poised to bring him back into the England fold for curtain-raiser at the refurbished Wembley Stadium—a friendly against Brazil. Somewhat fortuitously the coach had agreed to do a question and answer session at a dinner I had arranged at Durham City Golf Club where I am a member, and his cagey response to one of the member's queries about Beckham's possible return, especially after I had touched on the subject while playing 18 holes with McClaren earlier in the day, rang more than a few bells.

To be fair, McClaren would not elaborate enough to put the icing on the cake with a definite yes and we danced around the subject quite a bit until I asked, 'Would I look stupid if I wrote a story merely hinting it was a possibility?' His laconic shrug of the shoulders was enough for me to run the tale.

Beckham had disguised his true feelings when he reacted to being axed by stating, 'I can fully understand the manager wants to make his mark and build to the next World Cup. I'm proud to have played for my country for the past ten years and my passion for wanting to represent my country remains as strong as ever.' But he opened up to me in that second LA get-together, confessing, 'When I sit down and look back at that time, it was hard, really hard, probably the worst experience of my career.

'As a footballer, when people start questioning your ability, it's going to be tough. But I always knew if I worked hard and showed enough commitment, I would have a chance of getting back in the England squad.'

While mindful of critics who counted his mounting caps tally with growing disenchantment and simmering anger, especially when they continued under Fabio Capello, Beckham made no apologies for it. He came off the bench in the 87th minute against Belarus to pass Sir Bobby Charlton's 106 and became the third-most capped player in English history. At our meeting at the Home Depot Centre after he reached 114, overtaking Bobby Moore's record of 108, again after a substitute's role against Slovakia to become the most capped outfield player, he told me, 'I never expected to reach a hundred appearances for England. I know there are critics out there who ask if I should be given a cap for 15 minutes of football but I've started 100 games out of the 114, fifty of them as captain.'

He added, 'I try not to think about any of the criticism. Obviously, it's hard at times because there is a lot of it but I just do what I love doing and what I know I do best, which is to play football.' And he was not ashamed to target Peter Shilton's all-time record of 125, observing, 'I'd be a liar if I didn't say I'd love to reach it.'

It was not to be. The so-called purists would have been satisfied when the Achilles tendon injury he suffered playing for Milan in March 2010 ended his international career when he was just ten games short and ruled him out of the World Cup in South Africa.

What was even worse, for months even his competitive playing days looked to be over. And though, following a successful operation performed by the famous Finnish surgeon Dr Sakari Orava, he was eventually able to confound those who muttered 'good riddance', in our final interview just before his victorious farewell to LA Galaxy, Beckham recalled his anxiety as he was about to go under the knife. 'Suddenly, I thought, "this is going to be a tough one to come back from". But I did. I had a lot of positive people around me and I knew, once I got my fitness back, I'd be all right.'

I had been worried about being able to see him after arriving at the Home Depot a day after Beckham had attended what was to all intents and purposes his final media call. But again, Oliveira turned up trumps in arranging a meeting. Still, it was with a certain amount of anxiety that I stood at the head of the long corridor leading down to the Galaxy dressing rooms, hoping to catch sight of him, and that was when I felt a tap on the shoulder. 'You waiting for me?' he smiled when I turned around. And we got the job done.

Of course, such a glittering, if much-maligned career, could not possibly end anti-climatically and I was thrilled to shake his hand and congratulate him on the pitch after he helped Galaxy win the MLS Cup on December 1st, 2012. As I wrote in The Mail On Sunday, carp as they might, his deriders cannot dispute he is still the most recognized footballer on the planet.

And he offered his own fitting postscript when he told me, 'I'm very proud of what I have achieved in my career. I'm doing something I have always wanted to do as a young kid. To be able to do that still at 37 years old makes me feel really good.'

I was made fully aware of his intention to pull down the curtain on his days as a player after his short, again successful, spell with Paris St Germain on May 16th, 2013, but was sworn to secrecy. Unfortunately, much as I'd hoped, the text I received before the world was made aware of it came too early in the week for any revelation in my newspaper. Still, as I say, you can't win 'em all, unless of course you're David Beckham!

CHAPTER SEVENTEEN
LIVING THE FAIRWAY

Being at the sharp end of many big football stories involving the game's iconic personalities has had its moments and its memories. And if competing for back-page leads against top-class news-getters has produced pressures and emotions—great when you get one; gutted when you're stuffed—the over-riding satisfaction comes from covering the most popular sport in the world.

So why then am I just a teeny-weeny bit envious of colleagues who write about golf, especially those who chase the sun around the world covering not just the majors but the tournaments ranked just below them in importance. Having been fortunate enough to report on all four majors at different times I can vouch for the dedication, knowledge, creative talents and professionalism of guys who have a unique relationship with the people they write about. I'm talking about genuine friendships with golfing immortals.

When I became involved as stand-in golf reporter for The Sun and later acting as leg man for Frank Clough at Opens, I was in total awe of the mutual regard, not say esteem, between legendary scribes such as Peter Dobereiner, Michael McDonnell, Michael Williams, Renton Laidlaw among others, and the likes of Jack Nicklaus, Arnold Palmer, Gary Player et al. Such respect was borne out of the acknowledgement that giants who played the game were fully aware those who wrote about it knew what they were talking about.

All right, they were an elitist bunch, a journalistic royalty if you like; gentlemen covering a gentleman's sport, taking their cue from its hierarchy, establishment figures, who without question justify their status of almost total infallibility by the way they rule, but who remain a throw-back from the days when it was played only by the rich and famous. But they were never less than kind to this greenhorn, offering advice and guidance when I needed it—which was often.

The European tour was far from the behemoth it now is when I got involved. The prize money was a fraction of what tournaments offer today but there were more UK-based events and there was plenty to do covering The Dunlop Masters, The Coral Welsh Classic, The Jersey Open and The Greater Manchester Open, which were a breeding ground for golfers who went on to become the best in the world, not the least of whom was Sir Nick Faldo.

The Jersey Open at the La Moye course was a fun event, run by the island's Tourist Board, whose hospitality was limitless. If ever there was a bungfest, this was it. Unfortunately, on my first trip there I did not appreciate how generous they could be. Suffice to say, I had already raided the duty-free cheap booze shops in King Street, St Helier, when the farewell bung was dished out—wine, whisky, gin, perfume, you name it. I needed a Pickfords van to get the bags and luggage to the airport, where my burden problems were compounded when I met up with pro golfer Carl Mason whose flight to the main land had been seriously delayed.

The event's four-day format began with a two-day pro-celebrity competition, which opened with my journo colleague Mitchell Platts, who later became the European tour's Director of Corporate Affairs and Public Relations, partnering Mason in a four-ball which also included Bernhard Langer linking up with Margaret Thatcher's son, Mark. I had the honour of caddying for Mitch.

I have two outstanding memories of that day. The first when Langer's ball strayed close enough to an adjoining fairway for the celebrated German to fall foul of that brilliant Irish comedian Frank Carson, strolling in the opposite direction. It was too good an opportunity for Carson to miss. 'Are yoo Bernhard Langer?' he called in that familiar Belfast brogue. Langer nodded sheepishly. 'Was it yore father that bombed our fish shop,' cackled the comic, before marching on amid hoots of laughter from his following gallery. If facial expression could combine a smile with a wince, Langer managed it on that occasion.

The second, when Master Thatcher, apparently concerned that Mason was not exactly setting La Moye alight, offered him advice on how to improve his swing, later earning the Prime Minister's son a stinging rebuke from the normally phlegmatic pro. 'Could you believe that?' he declared after we repaired to the airport bar. 'What a fucking plonker.'

I was far from recovered from our session when my plane landed at Newcastle, stumbling from the luggage carousel with enough bottles of hooch on my trolley to start an off-licence business. The predatory customs officer must have thought it was his birthday, especially after I elected to go through the green channel. It was a fair cop, and if he threw a party with every bottle he confiscated, good luck to him. I was just relieved he did not pursue his prosecution threat. The warning against future transgressions was as sobering as an ice-cold shower.

My first encounter with Faldo was at the 1976 Greater Manchester Open at Wilmslow. We started on the right foot and became reasonably friendly in the early part of his career. I lost that contact when I came off golf before having a run-in when he refused me an interview after I joined The Mail On Sunday, a rebuff which subsequently, and to my eternal regret and shame, led to me behaving disgracefully at an official dinner during the 2008 US Masters week at Augusta.

Faldo had already been accorded a level of expectation similar to that subsequently achieved by Rory McIlroy, when, as a precocious teenager, he joined the European tour shortly before turning professional. One of his participated tournaments was the 1976 Greater Manchester Open played at Wilmslow Golf Club. The future three times Open and thrice Masters champion Faldo may have had an inconspicuous knock but, if he had scored as well over the Cheshire parkland course as he did on a visit to a local nightspot, he certainly would not have had to wait until he won the Skol Lager Individual

Championship at Gleneagles a year later for his first tour success.

After joining Mark McComack's formidable IMG group, he was allocated a personal manager. John Simpson (a lovely bloke) was handed the job of catering for his young client's every need. And, with a little help from me, he certainly seemed to satisfy one in particular that weekend. Becoming acquainted with both in the course of covering the tournament, I happened to mention to Simpson I knew the area pretty well having lived in nearby Cheadle Hulme during the sixties, and it prompted him to inquire whether I knew of somewhere Faldo could enjoy a relaxing evening.

He hardly had to mention the required scenery and I knew just the perfect place. Bredbury Hall, near Stockport, had a reputation for attracting the loveliest ladies from the Cheshire set and surrounding area. Let's just say the pair of them were more than happy with my recommendation.

Reverting to covering football, I did not see a lot of Faldo apart from when I was drafted in, both working for The Sun and later after moving to The Mail On Sunday to help out at the bigger golf tournaments. When our paths crossed, there was always recognition and courtesy and I applauded his elevation to become the world's top golfer.

So, it was with a degree of confidence that I responded to the inquiry from MOS sports editor, Roger Kelly: 'How well do you know Nick Faldo?' I told him 'well enough' when he mentioned Virgin had offered a free flight to Orlando, Florida, and it would be an excellent opportunity to get an exclusive one-on-one interview with the great man.

My mission became less than impossible when a little research revealed one of the assistant pros at the Lake Nona complex, where Faldo lived, hailed from my neck of the woods in the North-East and when I eventually arrived at the gates he was waiting to greet me and, having been assured there would be no problem with Faldo, chauffeured me to his residence.

And that's as far as I got!

After ringing the bell, the door was opened by a female staff member. I told her who I was and would it possible to speak to her boss. She disappeared to pass on the message, returning to say Faldo was very busy and did not have time to see me. 'Could you please tell him I've flown in from London and I wouldn't take up more than half an hour of his time,' I pleaded. Back she came to repeat her earlier message, adding that he had said I should have arranged an interview through the proper channels.

Of course, he was quite correct. It was just a case of ego getting in the way of eagerness. I wanted to let the boss know Faldo and I were still buddies—kind of! But that wasted trip rankled, and over the years festered into animosity, although it was mild comfort to learn the vast majority of people involved in golf also reckoned he was a bit of a prat.

And so, it came to pass that Mr Faldo and myself were among the guests at the swish European Tour dinner held annually on the Tuesday evening of Masters week at the magnificently palatial Augusta Country Club, which adjoins the much younger but nevertheless better known Augusta National Golf Club, home of the first major tournament of the year.

Like millions of others, I had drooled annually at the television images of what is surely the most famous golf course in the world, hardly daring to imagine one day I would actually go there. But the love affair was consummated in style in 2004 when The Mail on Sunday sports editor, Malcolm Vallerius, handed me a four-day Masters pass as well as flights and accommodation in one of Augusta's smartest hotels by way of a retirement present.

And I loved it so much, exploiting all the mental pictures of holes that used to banish my winter blues with names such as Pink Dogwood, Flowering Crab Apple, Yellow Jasmine; not forgetting Amen Corner and Golden Bell, the famous par three 12th hole over Rae's Creek, that I went back again the following year—and again, and again! In fact, I almost became a regular in the late soul star James Brown's hometown until my last visit there in 2012.

For that I was grateful to Vallerius, who paid for my flights; to the paper's Irish sports editor, Jack White, who arranged my accreditation to concentrate on the Irish players and last, but certainly not least, to the Sun's golf correspondent David Facey who allowed me to kip down on a divan in his condo for the price of a dozen bottles of white wine (which we guzzled in a nightly ritual) and a couple of dinners.

They were momentous weeks combining a golfing paradise with social activity, spent mainly in the company of Facey, Jim Mossop and Martin Hardy, formerly the Daily Express's golf man, before joining Chubby Chandler's International Sports Management group which handled top golfers such as major winners Darren Clarke, Louis Oosthuizen, Charl

Schwartzel and, for a time, Ernie Els and Rory McIlroy, as well as Lee Westwood among others.

But, if I blamed too much social activity for going completely over the top in my confrontation with Faldo, it would not come even close to excusing my behaviour. Suffice it to say, after arriving the previous evening and immediately hitting the sack, I woke up on the aforementioned Tuesday full of beans. After an idyllic breakfast of oatmeal and bacon and eggs on the clubhouse balcony overlooking the lawn; a leisurely stroll around the luscious golf course; a couple of beers in the clubhouse bar followed by barbecue lunch on the lawn washed down by a voluptuous Shiraz, I was off and running. And this perfect day was to be topped off by a superbly entertaining evening at the European Tour dinner.

Showered, jacket and tied, it seemed criminal not to join Facey in tackling the bottle of Californian Chardonnay which had been chilling in the fridge back at the digs, by way of an aperitif—several aperitifs in fact.

So, by the time I was proffered the obligatory Sundowner standing on the white-painted balcony at the Country Club, it became a priority to try, as desperately as I could, to disguise the fact I was already three sheets to the wind. A sensible person might have feigned illness, made an excuse and left. But this was not an occasion for sensibility. This was my mate Mossop's Masters swansong. After covering the tournament for nigh on thirty years he had been cast out by the Sunday Telegraph. This was to be his last visit to Augusta and Mitchell Platts had organised a special farewell presentation as part of the evening. I was certainly not going to miss that.

The function was running smoothly. My wine intake slowed down enough for me to engage in conversation with a minimum of gibberish. But the damage had been done. Mossop returned to our table after receiving warm applause for a dignified and typically witty trip down the memory lane, and then it all went downhill.

One of my table companions, John Paramor, now the Tour's chief referee but someone I'd known since my rookie golf reporting days, mentioned it would be nice if one of Jim's colleagues could say a few words about him. Foolishly, Jim and I having been friends since we were both trainee journalists, I decided that should be me.

Staggering to the centre of the room, I lurched into a tall plant-stand on top of which perched a pot containing a luxuriant example of Georgia's finest flora and fauna. The stand went flying, spilling plant, foliage and soil all over the carpet. It got worse. I then launched into a drunken, expletive filled speech about how long I'd known Mossop; what a top guy he was and what a shower of shithouses the Sunday Telegraph were to let him go.

It was not a complete disaster. That's because there were enough of my colleagues inebriated enough to engage my tomfoolery with raucous encouragement. But there were those who clapped slowly and quietly as I made my way back to my table where there was a dutiful back-slapping welcome.

Now you would think, having probably escaped the total wrath of the tour hierarchy who might have excused my antics as mildly amusing slapstick, I might have called it a night. And I would have done so, until I spotted Mr Faldo. Six times major winner, the most successful golfer these shores had produced, captain of the forthcoming Ryder Cup team; he may have been all of these, but to me that night, he was just the arsehole who would not give me an interview after I'd flown all the way to Florida, especially after I'd furthered his social pleasures in Bredbury Hall. And I was not going to miss this opportunity to let him know about it.

The confrontation was short and not particularly sweet; I don't think Faldo managed to get a word in edgewise until I was ushered away. But it was done. Satisfaction was mine. He knew he couldn't mess with me and I'd got a major monkey off my back.

The following morning—even before the massive hangover erupted like the climax of the 1812 overture—I realised just how abominably I'd behaved the previous evening. Possible reassurance from Facey evaporated with him pulling no punches about how he thought the powers that be would react to my performance. No amount of humble pie would be enough to get me out of the shit.

Grovelling apologies to Faldo, the European tour chief executive George O'Grady, my friend Mitchell Platts were needed, and the sooner the better. Mossop joined me on the lawn in front of the clubhouse where the great and the good of golf's officialdom congregated, and among them, Sir Nick chatting with a group of friends and associates.

We waited until my target walked away before I made my move. Unfortunately, Faldo saw me coming and quickened his pace towards the clubhouse entrance; but not quick enough to avoid this pursuer. 'Nick, can I just take a minute of your time to apologise unconditionally for last night,' I stammered, having finally persuaded him to stop.

'My behaviour was reprehensible and far from it being an excuse, I'd had a lot to drink.' Faldo looked down at me, half smiled and simply remarked, 'Had you... I hadn't noticed!' I suppose it was a half acceptance of my remorse but there were no repercussions when we met up again during his disastrous captaincy of the Ryder Cup team at Valhalla later that year.

And the Tour officials were more than beneficial when it came to deciding what would be a fitting penalty for my antics. Their one-year dinner ban was hardly a punishment that fitted the crime but I suspect their leniency may have something to do with the popularity of a bloke whose personality hardly matches up to his prowess.

He did himself no favours with the European players at the Gleneagles Ryder Cup when, commentating for American television covering the golfing spectacle, he questioned the attitude, character and talent of Sergio Garcia at Valhalla, one of the team's most committed members, describing him as 'useless'. It didn't win him many friends but it did further influence a few people's opinions about his crassness.

CHAPTER EIGHTEEN
THE GLORY OF RORY

For every pompously pretentious golfing prima-donna there are countless others who celebrate their endowment of prodigious ability and dedication with commendable gratitude and indeed humility. At least in my limited experience of covering the sport, I learned, with notable exceptions such as Sir Nick Faldo, Colin Montgomerie and a comparative non-entity called Ronan Rafferty (all right I'm biased; all three at one time or another dismissed my requests for an interview with brusque contempt) the more talented the player the better he was to deal with.

For instance, in spite of all the high stakes involved, both Lee Westwood and his pal Darren Clarke play golf with smiles on their faces. This probably had a lot to do with being stabled in the International Sports Management team headed by that larger than life character Andrew 'Chubby' Chandler, who has made a much better job of harnessing the talents of major winners such as Clarke, Rory McIlroy, Louis Oosthuisen and Charl Schwartzel than when he relied on his own prowess between tee and green which was his wont when I first knew him as a journeyman pro.

Chandler also had a three-year association with McIlroy after he turned professional in September 2007. I first heard about the lad from Hollywood, County Down from a friend and photographer colleague of mine at The Mail on Sunday. Big Ian McIlgorm, no mean golfer himself, kept banging on about this schoolboy wonder who was ordained to be the best in the world. 'I'm telling you, Cassie; this kid is gonna be better than Tiger Woods.' The big fella never held back in his gushing admiration of his fellow Northern Irishman.

It was something of a labour of love when, eventually making his acquaintance and that of his dad, Gerry, I was given the green light by his personal manager, Stuart Cage, to write about them, with the extra pleasure of doing it after I'd walked the course with them at Carnoustie in the 2007 Open Championship where, at just 17, he recorded his final triumph before turning pro by winning the silver medal for the leading amateur.

And our paths crossed regularly at the big tournaments. McIlroy Snr. seemed as regular as a three-leafed clover and at the same time as rare as a four-leafed one; unassuming but proudly bullish— anybody's dad really. It would be as good an indication as you could get how McIlroy junior's talent was first seeded, nurtured and finally brought to bloom.

Quite simply, Rory is just a chip off the old man's block, as ordinary as toast, albeit heavily smothered in the finest Beluga when it comes to golfing ability.

From a personal point of view, it was more than interesting that, as a member of Europe's Ryder Cup team, he renewed an acquaintance with Sir Alex Ferguson before and during the tournament, particularly remembering my role in the pair of them meeting in the first place. Little more than four years before Fergie was recruited by captain Paul McGinley to give his team a pre-tournament pep talk at Gleneagles, the young Irishman had good reason to thank the former Manchester United manager for providing the inspiration to go on and win his first big tournament in the USA, especially at a time when his morale was at its lowest ebb following a missed cut at his second Masters.

After an Augusta baptism of fire in 2009, McIlroy was desperate to bury the memory of a debut which had been memorable for all the wrong reasons. His magical journey to what (alongside St Andrew's) probably ranks as one of the world's most iconic golfing venues, was spoiled by being called before the rules committee, whose inquiry into a possible violation after TV cameras had picked him up kicking the sand after he had left his ball in the bunker adjacent to the 18th green, lasted long into the evening.

For those of us covering the tournament, delaying our departure from the course until a four-hour adjudication cleared him of any rules infringement was a minor inconvenience inasmuch as we had to temporarily postpone the social delights of the Washington Road strip.

But for 19-year-old McIlroy and his connections it was an enormous relief not to be booted out. It would surely have put the cap on a miserable finish to an eventful round in which he put himself on the heels of the leaders by eagling the 13th only to come perilously close to missing the cut by dropping five shots in the last three holes.

Move the calendar on twelve months to an older, maybe a little wiser and a certainly more ambitious Ulsterman. But, sadly in terms of performance, it turned out an even less successful trip down Magnolia Lane.

In fairness, the lad had been receiving treatment for a back problem but rounds of 74 and 77 hardly lifted his forlorn demeanour as, having paid the penalty of an early exit, he headed for his Hollywood home, ready to fling his clubs into Belfast Lough.

'I don't know what is going on,' he moaned. 'I am getting frustrated very easily and getting down on myself. I think I need to go home and get my head sorted. The whole game is getting to me at the moment.

'Maybe I just need to sit down and tell myself I am only 20 and things are actually going well for me. But I expected better from myself.

'I am supposed to play at Quail Hollow in a couple of weeks but I might need a bit more time to let this injury clear up. I just need to take a bit of a break and come back with a refreshed attitude.'

McIlroy needed friendly advice—and quickly. 'If there's something weird and it don't look good, who ya gonna call?' I decided it was a case for football history's most famous psychobabble ghostbuster. I thought of getting Rex Kramer (Airplane lovers will remember him) but, if there was one man who could rid him of his mental demons, it was Sir Alex Ferguson.

I made the Manchester United manager aware of McIlroy's plight via a transatlantic phone call. My timing could have been a touch better. The previous weekend United had been knocked off the top of the table, losing 2-1 at Old Trafford to title rivals Chelsea in a game which turned out to be the crucial championship decider.

Four days later, again in front of their home supporters, Fergie's team were dumped out of the Champions League at the quarter-final stage when they lost on away goals to Bayern Munich.

I'll admit I was nervous as I waited for that familiar Scottish 'hullo'—it was early afternoon in Augusta; late evening in England. I need not have been worried. 'Leave it to me. I'll give him a call,' was his immediate sympathetic response. And he did. And I had a cracking exclusive on the Sunday—a tale which proved of mutual benefit to an Englishman, Scotsman and Irishman!

McIlroy was more than surprised to hear his idol's voice on his mobile. Fergie said later: 'I mentioned it hadn't been a great week for either of us but, like me, he would bounce back.

'We're both too good at our jobs for that not to happen. You never make rash decisions when things have gone against you. I told him, "Get back out there and show everybody what you can do."

And get back out there is just what he did. Two weeks later, McIlroy won the North Carolina tournament he intended to watch from his armchair by four shots from the Masters champion Phil Mickelson, clinching his first PGA tour victory by shattering the

Quail Hollow course record with a ten under par 62 final round.

In fact, Fergie and his young pal became something of a habit with each other, particularly when McIlroy needed post-Masters commiseration. It certainly became a source of name-dropping piss-taking at my expense among the British and Irish contingent in the Augusta Media Centre, particularly when his third attempt at winning the green jacket in 2011 ended with the biggest nightmare of all.

Standing on the tenth tee with a two-shot lead on the final day, McIlroy's drive almost disturbed the Sunday afternoon barbecue in one of the white-painted gems of palatial real estate deep in the woods bordering the left side of the fairway. It was the prelude to a calamitous three holes approaching and around Amen Corner which handed the jacket to his Chubby Chandler team-mate Charl Schwartzel, who proudly sported golf's most famous menswear at Chubby's celebration later that evening.

This time Fergie needed no prompting from me to get in touch. 'I really felt for the lad,' he told me. 'It was heart-breaking seeing him suffer.'

Prophetically, he then observed, 'There's no doubt he'll put what happened behind him because he's got real talent. He didn't need me to jolly him along but I just wanted him to know he has everybody at United behind him.' Two months later McIlroy plundered the US Open at Congressional in Maryland by eight strokes; the first of his four majors to date.

And you can have your house on future transatlantic calls between the pair becoming obsolete. When Rory McIlroy does win the Masters—as he surely will—don't be surprised to find a certain Glaswegian knight of the realm among his Augusta gallery to help him celebrate.

'Clubs' for me, growing up in a background where finances governed one's sporting participation—school provided the opportunity to play football and cricket; the backstreets added the extra curricula activities—were places where your dad, granddad, uncles and cousins enjoyed their pints, darts and dominoes.

So, for someone who came late to appreciate and enjoy golf (playing it at a lowly standard) and then, like some starry-eyed fan, meeting and writing about the legendary superstars who dominated the tournaments, it was dreamsville.

I am not ashamed to describe the thrill of a one-on-one interview with Jack Nicklaus, sitting on opposite armchairs when he came to the Algarve in Portugal to publicise a course he had designed.

Or having Arnold Palmer—on tape—ordering a steward to let 'Bob' through the wicker gate that leads up to the Turnberry Hotel so we could conduct an interview 'on the hoof'.

Or Seve Ballesteros asking if I didn't mind him postponing our interview for an hour in Killarney Golf Club while he had lunch, '…but I would delay lunch, if you are in a hurry,' he smiled.

Oh yes, and comparing the delights of Blackpool's Pleasure Park with similar attractions in America with Tiger Woods no less, as we shared a courtesy car ride to Royal Lytham and St Annes Golf Course, now thereby hangs a tale!

I had arrived at the course on the afternoon of Tuesday of the 1996 Open week to pick up accreditation; too late to check in at the Grand Hotel in Blackpool and still get back in time for the annual Association of Golf Writers' dinner, traditionally held in the R and A tent at the Open venue.

I decided to leave my car in the media parking lot, attend the dinner and grab a taxi to the hotel later on. Fine, until the following day when I had to be at the course before lunchtime. After all it was Wednesday (Bollinger tent day) and I couldn't get a cab for love nor money.

That was when I spotted the courtesy car parked outside with its female chauffeur waiting in the lobby. After establishing there was only one golfer to be ferried to the course, a spot of cajoling found me in the back seat waiting for my travelling companion—none other than Woods, who was playing in his final big tournament as an amateur.

Introducing myself, we shook hands and off we went down the Promenade, chatting away to each other about this and that until we passed the Pleasure Beach. 'That, Tiger,' I informed him pointing out the Big Dipper, 'is probably the biggest of its kind in Europe.'

It wasn't quite him mentioning that in the US they have bigger sauce bottles than Blackpool Tower, but he did have a wide grin when he said the Dipper was nothing compared to what there is where he came from. After we arrived we shook hands and I wished him the best of luck; he probably would have won the amateur's silver medal anyway.

The next time I saw him was a year later at the Royal Troon Open. I even asked a question at one of his press conferences. He didn't remember me. I was hurt!

But not half as much as Jimmy Tarbuck was after he read his so-called Open diary in The Sun after the first day of the 1983 tournament at Royal Birkdale. What appeared under the heading 'Tarbuck's Diary' had precious little to do with what he thought would be published after our exclusive interview.

The comedian, himself a keen golfer, had been bought up by the paper to offer his thoughts on each day's play. He may have been one of the top comics of his day but put him in the company of the stellar names of the fairways and he was just as huge a fan as the next man.

It was down to me to put his words in the paper but he relished the idea of talking about his idols. It was a pleasurable job, especially when it meant hob-nobbing with one of the biggest stars of show business. Tarbuck launched into his role with a will, waxing enthusiastically about an opening day leader board which had Craig Stadler leading by three strokes from Tom Watson, with Nick Faldo and Sam Torrance breathing down their necks.

It was all serious stuff, and that was the problem; it was too serious for the indefatigable Sun editor, Kelvin McKenzie. My Open colleague, Frank Clough, took the call on our desk in the media centre which sparked hours of personal anguish. The voice on the other end of the line spoke in decibels:

'Okay, I'll tell him,' said Frank. Putting the phone down, he turned to me. 'That was Kelvin. He doesn't like the Tarbuck stuff. He said he thinks it's fucking shit. You're gonna have to do it again.'

My problem then was to find the London Palladium's answer to Henry Longhurst—no mobiles in those days either. I'd interviewed him before he went out for a round at nearby Hillside. Hopefully he would still be around either the course or the clubhouse. He wasn't!

I reported back to Cloughie who passed on my predicament to the desk in London. Ten minutes passed and the phone rang again. 'It's Kelvin,' he said passing it over. 'He wants to speak to you.'

Actually, I didn't need the phone; I would have been able to hear him all the way from London to Southport without it! 'Cass, this is fucking rubbish,' he bawled. 'I don't want Tarbuck thinking he can write about golf; I'm paying people like you to do that. I want him to be funny. I want a laugh a line.'

Vainly I pointed out that I had searched high and low for Tarbuck without success. 'Right,' he said. 'You fancy yourself as a bit of a comedian. You'll have to fucking write it—and be quick about it. I need it within the hour!' And down went the phone.

I suppose I felt like a bit like Sydney Carton before he knelt on the guillotine. It was awfully difficult to crack jokes when your backside is hanging out of your trousers—and hopefully I've done far, far better things than I did then. I remember beginning with a line about Greg Norman being sent to Coventry, which was a bit of a tale from the first day.

'They'll be thrilled. They've sold half their team,' I trotted out. And it went from bad to worse. Was Tarbuck amused? Well the writ that landed on the boss's desk would seem to indicate that was hardly the case. His threat to sue the paper for damaging his

206

reputation was placated by a substantial financial compensation. Needless to say, Tarbuck's Diary lasted one day.

But even that was far from my biggest memory of that weekend on the North-West coast. Surviving the Tarbuck episode by the skin of my teeth, Frank and I covered an exciting second day of the tournament which ended with top names such as Stadler, Watson, Faldo and Lee Trevino at the top of the leader board. Then, it was relaxez-vous; dinner, wine and drink. The following day was Saturday, the day daily men like us put away their pens; our day off.

The bar in the Prince of Wales Hotel was still bouncing in the early hours when I spotted Cloughie, who had declared some time earlier, lurching through the crowd in my direction. 'We're going. We're off to the sixth green,' he announced.

Mild protests that I was enjoying the company and was far too pissed to move on to some disco were silenced by my colleague snapping, 'It isn't a disco, you pillock. We're going to the sixth green at Birkdale. Somebody's dug it up.'

It was another prime example—whenever the unexpected arises—that sports journalists can switch to becoming news gatherers in a trice. Drinks were jettisoned as the troops were quickly rounded up. Those who had gone to bed were quickly roused; that is apart from The Mirror's Ron Wills, who had obviously lapsed into a state of total unconsciousness judging from his lack of response to us banging on his room door.

After piling into taxis to try and get as close to the scene as possible, the cream of golf writing talent together with lesser mortals such as I, found ourselves sartorially unprepared; climbing, scrambling, slipping and sliding over sand dunes in pitch darkness to try and get to where the black night was illuminated by a barrage of floodlights around the green in question.

Of course, the whole area was cordoned off with an army of security guards surrounding it, but we did manage to see that the green was seriously damaged and probably out of commission as far as the tournament was concerned, although, as it transpired, the R and A were able to make contingency plans.

You had to wonder where the security was earlier when friends and supporters of a bloke called Dennis Kelly, protesting he had been wrongly convicted of murder, sabotaged the putting surface by digging holes in the turf and daubing 'Free Kelly' messages with paint all over it.

Anyway, there was no sleep on a night when golf made the front and back page splashes in all the papers—including The Daily Mirror. Ron, entirely oblivious of all that had gone on, woke up to see his by-line under a screaming headline on the front page; phoning the story to his newspaper was a joint effort to make sure he wasn't left out.

I remember Tom Clark, the Daily Mail sports editor waiting for us when we got back to the hotel organising a champagne breakfast—just what we needed (following a refreshing shower) to kick-start another day-long session.

Frank and I did what came naturally to us on Saturdays; a visit to the exhibition tent when it was an exhibition tent, packed with stands tempting punters to buy anything from half a dozen balls to a world cruise.

And the more go-ahead exhibitors usually recruited a couple of attractive promotion girls to help with the sales pitch.

It was on one such stage that we loitered for a glass or two to enjoy the scenery. We were there when who should walk past but the aforementioned Mr Wills, feeling extremely chipper after seven or eight hours in the hay. Ron eyed Clough and Cass, bubbly in hand, enjoying the close attentions of a couple of stunning blondes.

And that's when he made his big mistake. Looking at the pair of us in mock disdain, he declared, 'It's nice to see the professionals at work.' Quick as a flash, Cloughie retorted, 'Well if you'd been on the sixth green at four o'clock this morning, you would have, wouldn't you Ron!' A classic put down which Wills graciously acknowledged with an airy wave as he continued on his way. Tarbuck would surely have been proud of it.

CHAPTER NINETEEN
BIG MAL AND BESTIE

I encountered Malcolm Allison late. More's the pity. Initially I thought him arrogant, self-centred, contemptuous and downright ill-mannered. Latterly I learned what a terrible judge of character I was!

Based in the North-East our paths did not cross that much but I well remember attending my first after-match press conference with him when he was Joe Mercer's first team coach at Manchester City. By then, because of his reputation as a larger than life character whose off the field notoriety mirrored his brilliance as an innovative coach, he had amassed an army of media sycophants who hung on every syllable he uttered.

They were a devoted bunch who thirsted for and then responded with uproarious mirth whenever he dropped even the most remotely amusing quip. And woe betide any newcomer who, for any reason, fell victim to his legendary put-downs. I always felt that Kenny Dalglish resented even the mildest intrusive question about his team's performance, reacting with near hostility; with Allison it was a smile, a nod or a wink, or, after making sure his throng of cohorts was on the case, a pause. And with me, it was a pause—a long, long, long pause.

If I cannot exactly remember my question, I won't forget his answer or, to be more precise, his non-answer! Having listened to him respond positively to a number of questions, I chanced my arm with something like an inquiry about whether he thought the opposing team (it was probably Newcastle or Sunderland) should have had a penalty.

Barely looking in my direction, he remained silent. It was almost as if he hadn't heard the question. Foolishly, and feeling a hot flush rising from my toenails, I further pressed him about the incident; again silence, broken only by audible titters from my colleagues, until after some delay he suddenly piped up with some remark of little consequence.

It seems I had been given the usual cold shoulder treatment Allison reserved for freshers; those he did not recognise at his press conferences. It was all in good fun and the laugh was on me, but I still came away thinking he was a supercilious arsehole.

Like I said, I could not be more wrong as I began to learn some months later when he and I did the first of several Q and A's at various sports dinners. We recounted the after-match conference episode and his explanation that it was 'just a bit of fun', which incidentally, now an eager recruit in his sycophantic army, I witnessed more than once later, sharing the comedy at the hapless victim's expense.

Allison—albeit with his City mentor reining him in when he needed it—and Mercer provide nostalgic memories of a golden age of British statesman-like managers who seemed as permanent at their clubs as their famous football strips. Men like Bill Shankly, Matt Busby, Bill Nicholson, Harry Catterick, Dave

Sexton, Joe Harvey and Alan Brown all enjoyed lengthy periods operating simultaneously at the top level. They worked for tolerant local businessmen who were nevertheless as desperate for their clubs to achieve success as the monolithic billionaires who run Premier League clubs today. It was just that the price of being less than successful was not as high.

There is little doubt that some foreign managers have enhanced the top division but there are none more innovative than Allison was. Whether addressing a top level coaching course or just talking to some spellbound individual in a bar, his tactical knowledge was mesmerising. On a personal level, there were the times he would explain to me how and why a goal should or should not have been scored; gush enthusiastically about what he suggested was an undefendable set piece whether from a free-kick, corner, or even throw-in, and then throw up his hands in abject surrender when I failed to grasp the intricacies of his theory, usually by looking totally vague when he would pose what he felt was a relatively simple question.

There were many champagne moments like that, particularly after he became Middlesbrough manager in 1982. He lasted 18 months at a club so beset with financial problems he was unable to put his stamp on it—well, up to a point. Because there was one all to brief successful spell just after he took over, the hilarious consequences of which had to remain secret at the time but can now be revealed.

Although his appointment was not franked until October 23, Allison had assumed control after Bobby Murdoch was sacked a month earlier with the team rock-bottom of the Second Division with two only points from seven games. The improvement under him was immediate, with four wins and four draws in the next eight games lifting them up to just below halfway. Of course, he revelled in becoming big national news again, with journalists queuing up for interviews and comments. But our friendship kicked in when he made me an offer I just could not refuse.

'The secret is in our dressing room preparation for a game,' he confided. 'If you like, you can come in before our next game; watch what happens and write about it.' Of course, I jumped at the chance. As instructed, accompanied by Sun photographer Keith Perry, I turned up at Ayresome Park's home dressing room door about three-quarters of an hour before the 3pm Saturday afternoon kick-off time. The opposition, Blackburn Rovers, in a similar league position, were not expected to be a problem.

I got on well with most of the players so, albeit with a bit of piss-taking jocularity, they readily accepted our presence in the room while they got into their strips. Then suddenly, about five minutes before going out, Allison's booming voice silenced the conversational buzz. 'Right lads. On your feet,' he bellowed. Instantly the players shot off their seats and stood facing each other, granite-faced. At another command from the Boro manager they threw their arms around each other's shoulders, teeth clenched and eye-balling those opposite like they were mortal enemies. Perry's camera motor was rat-a-tatting like a machine gun while I made feverish notes. 'Are we better than them?' thundered Allison. 'Yes, boss!' they thundered back. 'Are we gonna make them wish they'd never came here?' 'Yes, boss!' And so, the verbal storm went on until he blasted the final challenge: 'Right! Let's get out there and win this football match.'

And out they went, and peace and quiet replaced an atmosphere that crackled with indescribable emotion. Perry and I looked at each other. 'Brilliant, just fucking brilliant,' was all he could manage. I was tingling. Without question, if the big man had thrown me a first team shirt I'd have gone on the pitch and kicked shit out of the nearest opponent. I made a few more notes and my colleague checked his camera before we parted; him to his spot behind one of the goals; me to the press box, five minutes away at the most.

By the time I sat down Blackburn were one up. Not long after it was two. And when the referee blew a merciful final whistle it was five, with a single goal reply from Middlesbrough. Big Mal's expression of total disbelief after the match was a picture. 'I think it might be better if we bin that piece, what do you think?' he smiled. And another potential exclusive never saw the light of day.

I'm not sure whether Allison's pre-match ritual went the journey but it was typical of the routines and superstitions managers will resort to if they believe it will get them a good result. It's all bollocks of course but they illustrate the lighter side of the game as well as providing amusing material for noted after-dinner speakers such as the sadly missed Howard Kendall and some of his championship-winning Everton players. The story goes that Kendall, believing it would improve team performances, decided on a bit of team bonding by taking his players to lunch every Monday. And it worked, at least for a while.

Anyway, after a couple of defeats, he addressed his players again. 'Lads, I've decided that having these Monday lunches isn't working any more so I'm stopping them.' Then followed a theatrical pause before a wink and, punching the air, he bellowed, 'Starting next week, I'm switching them to Tuesday!'

I suppose it was appropriate that a relationship which started with me being cringingly embarrassed should have a similar finale, although this time it was not totally down to big Mal. He had asked me to join an exalted company of after-dinner entertainers at a benefit function in Manchester in his honour including George Best and Rodney Marsh with the infamous comedian Bernard Manning winding up (literally) the evening in his own inimitable style.

Not for the first time, I was thrilled and not a little over-awed to be sharing a top table with Best. I saw little of him in the flesh in his glory days at United but I got to write about him when his playing career was in decline, but not enough to prevent him signing a £2,000 pay as you play deal with Scottish club Hibernian.

I was indebted to his great friend and Daily Mail columnist Jeff Powell for effecting an introduction in an Edinburgh hotel on the evening before his Hibs debut in November 1979. And, if I say it was in the hotel bar, I should quickly add that Bestie was as dry as the desert, drinking only coke. Which was in complete contrast to me knocking back large gin and tonics like there was going be a world shortage of Gordons.

And then it became my turn to buy. 'Same again, lads. Sure, I can't tempt you, Bestie,' I slobbered. Bestie shook his head and, with a disdainful nod in my direction, observed, 'Don't you think you've had enough.'

The comment pierced my inebriation with enough accuracy for me to make my excuses and leave. Well, you would, wouldn't you? But there were more than a couple of subsequent evenings when we did Q&A's at sports dinners in the North-East. He had a captivating personality; full of fun, without any edge. A real pleasure to get to know.

Anyway, the running order for the Allison fundraiser was not set in stone but we were given approximate starting times and speech lengths. Best and Marsh, doing a question and answer session were allotted half an hour; I was told 15 minutes and Manning got as long as he liked.

The problem was the comedian's starting timing had to be precise. He rarely attended such functions; typically, he would ask for and be given a precise time to stand up and anybody who encroached on his territory was unceremoniously bulldozed out of the way—on this occasion it was me. I blamed George and Rodney. Their patter was so brilliant they were worth the price of the ticket on their own. They delivered the goods with a combination of wonderful anecdotes and hilarious repartee which had the audience in stitches.

But they went on and on, until after about an hour or so, and to rapturous encores from the dinner guests, they reluctantly sat down. And then it was me. It was a bit like following champagne and caviar with bread and jam. But it was a sympathetic audience and, no doubt out of the respect they had for Allison, I managed to get a few early laughs, enough anyway to march purposefully on. I was roughly about five minutes into a speech which I'd agonised over for a week or so, when there was a roar from the audience which I knew had sod all to do with my last punchline.

I felt a tap on my shoulder and, as a hand grabbed the microphone, I turned around and there was the man himself. 'Fucking sit down, son, and let a pro take over,' said Manning. And, of course, that's exactly what I did amid hoots of derision and laughter at the expense of another victim of his withering character dissection. But I did still manage to squeeze a laugh out of the dinner guests at his expense.

Bashing his pockets in a mock search, he announced he wanted a cigarette. Still on the mike he nudged me and declared, 'You haven't got a fag, son, have you?' I replied, 'Sorry, my friend, I don't smoke.' 'Glad to hear it, son,' he said. 'Smoking will kill you.' 'That's okay, mate,' I cut back. 'I've died already tonight.' And let me tell you, he did not like it.

I learned at a very early age never to take on accomplished funny men who delight in swallowing and then spitting out loud-mouthed hecklers. Inebriated one night in a cabaret club in Newcastle, I challenged the late, great Max Wall, who then clinically cut me to pieces, finishing with, 'I'm truly sorry, sunshine. If I've offended you, believe me!'

I have since been fortunate enough to share a top table with many brilliant comics such as Mick Miller, Jimmy Bright, Johnny Casson, Bob 'The Cat' Bevan, and I've already spoken of my admiration for Bobby Pattinson. I have the highest regard for those who just want to make people laugh. It's a lot more difficult than you think.

However, there was one guy who tried to embarrass me to get some cheap laughs and probably wished he hadn't. I mention it sadly, not only because Lennie Bennett is no longer with us having died in tragic circumstances at a comparatively early age, but also remembering he began his working life as a reporter on a local paper in Blackpool before achieving fame as a comedian and TV game show host.

Bennett provided the cabaret entertainment in a Liverpool club where I, Joe Melling and two other great journalistic colleagues, John Donoghue and Tony Hardisty of The Daily and Sunday Express, repaired to after covering a midweek football match on Merseyside. Two things were important in dictating the course of events that evening. One; I looked a right prat. At the time, I had pathetic affectation about having long hair; a droopy moustache and pair of bluish tinted horn-rimmed spectacles. And two; the room was less than half-full and the atmosphere bordered on funereal.

Mindful of our table on the edge of the stage we maintained the best of order, reacting cheerily to Lennie's gags and funny stories, but his was a thankless task; the audience was big enough only to offer him hollow laughter. Most comics would have struggled and, even in a city where there's said to be a comedian in every household, audience encouragement was in short supply that night.

But then Lennie decided to get personal, walking across to our table, he leaned over to me and, microphone in hand, cackled: 'Just finished your welding shift mate?' I let it go, but he persisted with a few more snide comments until I decided enough was enough. 'Look, Lennie,' I said. 'We're here having a nice night; we're enjoying your act and we appreciate your difficulties so there was no need for the insults. I now want you to remember you started it.'

Much of his material was not particularly original so I deliberately killed a few of his punchlines before he got to them. He had a nightmare and, in spite of his boorish behaviour early on, I didn't enjoy watching Lennie die on his backside or when he came over before he walked off to say, 'Thanks a fucking bunch, mate.' But we did exchange pleasantries some time later when he was a guest at the Football Writers' Association dinner. To be fair, when I mentioned that Liverpool evening, he just smiled dismissively and observed, 'Sorry, sunshine. I can't remember that at all!' It was just what I deserved.

It's almost boastful to say one has been ridiculed by the best. I'm just proud and fortunate to have even acquainted with such sporting icons as Malcolm Allison. A larger than life character in every sense of the word.

CHAPTER TWENTY
GAZZA

As I have already alluded to in an earlier chapter, if I could nominate one major change in the job of reporting football over the past fifty years it would be the polarisation of relationships between journalists and footballers. Today's scribes will never be able to experience the closeness that created the bond of trust which, I am delighted to remember, I enjoyed with many, many iconic football personalities.

It would be extremely unlikely in the current climate of sensational and website journalism to become close enough to big name footballers to be able to turn a blind eye (as we did) to what they might get up to in their leisure time. Great contacts were made in bars and night clubs simply because newspapers never found out about their social activities. Tweeting was avian talk.

I remember one top Newcastle international footballer pulling me after Saturday game and pleading with me to call him around seven o'clock that evening. 'Make out somebody has let you down as a speaker at a dinner and you are desperate for a last minute stand-in,' he said. I had no doubt he was looking for an excuse to indulge in a little extra-marital hanky-panky but I readily agreed to make the call.

Trouble was, I was getting into my regular after-match drinking session in the local when I noticed the time; 7:15pm. The only phone in the pub was behind the bar. 'Jack, any chance of a quick local call on your phone,' I wondered of the landlord. 'Sorry, mate, personal use only. If I let you, I'll have to let others use it. You'll have to use the call box across the road,' he said.

Sod's law kicked in when, after risking life and limb in a mad dash across the traffic-riddled main road, I found the kiosk occupied by someone who had me standing there for at least ten minutes before I could get in and grab the phone. 'Look, mate, it's me. Sorry I'm late; couldn't get to the phone,' I blustered. 'Who is it?' responded the player. 'What do you want?' He sounded prickly. 'I'm calling you as arranged. What do you want me to say?' I said obligingly. 'Hang on.' Then I heard him call to his wife, 'It's Bob Cass on the phone. Someone's let him down for some dinner and he wants to know if I could help him out. He knows it's last minute but he's desperate because he says the whole dinner could be up to Swanee.'

I hear the player's wife say, 'They always do this to you because you're too soft. They take advantage of you.' Then he comes back to me, 'You're out of order to come on this late. You can fuck off.' And down went the phone.

I wasn't happy. My evening in the pub had been interrupted by standing outside a phone box in the cold—a point I made quite forcibly when I saw the

221

player after training a few days later. He smiled, shook my hand and said, 'Sorry pal. I had to put a bit of a show on for the missus.'

I have always believed the camaraderie enjoyed between players and staff of Sunderland and the journalists who followed them throughout their journey to the final contributed to the FA Cup success in 1973. We stayed at the same hotels, dined in the same restaurants, drank and sang in the same bars. There was no demarcation, no us and them. We took the piss—and had it taken out of us. It was the same covering Newcastle United and, for that matter, any journo involved with any of the clubs, large or small.

The beginning of the end of my time with The Sun was the result of me refusing to comply with an edict from the editor Kelvin Mackenzie to dig for dirt stories involving footballers. Sports journalists became answerable to news desks and, on the day the paper led the front page exposing an England international's dalliance, I took a call from Ken Tucker, the Northern news editor, ordering me to root out similar tales. Did he give a toss about burning the kind of contact who could provide football-linked exclusives? Not a chance. Anyway, as I told him, as far as I knew the area was as pure as the driven snow.

Of course, the importance of contacts has been nullified by the social media offering stories on a velvet cushion. Twitter and other networking services, conveniently engaged by sporting personalities from the highest to the lowest profile, have created a level playing field which means journos no longer have to rely on personal relationships to get their tales. Who needs a contacts book when you can become a subscriber?

Which is just as well because what opportunity there is for conversation with players is normally restricted to after-match mixed zones, press conferences or one-on-one interviews set up corporately to publicise a guy's sporting suppliers or favourite charity, all conducted with an inevitable media officer standing by.

One should never take for granted being able to report on England, particularly of course in major tournaments like the World Cup and the European Championships. It is something to be proud of, especially when you get involved in big stories and they don't come any bigger than the day Paul Gascoigne ripped his international career to shreds!

Gazza and I go back a long way, to the days when he collected enough rejection slips to light a bonfire before he signed schoolboy forms for Newcastle United, the club on the other side of the River Tyne from where he was born—ironically on the same date as my birthday—in Dunston, Gateshead. And, watching him in junior matches, you didn't need to be the most discerning football judge to quickly realise the clubs who turned him down had somehow detected a lump of coal when they were looking at a diamond.

He was just a daft kid even then; full of mischief, a habitual practical joker, but warm as toast and as open as a book. And God, could he play. And if, subsequently, notoriety has become his best friend— sharing much in common with priceless soccer talents such as George Best, Malcolm Allison and Stanley Bowles among others—he has been characterised as a

223

flawed genius. In my experience, the lad does not have a rotten bone in his body. No doubt there are those who would offer a contrasting opinion which they may be well justified in voicing. Nobody's perfect.

Whatever judgement, comment or observation (call it what you like) has been made about Gascoigne's drink-fuelled dive into the pit of despair, he could never be accused of lacking emotion or passion, however much, when spectacularly misguided, it has led to his downfall.

Never was that more evident than when, for the second and ultimately final time, his shattered international dreams put him on the front page of every newspaper. Back in 1990 he tugged the nation's heart strings following his tearful reaction to a World Cup semi-final booking against West Germany which meant he would have been ineligible to play in the final had England got there. Eight years later such sympathy was in short supply when he responded to Glenn Hoddle's decision to leave him out of his squad for the World Cup tournament in France by wrecking the England manager's hotel room in La Manga.

And yet it all could and should have been so much different. Because less than 24 hours earlier I was privy to information that Gascoigne would be very much part of Hoddle's final choice. And why not? He had been a regular in the build-up matches, helping England win the Tournoi de France in 1997 and making an important contribution to the goalless draw against Italy in Rome's Olympic Stadium which guaranteed England's participation in the final stages.

But there was no question about the burning topic of the day; was Gazza in the squad or not?

Tantalisingly, Hoddle decided to bring his announcement forward a day earlier to Sunday May 31st at the team's training quarters in La Manga but he was keeping his cards very close to his chest, which was no good to Sunday paper men like Joe Melling and myself. We needed a steer from somebody on the inside.

It was decided I should be despatched to Frankfurt on the Saturday where Hoddle's number two, John Gorman, and his fellow back-room staff member, Glenn Roeder, had gone to run the rule over group rivals Colombia in their friendly against Germany. Not being a ha'porth interested in the game, my sole brief, knowing the pair of them, was to try and make contact and hopefully get my card marked.

I had known Gorman ever since his younger days as a full back at Carlisle United and Roeder as a player at Newcastle United, so when they agreed to meet me for dinner after the match it was a giant step in the right direction. There were bits of chat about Colombia's danger men which would come in useful in the eventual build-up to the game, but nothing about Gascoigne. We hadn't even danced around the subject, with me wondering how I was going to broach it and the clock running down towards contacting Melling who was waiting in La Manga to write what would be an exclusive 'in' or 'out' story.

It was almost shit or bust time when Gorman suddenly piped up, 'Go on then, ask me the question then. You want to know if Gazza is in or out, don't you?' Needing no further encouragement, I did ask the question and received an immediate answer in the affirmative; Glenn Hoddle would be naming Paul

Gascoigne the following day in his 22-man squad for the World Cup final tournament.

It was more than a tad fortuitous that, by the time the news was related to my colleague, it only managed to make an edition read by anybody other than a man walking his dog within spitting distance of Trafalgar Square.

I would have been in transit from Frankfurt to Newcastle when it all kicked off in La Manga that Sunday. Suffice it to say Gascoigne snatched failure from the brink of triumph, blowing his selection—and his England career—with his unacceptable behaviour, allegedly after he had been drinking on the golf course that day.

I was fully engaged in domesticity on the Monday, having first been informed by Melling how his 'exclusive' had all gone horribly wrong, and then reading all the lurid accounts of Gascoigne's antics in the papers. I was actually pushing a supermarket trolley when my mobile started ringing. 'Bob, it's John Gorman. Really sorry about what happened, but you have to believe me, it was right. Gazza was in the squad when I told you.'

Believe him? Of course, I did. It was just a bad day at the office for a couple of Geminis!

CHAPTER TWENTY ONE
BIG BOOBS

We've all dropped clangers, made mistakes or written stories which for some reason or other have been so far off the mark it becomes an embarrassment. Some consistently get it wrong, usually because they pick up a glimmer of a tip, get out their kite and head for Hampstead Heath. My MO is never to write a tale unless I've got cast-iron information to back it up, but sometimes it still goes wrong; like the one which kicked off one particular year in disastrous fashion.

I was where any red-blooded Northerner would be at around half-past eight on New Year's Day morning 1970—in bed, comatose. After all, hadn't thirteen hours or so earlier begun the traditional Hogmanay festivities; dinner, dancing... oh yes, and more than a few alcoholic beverages; activities which kept the party people occupied in various houses until three or four in the morning.

So, it was with a measure of annoyance that I found myself being shaken awake by my wife, Janet, who told me someone from the Sun sports department was on the phone. In a state which bordered somewhere between somnambulism and death, I picked up the receiver. 'Hey, Cassie. Colin Hart here.

We want you to go to Edinburgh,' said the voice of the paper's esteemed boxing writer who was doing a shift on the desk. Harty—bright-eyed and bushy-tailed after obviously enjoying a full eight hours kip—chirped, 'No, I'm not taking the piss, pal. We're told Peter Marinello is going to sign for Arsenal and we want you to go up there and do the tale.'

Marinello had become the pin-up boy of Scottish football. As a superbly talented winger with Hibernian, his boyish looks and long black hair had even labelled him the new George Best. He was due to play in the traditional New Year's Day 'derby' against Hearts with the Gunners ready to fork out a record six figures for the first time in their history to get him.

Driving was out of the question. My head was ready to burst wide open. I was plainly still under the influence; staggering around like some drunken dipsomaniac. Fortunately, Janet checked the trains and found one which would get me into Edinburgh in the early afternoon; the problem was reaching the station with her a non-driver and not a taxi to be had. There was public transport to town which meant a mile walk to the bus stop, but with time running rapidly out for me to catch the rattler, it was the only option.

Anybody who has been to Durham will know the station is at the top of a steep bank, which became like a climb up the north face of the Eiger after I'd arrived at the bottom just in time to see my last hope of getting to Edinburgh on time approaching the platform. But crawling the last few yards on all fours and having to be lifted bodily into the carriage, I made it, although it was Berwick before I was finally able to get off the floor and grab a seat.

The stroll from Waverley Station to Easter Road—no taxis there either—was eventful, with any number of cheery Scots offering me a tipple from their whisky bottles which I respectfully declined. So much so that when I reached the ground I was ready to do the job. And when I spotted Gordon Clark, the Arsenal chief scout and a good pal, in reception, I knew it was going to be a lot easier than it might have been.

As it happened, with Marinello missing the game because of a sore throat, the only thing worth remembering about the afternoon was when Peter Cormack, who later had a great career with Liverpool, got himself sent off for kicking an opponent up the backside.

But Clark told me he was due to meet the player's people after the game and we arranged a rendezvous later at the North British Hotel near the railway station. Job done—or so I thought. He was superb, keeping me informed of everything that occurred during the transfer negotiations, and it soon became clear that it was far from a done deal. Tottenham Hotspur, whose manager, the legendary Bill Nicholson, was also at the game were waiting in the wings ready to pounce if their North London rivals came unstuck, and with the Gunners man to-ing and fro-ing to meetings with Marinello and his clan and getting more and more exasperated by the minute, that's how it began to look.

'They're playing silly buggers,' he said. 'I'm going to give it one more go, and then I'm off back to London, deal or no deal.' And he assured me he would be back at the hotel in time for me to catch the last train back to Durham.

This was certainly not according to the script. Arsenal had agreed terms with Hibernian the previous week when Marinello had visited Highbury. Clark was only supposed to be going up to Edinburgh to formalise the transfer and return the same day with the completed papers. But when he did return it was only to tell me, 'It is no further forward than when I came here last night. We have bent over backwards to satisfy the player and the club. The difficulty has nothing to do with us and it is now up to Hibernian to sort the problem out'.

He added that he would make one final effort the following day, but generally speaking his message was that the deal could be off. And that, with the added angle of Spurs waiting to pounce with a dramatic bid and snatch the player, was the theme of my back page lead in the following day's Sun under the headline, 'Spurs Are All Set To Step In'.

Marinello signed for Arsenal almost before The Sun hit the newsstands. If there is anything worse than getting it wrong, it is getting it spectacularly wrong. And I feared the worst when my doorbell rang that morning and I was handed a special delivery telegram which, when I opened it, confirmed my worst fears.

It was from Frank Nicklin, The Sun's indomitable sports editor and the message was short and simple: 'Fuck 'em, I believe you!' Superb, and it eased the pain over missing out on the tale.

Then there are those stories you bungle because you think you know more than the people involved; when a little patience and understanding works better than bull in a china-shop belligerence. As I have said, the football club closest to my heart is Darlington, sadly languishing these days so far from league action they merit coverage only in the local paper.

They were operating at slightly higher sphere albeit without troubling the footballing gentry towards the end of 1978 when they were looking to appoint a new manager. A guy called Len Walker, who was born in the town, had been in charge on a caretaker capacity and I felt had done enough to get the job permanently, an opinion I passed on to a boardroom contact when he told me they were considering applicants at an evening meeting. The only other serious runner was Billy Elliott (no, not the boy dancer), someone who made his name as an England international footballer long before his namesake hit the boards.

Elliott was certainly a serious contender. He had been part of Sunderland's back-room staff when they won the FA Cup, having been replaced by Bob Stokoe after a short spell as caretaker boss following the sacking of Alan Brown. During his time there, he was credited as the brains behind switching Dave Watson from a striking role to becoming a top class central defender, but there was clearly a personal agenda between him and Stokoe which only came to light when Elliott, who had been at the club for five years, was suddenly sacked barely a month after the Wembley win.

It was an acrimonious split which all came out at a subsequent tribunal, with the Sunderland manager citing poor player relationships and all manner of reasons why he got rid of his trainer-coach. But the tribunal ruled in favour of Elliott and awarded him a compensatory payment of £1,448 for unfair dismissal.

Such was the background to another major howler when the question of the next Darlington manager arose. I favoured Walker but, when I rang my contact to see if there had been any decision at the meeting, I was informed the majority decision was to appoint Elliott. However, there was a problem. 'He's told us he has been approached to take over at Sunderland, so we're waiting to see what happens there,' said my man. My immediate reaction was that this had to be the biggest load of garbage I'd ever heard, sentiments which I passed on to deep throat.

'Look. it's not that long since Billy took Sunderland to an unfair dismissal tribunal and won compensation from them,' I told him. 'There is no way they're going to appoint him as manager. Take it from me, he's trying to squeeze a better deal out of you. Just give the job to Lennie.' He did not sound convinced but promised to get back to me if and when there were further developments.

That call never came, but one that did the following day, informed me there was a press conference at Roker Park where an important announcement would be made. And still the penny didn't drop, nor did it until after I turned up at the ground and saw Andy Rowell, the Darlington secretary, standing outside. 'Hi, Andy. What are you doing here?' I asked. 'I'm waiting just in case Billy doesn't take the Sunderland job,' he replied.

Surprised? You bet I was. More like hit over the head with a sledge hammer. Of course, Elliott became Sunderland manager—a shock appointment which I could have predicted exclusively in The Sun had I been able to see the wood for the trees. If it wasn't for laughing, I could have cried my eyes out!

There was further irony. Walker duly took over at Darlington until he was sacked at the end of the 1978-79 season, and was replaced by—you've guessed it; Billy Elliott. Who, in fairness, had a great six months at Roker, almost winning promotion, but was still shown the door. What a managerial merry-go-round that was!

But I certainly didn't need Elliott's help to put the dunce's cap on after a game at Middlesbrough. It was all my own work. The Boro were playing Derby County in their Premier League days in a one-sided game which the Rams were on the wrong end of. Edition times demanded that I had to have a lengthy running report transmitted on the final whistle which meant—as you invariably had your head down, banging away at the keys on your lap top—that you could miss the odd incident in the match.

Anyway, this looked an easy match, Middlesbrough had coasted into a three-goal lead with two, including a penalty, from their Croatian striker, Alen Bokšić, when the referee offered the perfect intro by awarding the home team another penalty. Terrific! Bokšić strikes again from the spot; hat-trick! Job's a good 'un. That was until Hamilton Ricard strides up and smashes the ball into the net.

Okay, I thought, *Bokšić has scorned the opportunity to grab the glory, deferring to his Boro team-mate; a nice human interest tale*. But I was still bugged by the missed hat-trick and I awaited the reaction of the then stand-in Boro manager, Terry Venables, in the after-match press conference. The TV interviewers had first bite; platitudinous questions about the great win, individual performances, even that of Bokšić, but not one inquiry about why he hadn't taken the all-important second penalty.

And that was followed by my fellow scribes; same thing, nobody asking the obvious. So then it was my turn; stand by, my friends, I am now about to ask THE question which will deliver your match intros. 'Tel,' I opened up. 'Yes, Cassie,' answered a smiling Venables. 'Tel. What I want to know is, after Alen Bokšić had scored two goals, including a penalty, why didn't he take the second penalty and help himself to a hat-trick?'

'Why?' replied Venables. 'Why? Because he was in the bloody shower at the time!' Naturally my colleagues were convulsed with laughter. Head down doing the runner, I had missed substitute Ricard coming on to replace Bokšić. My mistake. But it didn't help when Ken Pollard, the sports producer from Tyne Tees Television whose cameras had covered the whole proceedings, came to me afterwards and said: 'Cassie, that was hilarious. You don't mind if we use that on our sports programme tomorrow?' 'Yes, I bloody well do mind,' I said, to which he retorted, 'Well bollocks to you, mate! I'm going to use it anyway.' And he did.

CHAPTER TWENTY TWO
BIG DEALS

It's an all too familiar question: where was anybody when the world was rocked by some cataclysmic event. For example, on that terrible 9/11 day in 2001, I was on the official Manchester United plane which landed in Athens for the aborted Champions League match against Olympiacos. When the news of John F. Kennedy's assassination broke, I was preparing for an evening of drink and dominoes in Darlington.

Somewhat less momentous, however pivotal it may have been in the history of Liverpool FC, was the transfer of the American president's namesake Alan Kennedy. But I well remember where I was when that went down; at home helping to set up his move from Newcastle United.

Once again, I was indebted to my journalistic mentor, the much missed Vince Wilson, a brilliant football reporter with The Sunday Mirror, not only in helping me get acquainted with Liverpool's legendary chief executive Peter Robinson, but also, crucially, assuring the man who, above all, was behind the major decisions which created the team's near invincibility in the seventies and eighties, I was someone who could be trusted.

And so, it came to pass that I took a call from Robinson one evening in July 1978. 'How well do you know Alan Kennedy?' he inquired. And, comforted by both my close enough association with the United left-back and my discretion, he requested, 'Could you pass on my number and ask him to give me a call?' No problem... Well, none you might expect.

I rang Kennedy at the home which, God love him, despite playing nearly 160 first team games for Newcastle and being tipped as a certain future England international, he still shared with his family. His mum took the call, informing me he was out but would pass on a message to phone me when he returned. Hmm... Newcastle has not earned its reputation as one of England's most pleasurable night-life cities for nothing, and you cannot blame any 23-year-old footie star, single and with a season of disciplined training ahead, and a few quid in his pocket, lapping up the delights of the Quayside.

And that's what young Kennedy was about that night. I know this because I was wakened by my phone blasting me awake at around two o'clock the next morning. 'Cassy, me mam's left a message for me to ring you. What's it about?' he blubbered. I told him about the Peter Robinson call and passed on his number, pleading with him to wait until the morning before getting in touch. Wasted words.

And if it came down to a matter of two choices: one; deciding to pursue a player who made a habit of disturbing folk's slumber, whilst clearly alcohol induced; or two; being taken with his keenness not to let his golden chance to join Liverpool slip by; the consummately shrewd Robinson made the right one.

Alan Kennedy signing for £330,000 on July 13 was a Sun exclusive and what a good deal it turned out to be. The left-back made 251 first team appearances for the club over a period of eight years and twice scored the goals which took the European Cup to Merseyside in 1981 and 1984. We still laugh when we recall the time his hopes of joining Liverpool and subsequently joining the ranks of the great heroes of the Kop might just have all gone up in smoke.

It's great to look back on major transfer business you were involved in; the intriguing insider dealing, the secrecy, the satisfaction you get when you're one step ahead of the rest of the journo posse. That was certainly the situation with two centre-forwards who became Geordie legends: Malcolm Macdonald and Alan Shearer.

It was not so much Supermac's arrival on Tyneside that was any sort of revelation; Joe Harvey's inspired signing of the flamboyant, tank-like Londoner had been well aired before he made his theatrical entrance at St James's Park in a chauffeur-driven Rolls Royce. It prompted a remark from yours truly that he was the first player to turn up in his signing-on fee, which tickled him enough for him to mention it in his autobiography.

It was the start of an association which combined professionalism and warm friendship which has been long lasting. Okay it may have been founded on a weekly column which I ghosted for him in The Sun but, unlike Keegan, Macdonald was as open as a book away from the times we did business together. He was never out of our office in Newcastle, popping in for a coffee or a game of dominoes with myself and The Sun's North-East snapper, Keith Perry.

That pair's particularly close association was reflected in the excellent exclusive pictures Keith regularly supplied to the paper. One in particular I remember was after Supermac scored all five England goals against Cyprus on April 16th, 1975. I wrote the words but the picture of him with a crown on his head holding one of his daughters under the headline: 'My Dad is the King of England', made the piece.

Like Keegan later, Macdonald was a story-getter's gold mine. That was never more illustrated than when Newcastle were involved in the epic, unprecedented FA Cup sixth-round controversy against Nottingham Forest in March 1974—the notorious St James's Park pitch invasion which created sports headlines which ran for weeks.

United supporters created shameful scenes of violence and thuggery when they charged on to the pitch after Forest took a 3-1 lead with a controversial penalty awarded by referee, Gordon Kew, who also reduced the Magpies to ten men by sending off Pat Howard. The rest is history; a lengthy hold-up, an eventual 4-3 victory for Newcastle. The FA ordered a rematch at Everton's Goodison Park and a second replay after a goalless draw when Macdonald scored the only goal and put the Geordies in the semi-final.

What is not so known was the after-match panic with reporters crowding the passage leading to the Newcastle dressing room, desperate to catch deadlines with quotes from the match winner. Melling and I managed to battle our way to the front of the queue and I banged on the dressing room door. It opened a fraction with John Tudor squinting through the gap. 'Tude. We need to speak to Soops,' I begged. 'And we're up against it.' The door shut to reopen a couple of minutes later with Tudor beckoning to Melling and myself. 'Right, just you two and that's it.' Promising to pass on the quotes to the rest, we went in. There was no immediate sign of McDonald, but he emerged from the bath, stark naked, towelling himself dry.

And what a sight. No front teeth and so bandy-legged, he would never, as the saying goes, have been able to stop a pig in a passage. 'Mal, I've just got one question to ask,' I began. 'How the fuck do you pull birds?' But we did get the real quotes and we did pass them on.

I had become well-acquainted with Terry Neill during his time as manager at Hull City and he developed into a close confidant. He knew, therefore, he could count on my discretion when, after he had taken over at Arsenal, at his behest I spoke to Macdonald about a possible move to Highbury. Things moved swiftly on with the clubs reaching agreement on a deal which would end Supermac's five magnificent years on Tyneside and break thousands of United supporters' hearts into the bargain.

Neill flew up to Newcastle on a private plane, sorted out the nuts and bolts, and was then set to take him back south on the same plane. My reward, for my part in the deal and also because the player was still on The Sun's payroll, was to join them on the return flight and write an atmospheric piece about his sad farewell to Geordieland. Well, that was the plan, until we arrived at Newcastle airport and I saw the flimsy, single-propelled engine plane waiting to transport us. I have never been the bravest of fliers and it was the sight of the little Cessna added to the ferocious wind stretching the airport flags which made my mind up that plane was gonna leave without me.

Neill readily agreed to say he was not allowing me to fly back with them, a message I passed on to The Sun's sports desk and nothing was lost, but needless to say I still felt a bit of a wimp when all on board landed safely.

It was two decades later that Shearer completed a move which was surely written in the stars. He was as much wanted by the Tyneside folk he grew up with as it was his desire to pull on a black and white shirt with the number nine on the back. The fact his circuitous return to his hometown club from Southampton was via Blackburn Rovers and not Manchester United was due to the first of Sir Alex Ferguson's two missed attempts to sign one of the most prolific goal-scorers in Premier League history.

My special interest in Shearer's career was forged by the man who picked the pockets of a bundle of more fashionable outfits to persuade him to join the English club, which was just about as far away from his birthplace in Gosforth, Newcastle, as possible. Southampton's reputation for nurturing world-class football talent needs no polishing from me, but there have been few better examples than the golden nugget unearthed by Tyneside scouting Midas, Jack Hixon.

A respected sports broadcaster and journalist of my youth named Arthur Appleton once famously described the North-East as 'The Hotbed of Soccer'. Nobody underlined the truth of that more than Hixon—unfortunately for the two biggest clubs in the area, apparently oblivious to his talents, his discoveries attained football fame after packing their bags and heading all points west and south. Players such as Brian O'Neil, Ralph Coates and Dave Thomas to mention just three were recruited for Burnley and went on to play for England.

Hixon's day job, in the railway administrative offices at Newcastle Central Station, was an unusual vehicle for his loquacity. We met almost daily for a lunchtime pint or two and he was the most wonderful company whether waxing lyrically about his protégés or just putting the world to rights with his limitless grasp of the English language.

There were regular bulletins on Shearer's progress at Southampton. I was introduced to his dad, also called Alan, and we met on a few occasions when he returned home to spend time with his family. His move to Blackburn Rovers in July 1992 was no surprise, especially as I was involved when Fergie tried to hi-jack the deal. Unbeknown to me there had already been discussions between Manchester United and Shearer's representatives, but for one reason or another, negotiations had stalled, presenting Rovers with an initiative which put them firmly in the driving seat. It was a situation which the United manager attempted to influence by giving me a call. 'Could you contact Shearer and tell him we're interested. Ask him not to make any commitment with anyone until he's talked to us.'

I rang Shearer and passed on Fergie's message. 'You'll have to go back to him and tell him he's too late. I've agreed to join Blackburn Rovers.' His answer was brief and unequivocal. United not only missed out on an English record £3.6million transfer, Shearer's goals also enabled Rovers to pip their illustrious rivals for the 1995 league championship, spoiling what would have been an unprecedented sequence of five successive Premier League titles.

The United manager's intolerance of those who get on the wrong side of him is legendary; don't I know it! He was more than disappointed Shearer did not end up at Old Trafford four years earlier, so his second pursuit of the striker when he decided to seek a new challenge reflected the Scot's singular desire to get him in a red shirt. This time there was no hanging about; no need for any cloak and dagger nodding and winking. United made their interest known, but so did Newcastle United and Jack Walker was also ready to top any financial offer the others came up with.

It was a tough call for Shearer but, having had my card marked by Newcastle CEO Freddie Fletcher as well as my pal Hixon, I was pretty sure Fergie— again—and the admirable Rovers owner were both destined to miss out. On July 30th, 1996, the Magpies smashed the world transfer record by forking out £15million for a player born within sight of St James's Park; a kid they could have had for nothing.

But what was behind the headlines of such an historic deal? A good question which, furnished with precise detail provided by contacts on the inside, I was able to answer in a follow-up fly-on-the wall feature, albeit with a sprinkling of poetic licence, which appeared in that weekend's Mail on Sunday. And I'm proud enough of the tale to reproduce it in full as one of the memories of great days as football journalist:

'The twin jet engines of the Citation 2 aircraft whined into life. It was just after 10 o'clock in the morning and Blackpool airport was easing itself into another uneventful day.

A handful of airport workers didn't bother to glance up as the silver-grey plane taxied to the end of the short runway to begin its flight back to Jersey.

At precisely 10.07am the jet was airborne. Inside, occupying three of the eight passenger seats were Alan Shearer, Blackburn chairman Robert Coar and Shearer's agent, Tony Stephens. Shearer knew that the day would not only be the most important but also one of the saddest of his life.

Jack Walker had been more than just an employer in the four years and one day since he had paid the £3.6million it needed to take the fair-haired footballer from Southampton to the steel magnate's beloved Blackburn Rovers. He had been a good friend—almost a favourite uncle.

And, in a little more than an hour, as Shearer settled back in his seat and the Citation 2 swept in a wide circle over the Irish Sea and pointed its nose back towards its Jersey base, he knew he would be telling Walker that not even his mega-millions would be enough to keep him at Ewood Park. His two travelling companions on the plane Jack had bought to ferry him from the Channel Islands to Rovers' games had differing interests in the confrontation.

Blackburn chairman Coar was hoping a joint assault with Walker could persuade the 25-year-old striker his future was with Rovers. Stephens, Shearer's agent who, just a year earlier had successfully negotiated a new four-year contract for the player, was there to support his client.

At Jersey airport, high on the cliff above St Ouen's Bay, a limousine was waiting to whisk the party to Walker's farmhouse mansion, a 20-minute drive away at Mont Cochon, a rural area on the outskirts of St Helier. Over coffee—then lunch—and long into the afternoon they talked. But, in spite of Walker's cajoling, a deal to match and better any rival offer, Shearer could not be swayed.

The meeting lasted more than five hours, with Coar making his points, Shearer giving his explanations firmly but politely, and Walker at times throwing up his hands in exasperated frustration, before finally the two Blackburn officials were finally forced to accept 'no' for an answer. The former farm cottage, converted like many of its kind on Jersey into a sumptuous country residence overlooking a picturesque valley, had hosted many a happy social gathering but this time, when it was all over, there were only hand-shakes as well as mutual gratitude and good wishes. Each side shared total respect for the other's role in establishing Blackburn as one of the country's top clubs. Each recognised that the 1995 title success could never have been achieved without the former Lancashire sheet metalworker's financial clout, much less the Tyneside sheet metal worker's son's goals.

Reluctantly but with a measure of dignity and honour that is rare in what has become a tough, hard-headed business, Walker agreed to keep a promise that he would never force his prized possession to stay at Ewood against his wishes.

They said their goodbyes before the trio climbed into the waiting limousine for the journey back to an island airport bustling with traffic at the height of the holiday season.

At 8:51pm the Citation touched down at Blackpool for the second time that day and immediately the wheels were set in motion for the transfer deal that would stagger the football world.'

But the parting was to be exacted at a price and with a degree of ruthlessness that did little to foster cordial relations between Blackburn and their Lancashire rivals, Manchester United.

The enmity between the two clubs had been deep-rooted, fanned by minor incidents in recent meetings on the football field. Off it, Rovers had been upset by the continued speculation of United's interest in Shearer, culminating in the leaking of news of a £12m offer for the player.

There was even a suggestion that, had the player gone to Old Trafford, there could be a mass exodus of Rovers fans down the M66 to follow him. A fanciful prospect maybe, but one that Walker was not prepared to entertain. Wherever Shearer was going, and whatever his own personal ambitions; one place it was not was Manchester United.

Alex Ferguson, disappointed four years earlier when he made an unsuccessful eleventh-hour attempt to prevent Shearer joining Blackburn, was thwarted once again in spite of well-founded optimism that this time he would get his man.

The United manager accepted the situation. 'I can't complain. I have a smashing squad; it's a young squad with only a handful of players over 25,' he told me. 'We did the double last season and I believe there is still room for improvement.'

The Shearer deal, meanwhile, was moving on a pace. On the morning of Friday July 26th, the day following the Jersey trip, in accordance with Walker's instruction, Newcastle, whose interest in the player they could have signed as a schoolboy had been constant if less obvious, were informed he was available.

Coar spoke to United chief executive, Freddie Fletcher, and told him the price: '£15m—and no quibbling'.

The news sparked excitement and furious activity. Fletcher began a round of calls including club director Douglas Hall, son of chairman, Sir John Hall; Hall's boardroom colleague vice-chairman, Freddie Shepherd, and manager, Kevin Keegan, who was at Heathrow Airport about to board the plane that was to take him and his team on a three-match Far Eastern tour starting in Thailand.

When Sir John, on holiday in his villa near Marbella in Spain, was asked for his seal of approval, he charged: 'Do it'.

Keegan acted swiftly after taking Fletcher's call on his mobile phone. He pulled himself off the Bangkok flight, swore his number two, Terry McDermott, to secrecy and ordered him to take charge of the party.

The players departed knowing something was up but hardly guessing what it was all about.

The Newcastle boss rang Stephens and arranged to meet him and Shearer at a secret rendezvous—the home of a mutual friend in the north east—that afternoon. Douglas Hall, Shepherd and Fletcher were also present when, with a minimum of fuss, the player agreed to a five-year contract. Later that evening, Shearer rang his Blackburn manager, Ray Harford, and told him what had happened. Harford, as disappointed as anybody about losing his England striker, thanked him for his services and wished him luck. Keegan eventually left on Saturday, a day later than planned, along with a group of United officials after making arrangements for Shearer to undergo a medical on Monday prior to him joining his new team-mates in Bangkok the following day.

Ironically, Sir John was in England attending a rugby meeting when his son rang him to say the deal was done.

It was not until Monday morning that the United chairman spoke to fellow director Shepherd. 'He said are you standing up or sitting down and then confirmed we had spent the £15 million,' recalled Sir John. 'I told him, "Well done, now you have to make it work".' He added, 'It's always a bit of gamble but you do your calculations and if it is successful you don't know where it's going to take you. We lost out on £10m by not winning the title last season so, in effect we could quickly get the money back if we got there this time. But apart from that, signing Shearer has elevated Newcastle to being one of Europe's top clubs. Our profile has been raised tremendously.' Rovers chairman Robert Coar insists there is life after Shearer. 'You find yourself in a situation and then you move on. We were never a one-man band and it's up to us to prove it.'

But for Jack Walker the next flights north in his Citation 2 would never be quite the same again. The player who once took him high in the clouds had brought him back down to earth.

CHAPTER TWENTY THREE

METRO RADIO

My excursion into sports broadcasting was highly enjoyable; mostly a source of warm self-accomplishment without being the kind of ego aggrandisement others involved in current television programmes could be accused of; on rare occasions ground-breakingly serious. Oh yes, and constantly hilariously incompetent.

Although most of it, around 12 years, was spent at Metro Radio, the North-East commercial radio station, I cut my teeth doing match reports for the now long since defunct BBC Radio Durham. Although the demise of the station had little to do with my amateurish attempts to emulate such luminaries as John Motson and the late great Brian Moore, they could hardly have increased the listening audience beyond close friends and family members. Unless of course they tuned in because they'd run out of Prozac or other anti-depressants. Invariably they were guaranteed a laugh.

I had been recruited for Radio Durham by Alan Sleeman, the aforementioned sports editor of The

Journal who had managed to acquire a role anchoring a Saturday afternoon sports programme. I grabbed the chance to supplement a meagre income by doing reports from games involving Newcastle and Sunderland. These were done by telephone with the station's financial resources unable to stretch to more sophisticated means of communication such as lip-mikes etc.

Which was all fine, until and unless you were on the end of a poor line or the noise of the crowd made it difficult to pick up cues from whoever was trying to get to you. Which is what happened one afternoon when I was covering a game at Anfield, the home of Liverpool.

Now this story has been embellished, not to say hijacked, by others to the point of becoming apocryphal. But let me tell you, it actually happened, much to my eternal horror and embarrassment.

I had experienced difficulties phoning copy from Anfield with its centrally placed press box affording an excellent view of the pitch, but it was a nightmare when trying to hear and make yourself heard, especially with the Kop to the right was in full voice. Which is what happened on this particular wet and windy day on Merseyside.

Sleeman, in order to check audio levels, prefaced any pre-match scene-setting by asking what I'd had for breakfast or what the weather was like. That's what I thought he was doing when, above the singing, chanting, cheering and foot-stamping of a normal match afternoon at Anfield, I just managed to catch the words, 'What's the weather like over there?'

'Alan, its fucking pissing down, mate, but I can barely fucking hear you. Is that all right for level?' I shouted. Then I went cold. 'Bob, we are on the air,' he came back. 'Uuhh... Sorry, Alan. I obviously didn't realise that it's raining heavily here at Anfield...' And I've still never really lived that down, although it's now part of any after-dinner speech I'm called upon to do.

There were others, like when a sudden gust blew away my carefully prepared preamble, reducing me on air to bellow at press box colleagues, 'Grab that fucking paper somebody' before ending a splurge of bumbling gibberish by deliberately cutting myself off while I retrieved my notes.

How on earth all this evolved, a couple of years later, into joining the sports staff of the newly inaugurated Metro Radio, then broadcast from Gateshead, is anybody's guess, but I actually became quite adept at doing taped interviews and then, having been handed my own sports programme—an hour-long production of news and reports called Talking Sport which went out every Sunday evening—doing my own cutting and editing. It was all totally professional and creditworthy, albeit prone to the odd lapse.

It's fair to say the station's sports output did not exactly rocket into listening orbit. In fact, it was almost sabotaged on the very first day of broadcasting by an international crisis. That's when I was introduced to the supreme talents of the station's head of sport, Charles Harrison. Barnsley-born, his privileged public school background allowed him to sound like someone straight out of Debretts one minute and D.H. Lawrence

251

at his most basic the next. But Charles' affable, easy-going manner camouflaged his ability to meet any emergency head-on and deal with it and, in all the time we worked together, there was never a bigger emergency than the one he encountered on Metro Sport's first Saturday afternoon programme.

The station was launched on July 15th, 1974, providing a staple listening diet of popular music but with a vibrant newsroom which contributed regular bulletins, current affairs programmes and, of course, sporting items both local and national. Charles had prepared well for the first five-hour long sports programme, scheduled five days later on the following Saturday; with interviews, invited guests, breaking sports news from the various wire services, and time allocated for a listeners' phone-in. He himself was due to contribute regular cricket reports from a local Minor Counties match while I had been called in to fill a spot of about an hour talking about the North-East football scene. It was all hunky-dory until Turkey chose the birthday of Metro Radio's heavily promoted sports programme to invade Cyprus!

Now such events may be the stuff of history, especially when, in that case, it resulted in the divvying up of that beautiful island, but the effect it had on the launch was almost catastrophic. Suddenly, any reliance on wire services providing sports items—an intended source of discussion, opinion and phone-ins—went out of the window. The agencies sources became completely clogged up with what was happening in the Mediterranean. Of course, the news-readers stepped in at regular intervals and there was an option in the worst possible scenario to have music interludes, but Charles and the station management were desperate to maintain a sporting identity, so we decided to push on and make the best of a situation which worsened even more when Charles lost the line from the cricket and decided to hotfoot it back to the situation.

The taped interviews were used and repeated. My stint was extended to the whole of the five hours during which I waffled on about everything from penalty shoot-outs to the price of potted meat and when, inevitably, the phone-in callers slowed from a trickle to almost non-existent we had management and others coming on in various guises and using a variety of accents from pidgin English to corner shop Pakistani which, in spite of the anxiety of the situation, had us clasping our mouths to contain our aching laughter.

There was the odd nut case; one particularly offensive caller took advantage of the absence of any time delay to tell me to 'fuck off', which I returned in similar vein, 'and fuck off yourself, mate'. It was Casey's Court with no-holds barred and nothing was sacred, but we got through it and celebrated with some well-earned bubbly when at last seven o'clock came around.

Charles, consummately professional, was a far better broadcaster than he gave himself credit for. And his fledgling staff wasn't bad either. Operators such as Peter Slater and Bill Arthur went on to become highly successful in their own right. My input was on a part-time basis which received the blessing of my Sun newspaper employers.

But Metro was not the only additional perk. Before moving to the North-East, Charles had worked in sports production for Yorkshire Television and still retained his links with the company, especially when their outside broadcast team covered the European Tour live. His former boss Lawrie Higgins appointed him to organise a scoring system which made sure the commentators and the captions unit were aware of the players' scores at any time. I was one of a group of three or four recruited to help out; it was hard work involving long hours but it was also a lot of fun. Two particular occasions are stand-out memories.

Charles, who certainly knew his golf and enjoyed putting his money where his mouth was, persuaded me to join him in investing a few quid on a comparatively unknown Italian called Baldovino Dassù in the 1976 Dunlop Masters tournament at the St Pierre club near Chepstow. Dassù was a complete outsider whose chances were reflected in his 100-1 price in the betting market. We had a tenner each-way between us. To cut a long story short, our joint celebrations were more than a little OTT when Dassù rolled in a fifty-footer at the 72nd hole to beat a top American called Hubert Green by a stroke, prompting the pair of us to hug each other wildly while leaping up and down on the clubhouse roof.

And that was not the only memory of that trip to South Wales. Returning in Charles' car, which was unlikely ever to have had its bonnet raised, we broke down leaving us stranded late in the evening somewhere on the M5. Typically disorganised, my colleague had no means of rectifying the situation but fortunately I was an AA member and we engaged their relay system to get us home. Anybody who has endured similar misfortune will know what an interminably excruciating experience that was.

As its label suggests, if the vehicle cannot be instantly repaired—like this one—it is loaded on to a truck, with any passengers accommodated either beside or behind the driver, and transported via a series of relay station stops until the car finally arrives at its destination. On this occasion, the journey, including stops, from the south-west to the north-east took the whole of the night and more.

After waiting an hour or so for the first AA man to turn up we arrived in the early hours at the first station on the outskirts of Manchester, where it soon became clear we were not the only ones in trouble and we had to take our turn in a long queue. There were sparse refreshments and doctor's waiting room reading material, but the room was dominated by possibly the biggest tropical fish tank I have ever seen outside an aquarium—and it was absolutely crammed full of fish of all shapes and sizes. There were hundreds, shoving, pushing, bumping each other in what, to me, looked like an aquatic version of the Black Hole of Calcutta.

And it became a source of gallows-type humour as we whiled away the early hours before at long last came the call which would take us to our next station somewhere near Leeds. Just as we were leaving, another unfortunate and harassed looking couple were arriving. 'How long have you had to wait?' asked one. 'Put it this way,' I replied, 'when we got here there were only two fish in that tank!' They weren't amused.

Such moments of mirth were a feature of Metro's match reports and my hours of Talking Sport even though they were the exceptions in the serious business of covering the area's football teams. But the blunders stick in the memory more than the straight forward stuff. I cannot recall the opposition but one particular Newcastle match featured the greatest own goal I have ever seen—and my expression of Anglo-Saxon incredulity that went with it. The routine for live reports was standard stuff which, no doubt, continues today; regular insertions into the sports programme and keeping the studio in touch with incidents such as goals, sending offs, penalties and the like.

When there was anything, the studio came across and you described the incident while at the same time keeping an eye on what was happening on the pitch. And so, it was on this particularly gale-lashed afternoon at St James's Park. While I was describing the previous occurrence, the ball came to rest at the feet of a United midfielder by the name of Graham Oates—Sam to his friends—towards his attacking right, roughly in a position around the halfway line. Sam looked forward and sideways and, deciding any pass to a team-mate was not on, chose to play a fifty-yard ball back to his keeper, Iam McFaul, and all this while I am still talking about the previous play.

The ball sat up, inviting the broad right-foot sweep; the connection was perfect—a golfer would say 'right out of the screws'—the volley, pursued by a fierce gust of wind, was thunderous. Before an open-mouthed McFaul could move, the net behind him bulged with the power of Oates' effort and in mid-sentence, I just screamed, 'What a fuckin' goal!'

Another Cass clanger had entered the Metro Radio archives.

In spite of all that, I had a regular spot reading the sports bulletins in breakfast programmes, hosted by top broadcasters such as Bill Steel, but I was particularly chuffed when Charles handed me responsibility for the new Sunday evening sports magazine and I have to say my employers at The Sun, while they may not have appreciated just how much time I spent during the week in preparation, were brilliant in allowing me to do it.

It was mainly football orientated but cricket, golf, boxing and especially athletics were strongly featured as well. My interviewees over the years, either on tape or guesting in the studio, were a roll-call of the great and the good of local and national sports personalities. Some are particularly memorable for a variety of reasons like when Brendan Foster saved my skin after a loud-mouthed boast I could run a mile inside seven minutes.

It started when Brian Clough, the main speaker at a sports dinner, inferred that footballers trained harder than athletes. As usual, I regarded Cloughie's opinion as gospel and expanded on that view in a drink-fuelled discussion in the bar afterwards. Foster, naturally, took the opposite stance, telling me I was so ill-informed about the training programmes in either sport that I wasn't qualified to have any say at all. It was all light-hearted stuff, especially when the former world record holder and Olympic Games medallist set me up for challenge. 'Bet you couldn't run a mile in seven minutes,' he smiled. 'I'd piss it,' I retorted and in next no time with people clamouring to get a slice of the action, I was accepting wagers of up to around a hundred quid—a lot of money back in the seventies.

A few days later, stone-cold sober, I turned up at the Durham University Sports Complex at Maiden Castle where I had been allowed use of the running track. It took me a little more than a couple of laps to realise I would struggle to even complete the required four, let alone do them inside seven minutes. And I hardly felt any more confident when the day of reckoning came at Gateshead Athletics Stadium in front of BBC TV cameras and a nominated charity, now the beneficiary of the winning bet.

That's when Foster, bless him, came into his own. 'I'll pace you round, just stay close,' he counselled. And he did, even to the point of saving me for a sprint finish of sorts which got me over the line with over ten seconds to spare. Sometime later he came into the studio to launch the now world famous Great North Run which was inaugurated in 1981 and goes from strength to strength. I stayed fit enough to participate in the half marathon from Newcastle to South Shields three times, even managing to finish in under two hours in one of them. A rare period of self-preservation which did not last long enough.

Fortunately, Talking Sport did achieve a respectable following. In fact, I remember Alan Shearer once telling me he never missed a programme as a kid. He and others would hopefully have enjoyed what I always tried to provide, which was entertaining topical craic, even if sometimes the best laid plans went awry. For example, who could possibly have anticipated an interview with former top referee George Courtney could have ended up as one of the main items on Metro's chronicle of bloopers? But it did.

The chat with George, ostensibly about his notable career as a match official with anecdotes about some of football's stellar names, was filling the final quarter of the programme, scheduled for about twelve minutes. He was ushered into the studio while the commercials were on, ready to sound off when they were over. Now, I should point out at this stage that I had a TV set close by, obviously with no sound, which enabled me to check any teletext stories which may have been of interest. In came George and took his seat around the round table in the middle of which was the light which signified whether or not we were on air.

I was explaining to my guest that when the red light came on we were live, which would be in a couple of minutes after the commercial break was over when, without any warning, the text disappeared from the TV screen which was then showing the regular Holiday programme. And it just so happened the subject being portrayed was an item promoting naturism. Fatal.

George turned his head to catch sight of a busty lady playing volleyball and, at the precise moment the red light came on, the first words my listeners heard from the top FIFA whistle blower was, 'Have you seen the size of her tits!', followed by, and with a look of sheer horror on his face, 'That didn't go out live, did it?' Vainly I tried to rescue the situation. 'Well if you're listening to us and watching the Holiday programme at the same time, you have to agree with my studio guest, top referee, George Courtney.' The ensuing interview was hardly as memorable as its introduction.

A more intentional leg pull was the mock interview I did with Bill McGarry, a highly successful and well-respected manager with Wolverhampton Wanderers in the seventies but unable to repeat it when he was in charge at Newcastle for three seasons. It's fair to say Bill did not have the greatest sense of humour. When a leading journalist once described him as a 'fearsome character when crossed', it just about summed up the dour personality of a man from the Potteries who lived for little else outside football. Inevitably, as with many of the game's leading lights, Bill had his mimics and none took him off better than John Richardson, formerly of The Sunday Express.

So much so that when Bill took a job in Zambia after getting sacked at Newcastle we decided to stunt up an interview with Ricco doing his famous impersonation of the former United boss. It was a case of anything goes with background jungle noises such as screeching birds, trumpeting elephants, roaring lions, native drums—nothing was left out. And above it all I had Ricco on the end of a local telephone line, trying to make himself heard as Bill McGarry. Suffice it to say trying to keep a straight face was impossible, but with a final 'great to speak to you Bill' above another defining screech, we ended the conversation.

It was great fun but we kept up the pretence without revealing it was all totally made up. And we got away with it. So much so that the following day when I happened to be at St James's Park, Joe Harvey collared me. 'Hey, Cassie. I heard that interview you did with McGarry yesterday. He sounded pissed to me'. I didn't have the heart to tell him the truth.

But there were more sombre moments, and none grimmer than the announcement I had to break into the programme on January 4th, 1981. A newsflash came over the wires that a man was to be charged with a series of murders, principally in the Leeds area. It was my responsibility to inform my listening audience that the hunt for the infamous Yorkshire Ripper was over. A rather dubious claim to fame maybe, but a momentous one nonetheless.

My days at Metro ended when I was recruited by The Mail on Sunday to cover the whole of the Northern football scene including the North-West, and I didn't have the time to spend much of the week researching my material. Anyway, we all felt Talking Sport had run its course but it was a wonderfully fulfilling experience. And working with the redoubtable Mr Harrison was one of the great pleasures of my life.

CHAPTER TWENTY FOUR
HANDBAGS

I've had less than my share of punch-ups. In most cases whenever diplomacy could have transcended pugilism I have favoured the former. I am not a big chap and because of that, coupled with the fact I come from a long line of cowards, I have always contended that violence proves nothing. I hate the sight of blood, especially when it's mine.

I was always a little titch at school and fair game for a bit of bullying. I remember at primary school in rural Lincolnshire I was targeted by a farmer's boy called Billy Talbot, a fat lad who was as thick as a rhino's backside, smelt of manure and who took great delight in punching and prodding me at every opportunity. He would then cackle like a hyena, opening his mouth to expose the absence of his two front teeth.

I will never forget the day he warned me in the classroom he was going to give me a good thumping at play-time. Since the majority of kids in the school came from agricultural stock with a smaller percentage being there because our fathers were in the RAF and stationed locally—in my case first at Manby and later

Swinderby—the locals tended to gang up and treat us like fancy little Lord Fauntleroys.

Resolving to keep as much distance as possible between us, I managed it until, encouraged by his pals shouting, 'Go get him Billy!' He chased me around the field until I could run no more. That was when I turned and swung my right fist as hard as I could, catching him right on the point of his nose.

It wasn't so much that punch that stopped him or the follow-up left to his face; it was more the shock encounter with the cornered mouse which left him with a bloodied nose. I cannot recall Billy ever troubling me again.

Another image of school bullying which left an indelible memory came in my early days at the grammar school where I fell afoul of a similarly tubby miscreant called Tony Daley. Tony was an avid wrestling fan who, having attended local shows, would then seek me out to practise his expertise with holds ranging from a half nelson to the scissors, which involved him gripping me between his legs and squeezing until I could hardly breathe. Thank God, his lack of agility ruled out the flying drop kick!

That particular torment ended when a Good Samaritan schoolmate called Trevor Parfitt, who was a top sporting all-rounder and could look after himself, took pity on me enough to warn Daley off.

There were also a few skirmishes when I was in the army. I remember escaping from one massive confrontation in the Aldershot Naafi Club between soldiers from the Parachute Regiment and the Durham Light Infantry by climbing through a window helped by a red beret boot!

Joe Melling and I were involved in another close shave when we were in Jersey covering a mid-winter training break by Middlesbrough. The team and ourselves were staying at the Pomme d'Or Hotel on the harbour at St Helier, and on this particular day the manager John Neal had given the players an afternoon off to spend at their leisure.

That entailed hiring a minibus with the purpose of having a half pint of beer in as many pubs on Jersey as time would allow. Of course, my mate and I needed no second invitations to join them.

Now I don't know the number of alehouses there are on the island but I've posed the question to several people since: Leaving at around one o'clock and returning not much before midnight, how many did we visit? Answer… one!

The first one we visited served such great ale and had such a good atmosphere, we decided to have another, then another; and time just flew by.

And that's where most of us stayed, save for a couple of hours when all the players, apart from Welsh international midfielder John Mahoney, left for a couple of hours on a pre-arranged booze-buying trip. With the likes of six-foot plus central defenders Stuart Boam and Alan Ramage and the equally towering goalkeeper Jim Platt gone, it seriously cut down on our physical capacity which would not have been a problem had 'Josh'—Mahoney's nickname—not started to get involved with a heated argument with a group of regulars.

Josh, especially after he'd had a few, had a seriously wicked sense of humour which at times had been known to rub people up the wrong way. This was one of those times, and these were big people, four or five of them, and they were getting madder and noisier; and, in spite of futile attempts by Melling and myself to settle Josh down, it was obvious we were in serious trouble.

It had gone past the 'listen to me, pal... No, you fucking listen to me' stage with Mahoney, shrugging off both our efforts to calm him down. And with the opposition involving us in the confrontation, we were ready to adopt a musketeerial motto of one for all and all for one.

And that was just when the cavalry came over the hill. Had a fanfare of trumpets heralded the return of Mahoney's team-mates it would have been entirely appropriate. Whatever they felt at Mafeking, it was nothing compared to the relief of Cass and Melling when Boam, Ramage, Platt and the rest walked through the door.

Suffice it to say calm was restored by skipper Boam apologising on the Welshman's behalf; a general all-round handshake, followed by a raucous evening of drinking and singing. The locals even applauded Mahoney murdering Land of My Fathers.

But even that heart stopping experience paled in comparison to the evening when for once in my life I forsook all self-administered protectionist advice; when I actually stood up to be counted, and when I thought my foolhardiness would result, at the very least, in a hospital bed. It was the evening I took on the most fearsomely quirky character I have ever met in sport, Pat Van den Hauwe.

Covering Wales for The Mail on Sunday took me to Italy in June 1988 for an international friendly in

Brescia. Thanks to an Ian Rush goal, Terry Yorath's team had achieved an astonishing 1-0 victory against opposition packed with stellar names such as Franco Baresi, Paolo Maldini, Carlo Ancelotti, Roberto Mancini, Gianluca Vialli and Roberto Donadoni.

Celebrations were in order, for which management and back-room staff, officials, players and media alike repaired to the hotel bar. And it was fun until, thanks to Van den Hauwe, it all turned suddenly very nasty.

A native of Belgium but brought up in London, the defender became a cult figure at Everton where he was part of Howard Kendall's side which won the league title twice in three years in the eighties. Being born outside the UK but holding a British passport he qualified for any of the four home nations but turned down Bobby Robson's England invitation to join Wales at the behest of Goodison Park team-mates Kevin Ratcliffe and Neville Southall.

To say Van den Hauwe was complex was like suggesting Chaplin was mildly amusing. In his autobiography 'Psycho Pat: Legend or Madman?' he admitted being high on drugs, having links with the Krays and other criminal gangs and revealed how, while in South Africa, he dreamt he blew someone's head off with a 38 revolver when in reality he stopped short of pulling the trigger. 'I let the bloke walk away. It was a decision that probably saved my life as well as his,' he sagely intimated.

Well, when cowardice takes a back seat, why not step up to the plate with blind courage; after all, didn't David pick a fight with Goliath?

As the drink-fuelled frolics stretched into the early hours, one of the players, celebrating his birthday, opened a bottle of champagne and dispensed it among his closest company which included me. As it had been mine (my 50th no less) just the previous week, I felt reciprocation was in order and so I repeated the gesture, topping up the glasses until I got to Van den Hauwe.

Putting one hand over his glass, he snarled, 'I don't drink with press hangers-on', or expletive-filled words to that effect. For some stupidly idiotic reason I just snapped. 'Well fuck you, arsehole.' Instantly there was pandemonium with Van den Hauwe making a grab for me. Fortunately, there were plenty of people around to pull him away; enough anyway for my bravery to continue by muttering things like: 'Well, who the fuck does he think he is anyway?'

With enormous relief on my part, he responded to calls to shake hands and that appeared to resolve the matter until, a good half hour later, he sidled up to me and whispered menacingly, 'Right. You and me in the toilet, now!' And promptly headed for the gents. Panic-stricken, I followed him, with some crazy notion flashing through my brain that, before being knocked into the middle of next week, I would get a kick either on his shin or his balls.

He opened the toilet door; I went in after him. And then what happened was: he threw back his head, slapped me on the back and, roaring with laughter, shouted, 'We sure had them fooled in there, didn't we?' All I could say, quite appropriately as it happens in view of where we were, was. 'Jesus, Pat. You had me shitting myself.' And my heart was still thumping when Ian Gibb, a former Sun Colleague, popped his head around the corner and smiled, 'Everything all right in here?'

I believe Van den Hauwe had a change of heart in the twenty yards or so it took him to reach the toilet door. Maybe it dawned on him that I wasn't worth risking his football career or even a possible spell behind bars. I honestly cannot credit him for being subtle enough to fool me into thinking I was going to get a good hiding and then treat it as one big joke, not without an audience.

Whatever. It was an everlasting memory of Pat Van den Hauwe. 'Psycho Pat: Legend or Madman?' Well I'm not so sure about him being a legend!

CHAPTER TWENTY FIVE
MASTERS OF THE ART

'Bullshit' is defined by the Concise Oxford Dictionary as 'nonsense in an attempt to deceive'. Well, far be it from me to query such incontestable authority, but whoever came up with the interpretation has never been bullshitted by a world class bullshitter. It would certainly not have been the definition offered by my late mate, former colleague and brilliant football journalist, the sadly missed Joe Melling. He always maintained that, rather than nonsense, proper bullshit was eighty per cent truth. And he should have known that he was head and shoulders above the rest when it came to the noble art.

Many times I have listened in awe and astonishment at Joe's breathtakingly audacious rhetoric. Whether proclaiming football dogma in a manner so apparently fundamental it brooked no argument or contradiction, or, if it was necessary, engulfing the more gullible in such a tidal wave of flattery and cajolery it left them literally speechless, Joe was a complete master. Later, of course, he would wink at me or grip my hand in triumph at another contact made or potential headline achieved.

I've always suspected the foundations of such enviable talent were laid in his early days on The Daily Express where bullshit was accepted, nay demanded, as an essential item on a journalist's CV. I remember listening to Arnold Howe, Joe's predecessor as the North-East-based football man on the paper, coming out with all sorts of unbelievable tripe in a telephone conversation with someone on the Manchester sports desk. Arnold, bless him, rattled on about who he had interviewed, who he'd had lunch with, where he had been, where he was going. Then, putting the phone down and knowing that I knew that what he had just talked out was just the biggest load of bilge I had ever heard, he nodded in my direction and explained sheepishly, 'It's all right, the lads on The Express like a bit of bullshit.'

Arnold, bless him, was a great character. To coin a great North-East saying, he tore the arse out of life. He loved a drink, smoked like a chimney—Park Drive as I recall—and had a wide vocabulary of total vulgarity with a depraved sense of humour to match, surprising really since he was the son of a Church of Scotland minister! Typical of his recollection of the events of one particular evening was when he told me, 'I knew from a very early stage that I wasn't going to pull so I just concentrated on getting pissed.' And he could certainly do that.

I remember one occasion when I went to Scotland to cover a football match along with Arnold and others such as Doug Weatherall of The Daily Mail and Charlie Summerbell. Charlie was a one-off, a wonderful old character whose supreme writing talent surpassed not only those who undeservedly preceded him in The Daily Mirror pecking order but who gained respectful recognition from such incomparable wordsmiths as Ian Woolridge, and before him, Geoffrey Green. It was Newcastle United's first defence of their aforementioned Inter Cities Fairs Cup victory of in 1969. The Magpies had been drawn to play Dundee United in the first round with the first leg at Tannadice. The team—and the press—were all booked into Carnoustie's famous but sadly now defunct Bruce Hotel.

Not being a golfer at the time I have to say that, initially anyway, the famed Scottish town had little to recommend it in the way of entertainment—that is until Charlie suggested we visit the hostelry known as the Station Hotel. Dinner was taken at a leisurely pace until, at around ten o'clock, Arnold wondered aloud whether, knowing that Scottish pubs in those days called time at around 10.30, it was worth walking the half mile or so to the pub. At worst, it was a bracing stroll along a blackened road without even a candle's illumination, at best. As we plodded blindly in the pub's general direction, 'at best' wasn't even a consideration. And then bingo! All the doubts evaporated as if, on that long, lonely, deserted road, we had suddenly discovered Brigadoon. First of all, dark became outrageous light; and then the unmistakable sound of music, singing, laughter and chatter blasting out through open doors and windows. If there were licensing laws in Scotland, they carried little weight at the Station Hotel, Carnoustie.

Arnold and I needed no invitation to get into the swing of things to such an extent that a couple or three hours later, without recalling any attempt at all by the mine hosts to get rid of us drinkers, we staggered back into the night hardly able to stand up. Somehow, we managed to get back to the Bruce and into the twin-bedded room we were sharing where I went out like a light.

Now it's difficult to describe the next sensation I became rudely aware of; suffice it to say I was dreaming I was standing under a cascading waterfall with the torrents splashing all over me. It was cold and refreshing, as I, together with the unknown naked lady prancing next to me, caressed the moment—that is until the feeling of getting wet became very real and the idyllic fantasy took a definite turn for the worst. Jolted awake I opened my eyes to see Arnold, standing next to my bed and, still absolutely comatose, pissing all over my face. He wasn't asleep for long. Leaping out of bed I grabbed his shoulders, yelling, 'Good God, old chap! What on earth are you doing?' Or words to that effect.

Arnold lurched out of his slumber, looked at me and my saturated pillow and began wailing. 'Oh God, no, no! Don't say I've done it again.' 'Done it again? Done it again? What the hell do you mean, done it again?' I shouted before concern at Arnold's obvious distress set in. Then it all came out—all his 'previous'. 'I'm sorry, pal, it's the drink,' he blurted and then proceeded to confess to having performed similar nocturnal acts over his wife before being banished to a separate bedroom as a consequence.

His punishment that night was to swap his dry bed for my wet one and the following morning he was full of remorse. 'Am I forgiven?' he begged. 'Okay,' I answered, 'just as long as I can tell the other lads.'

Sure enough, his misdemeanour was the main topic of discussion over breakfast, triggering off further revelations that Charlie had also been a victim but had maintained a gentlemanly silence. I was in no mood to share such admirable tolerance, recounting the events of the night in detail which, stimulated by Arnold's increasing discomfort, became more exaggerated as it went on.

Of course, he joined in the humour of it all which was typical of someone who was himself a great story-teller with few reputations sacred. When he first moved to the North-East and feeling the need to make a few special contacts, he decided to take the Sunderland chief scout, Charlie Ferguson, out to lunch. Charlie was a colourful character in more ways than one. Rather than trying to appear inconspicuous as you would imagine a talent scout would, particularly when he might be on a secret mission to spot a potential signing, he favoured brightly coloured shirts and ties with absolutely no co-ordination at all. You could pick him out in the crowd at Wembley on FA Cup final day.

But his reputation for recognising embryonic football talent was unquestionable both for Sunderland and before that when he worked for Burnley. Having said all that, nobody had ever thought of wining and dining him until Arnold arrived on the scene so, not unnaturally, he jumped at the chance of a free meal. Perusing the menu in the dining room at the Roker Hotel on the seafront at Seaburn near Sunderland, he pointed to the word 'scampi' and enquired, 'What's this, Arnold?' Back came the reply. 'Well it's like prawns cooked in bread crumbs.' 'Hmm,' murmured

273

Charlie as he continued to pore over the menu before laying it on the table. Up came the waiter to take the order. 'I'll have scampi,' declared Arnold. 'What about yourself, Charlie?' 'I'll have scampi too,' said Charlie. 'But can I have it without the prawns!'

Arnold delighted in debunking people, especially those who tended to lead with their chins. One hilarious example of that was when, having of course been sworn to secrecy, he revealed how a leading sports television presenter contacted him and explained how he wanted a church wedding for him and his previously married and divorced fiancée but had been turned down by every vicar he had approached. 'Would you have a word with your father and put in a good word for us?' he pleaded. Arnold did so and the wedding duly went ahead in his father's church. At the reception, the TV man was typically effusive, desperately trying to demonstrate his gratitude with material reward that didn't interest the saintly Mr Howe senior in the slightest. 'There must be something I can do for you in return,' he insisted, before hitting triumphantly on what he believed was the perfect solution. 'I know, I'll get you on the Epilogue sometime.' A reference to the late night religious programme which in those days ended the day's schedule on Tyne Tees Television.

An absolute gem of wonderfully outrageous bullshit worthy of inclusion in any compilation. No more though than the observations of somebody who in his days at The Daily Mirror was one of the most read and respected northern football writers. He and I were among the press contingent consigned to Milan to cover Newcastle's match against Inter in the following season's Fairs Cup. My habit, especially in magnificent historic cities like that one, is to cram in as much sight-seeing as possible, and my mission on that particular trip was to see Leonardo Da Vinci's painting of The Last Supper.

It was my first time in Milan, and knowing that the Mirror man had been there before, I asked him about the Da Vinci masterpiece; had he seen it and, if so, could he tell me where it was. 'I certainly have,' he answered. 'It is well worth seeing and you'll find it in Milan Cathedral.' Off I went, trembling with an anticipation that changed to heart-thumping excitement when the taxi driver put me out in that magnificent Piazza del Duomo, allowing my first glimpse of the superb facade of the cathedral.

Two hours in that magnificent place of worship is hardly enough, but of Jesus Christ and his disciples breaking bread there was no sign. Eventually, giving up the search, I asked one of the guides if he could help. 'Ees not here,' he answered. 'Ees in convent Santa Maria delle Grazie—you must take taxi.' Buoyed with the certainty that, at last, I would locate what I was looking for, I headed for the convent where indeed Da Vinci painted the mural towards the end of the 15th century and where, through some miracle, it has remained virtually intact in spite of severe bomb damage to the building during the war.

Those who have shared my good fortune by being able to stand in that holy place and just immerse themselves in the spectacle and sanctity of it all might appreciate how I felt it was truly a hair curling on the back of your neck experience. Relaxed and finally accomplished, I returned to the hotel where that evening I bumped into the Mirror man again. 'Did you see the Last Supper?' he enquired. 'I did, and, like you said it was wonderful,' I replied, adding, 'but it wasn't in Milan Cathedral. It was in a convent called Santa Marie delle Grazie.' 'Oh,' he retorted. 'They must have moved it since I saw it!'

But there is 'art' and there is 'art'—and bullshit, when performed by a master like Joe, was not only an art-form but an experience not to be missed, and I was privileged to be so closely associated with such an expert. Inevitably, things rub off to the extent that, without blowing my own trumpet, I became quite good at it myself; certainly, good enough to take even Joe on the odd occasion. Later he would graciously acknowledge the particular wind-up in a manner which suggested huge personal satisfaction from my successful education.

In the end neither was able to bullshit the other and we delighted in being able to spot and denounce any attempt with tennis-like jargon such as 'Never try to out-bullshit the incoming volleying bullshitter.' It was a great game and just one of the many memories I shall store and treasure from a friendship that began in the seventies when I was with The Sun, and Joe, The Express, and grew stronger when we became colleagues at The Mail on Sunday. Our friendship lasted until he died after a nine-month battle with cancer on March 31st, 2004.

Not only were Joe and I the closest of pals—'those two are joined at the fucking hip' was the popular description of our relationship—we were also a terrific journalistic partnership. Together we cracked an abundance of exclusive stories, either working independently or sharing our contacts. If I say it myself, there weren't many—if any—better.

And yet we started out as keen rivals covering the far North football scene, based in the North-East. I had been with The Sun for some time when Joe was transferred from the Manchester office of the Express. We met in the press room at Carlisle United, then quite a successful team, who later, under their manager Alan Ashman, not only won promotion to what is now the Premier League but were actually top of the league after the first few matches.

Our friendship and professional liaison developed and blossomed over the next thirty years with mutual respect as its bedrock, and as its structure a shared appreciation that building contacts involved social camaraderie and total trust. And if that meant a few late nights after matches mixing with players, managers and club officials. It was all part of the job. A serious business but also a hell of a lot of fun.

One time, we both attended a Middlesbrough club function—I think it was their centenary celebration—at which many officials from other clubs were present. They included the notorious chairman of Burnley, a Mr Bob Lord, a local butcher who had a reputation for making mincemeat out of members of the media. Anyway, a point came during the evening when Joe and I, sufficiently fortified with vino, mischievously decided to put his demeanour to the test. 'Mr Lord,' we said, introducing ourselves. 'Bob Cass of The Sun and Joe Melling of The Express. Can we say what a pleasure it is to make your acquaintance.'

Lord's response was encouraging enough for the three of us to chat away for some time until as a parting shot, Joe declared, 'Well it's been really nice talking to you, Mr Lord. You're not at all like the person you've been painted.' Lord, smiling as he shook our hands with an exaggerated vigour, declared, 'Load of rubbish. Let me tell you lads, you can ring me any time you like.'

Some months later we were tipped off that Jimmy Adamson, then the Burnley manager, was in the frame for the job at Sunderland. A great story if it was true, but it needed checking out. Joe and I had joined up in The Sun's office in Newcastle. 'This is the test,' he said. 'Bob Lord told us we could ring him at any time. One of us is going to have to do it.' The task was decided by the toss of a coin and, if I say I lost, it was only because I called correctly. With quivering fingers, I dialled his number… a few rings… then a gruff, 'Hello. Bob Lord.'

Nervous, but trying to sound as if he was my best friend, I cackled, 'Mr Lord. It's Bob Cass. You may remember you met Joe Melling and me at the Middlesbrough centenary celebration.' There was a pause that seemed to last for ever. 'Mr Lord, are you still there?' I spluttered while Melling frantically mouthed instructions in my face. 'I'm here,' he replied darkly. 'Well Mr Lord, you indicated you would take a call from us if we needed to check anything out with you,' I pleaded. 'Yes, what of it?' He now sounded impatient and totally uncooperative. 'Well I've been told Jimmy Adamson might be getting the job as Sunderland manager, and I just wondered if there was any truth in it.' This time Bob's pause was an eternity, and then slowly he drawled, 'Mr Adamson will be appointed manager at Sunderland tomorrow morning.'

He followed this by stating, 'never ring me again,' before slamming down the phone. The Cass-Melling bullshitting master class had struck again and we celebrated with the grandest of high fives. Cue back page leads in The Sun and The Express.

CHAPTER TWENTY SIX
TEETHING TROUBLES

Would that I had the benefit of such experience when I started out as a junior reporter on The Northern Echo and Northern Despatch in Darlington. You could say in those days I was definitely an 'in' person, interested and innocent, but incipient, insignificant, insecure, inferior; in fear of the sack and anyone in authority, and certainly in absolute dread of the deputy chief reporter, Dick Tarelli, who within days of my joining the paper for a probationary period had decided I was incompetent, indolent and incapable, among many other freely voiced insults.

And I don't know why. His reasons could have had little to do with my input because all I was entrusted with was answering the telephone, cycling around the town's auction marts and fruit and vegetable wholesalers every Monday (market day) to collect the prices of livestock and greengrocery, picking up handwritten copy from reporters covering the local Magistrates and County Courts, and consulting two books to write a weekly paragraph listing the gardens that were open that weekend in aid of the Retired District Nurses Benefit Fund and National Trusts Gardens Scheme.

Soon, I was pedalling my bike the couple of miles or so from home to the office in Priestgate, twitching like the fried egg I had in a sandwich most days for breakfast. It didn't take a lot to deepen my insecurity. Even from the first day I had the distinct feeling I was in the job on false pretences. Mounting the stairs and walking along the long, narrow corridor to the rectangular reporters' room, I felt like a spare part.

After all, I had no pretensions to a career in journalism when mam persuaded me to let her write to a chap called Joe Wood, who was boss of the printing office at the paper, in an attempt to get me started as an apprentice linotype operator. I had left St Mary's just after my 16th birthday, having disappointed my dad in particular by managing only three GCE 'O' levels; French and English Language and Literature. Which only goes to show that, if you get lucky, even the measly and entirely appropriate consequence of a grammar school education wasted by wanton disregard for study and application can turn out to be just as rewarding as a portfolio of passes.

Lucky break number one came when Joe ruled that French and two English 'O' levels still overqualified me to follow in the footsteps of William Caxton. Lucky break number two was when he decided to pass on mam's letter to the editor of The Northern Echo, one Reginald Gray. Lucky break number three came when Mr Gray just happened to have a vacancy for a trainee reporter. Lucky break number four came when my non-existent alternative job prospects made it easy for me to accept the interview offer from the editor. And lucky break number five was the promise by Mr Gray at that interview to keep the vacancy open for another four months if I went back to school and added mathematics to my puny list of academic achievements.

In those days, with the blessing of your headmaster—in my case Father A.M. Cunningham—you were allowed another crack at the GCE examinations at the end of the autumn term. It was a toss-up of who frightened me most into breaking the habit of my schooldays and working hard: 'Reggie', as the editor was affectionately known, with his imposing frame which he managed to squeeze into an enormous high-backed armchair behind a ridiculously ostentatious leather-topped mahogany desk... or Mam and Dad, who somehow retained parental faith, that with a bit of effort, I might just make something of my life. Anyway, I achieved the maths 'O' level—just—and got my start at the Echo. Kitted out in new suit, shirt, tie and shoes that Mam and Dad subsidised courtesy of the credit club that was always the principle supply of wherewithal for working class folk like ourselves.

It would certainly have been a short-lived career, over and done with long before the gear had been paid for had Tarelli had his way. I was rescued when the first microcosm of bullshit suddenly glittered into my psyche. It so happened that his superior, the chief reporter—a kindly but tough Yorkshireman called Bill Myers, who could be as blisteringly cutting as he was benevolent—had two important roles on the paper. As well as directing reporting traffic by allocating jobs on a daily basis in the desk diary, Bill was the man responsible for covering Darlington FC in what was then the Third Division North, doing the daily team news and reporting their matches, home and away.

As a mad keen Darlington supporter, this presented an unexpected opportunity that I needed to grasp with both hands. Casually at first and with no apparent purpose, I would inquire how a certain player had performed. I might mention a few statistics like what club they had come from and for how much, and very soon I was tentatively venturing opinions on the matches; all good bullshit which would certainly have met with the subsequent approval of Melling because it was more than eighty per cent knowledge. Then I hit the jackpot.

Saturday afternoons during the football season had been spent helping out with simple chores while the production staff got out the sports edition. The aforementioned Joe Wood took a leading role and was in his element when calling out the football results, laced with a litany of hilariously mispronounced Scottish teams, such as Cowbeneath, Stenhousemanure, Patrick Thistle, Drumbarton, Hamilton Chemicals and Airyonions. It was different and fun, but it wasn't where I wanted to be, so when Bill asked me whether I would like to join him in the Press box at Feethams for a Darlington home match, I could not have been happier.

Bill made a nice few quid on the side doing freelance work on match days and he wanted me to phone his copy to various Sunday papers such as The News of the World, The People—even The Sunday Post. It became a regular duty for which he gave me ten bob (50p in today's money) which was a small fortune for somebody earning just under £2 a week.

But the petty cash was less important than the relationship evolving between myself and the chief reporter and besides, I was getting into Feethams without paying and without having to risk ripping the arse out of my trousers on the barbed wire whilst climbing over the fence at the bottom of Beechwood School football field, which had always been my previous means of free access.

Bill came up trumps when my six months' probation was up and a decision had to be made whether I was good enough to enlist in the three-year indenture scheme. My tears and his sympathy overcame Tarelli's negative recommendation and I was packed off to the Bishop Auckland office of the paper for further education. It's all water under bridge now of course and, looking back, I'm happy to say that such similar career complications have been few and far between.

Although in those early weeks I felt dwarfed and intimidated by what I believed were supreme journalistic beings, I realise now they were nothing special; just honest to goodness hacks doing their best to earn enough to pay their mortgages, the hire purchase on their cars, and have a bit spare for a fag, a pint and a couple of weeks' holiday. They never had to worry about being scooped because there were no opposition papers and it was all diary stuff anyway—that is until life was suddenly spiced up by an unforeseen death, whether it be as a consequence of an accident or, less frequently, murder. It was then an altogether different so-called bumpkin sprang into action and you were taught lessons in bullshit and opportunism that were never part of any curriculum that I encountered in those three years on the Westminster Press group training scheme. Naturally you learn most from experiences which make the biggest impact and the day I discovered, when the price is right, newspaper loyalty can be a cumbersome liability, is one I'll never forget.

Ironically, and though it was quite definitely far from the object of the exercise, it was my old adversary who significantly improved my education. I had met the love of my life, Janet, at a parish dance in Darlington and our courtship consisted of exchanged visits, she catching the train to Bishop Auckland or me doing the reverse trip. I was no Hannen Swaffer, although by this time operating in a four-reporter office, I was covering courts and councils, but even still wet behind the ears I had to put up with a few leg-pulls from the folks back home. I guessed it was just another wind-up when I turned up at Janet's house to find her dad standing on the doorstep and asking me where I'd been wasting my time when somebody had been murdered in the next street.

It only needed a confirming nod from my future wife to convince me he wasn't kidding, so off I went like a bat out of hell through the back-lane linking Eldon and Lansdowne Streets to discover a bustle of police activity outside a house barely two minutes away. It was a stroke of unbelievable luck that a policewoman I'd met and got to know collecting court copy was standing guard outside the door. 'What's happened?' I enquired hopefully. 'You'll get me shot,' she whispered, and then, glancing furtively around, confided, 'There are two dead, a woman and a little boy, and a little girl has been badly injured. Now buzz off.'

Sadly, hard news is often borne out of tragedy and this was a shocking, heart-rending story of a wife and baby son who were battered to death by her husband's workmate, who had broken into their house intending to steal his holiday pay. But the discovery of the bodies was my first ever major scoop, and I had to deal with it. Heart thumping, I raced down the street to the nearest public telephone box to call the office—no mobiles or even house phones in those days. 'Northern Echo,' said the voice on the switchboard. I managed to stammer out, 'Chief reporter Mr Myers please.' 'Mr Myers is on a day off. His deputy Mr Tarelli is in charge today,' came the slow, measured reply. 'Could I speak to him then?' I asked. 'Who's speaking?' The operator's calm was driving me to apoplexy. 'It's Cass of Bishop Auckland,' I screamed. 'Hold on please.' And then the familiar sound of the extension ringing. 'Reporters.' The tone was familiar, a young voice minding the shop; I'd been there. 'Mr Tarelli, please. It's Cass of Bishop Auckland.' 'He's not in just now. Can I take a message?'

The frustration was sending me over the top. 'I need to speak to him urgently. Do you know where he is?' I bawled. 'I think he might have gone to the library.' The voice was now riddled with uncertainty at having to spill the beans over what everybody in the reporters' room knew had become a regular habit for the deputy chief reporter. The Public Library across the road in Crown Street housed records from the year dot and was an ideal place for researching background. You could also get a decent cup of coffee there brewed by friendly librarians. 'Would you please get him now? I'll wait,' I insisted. 'But there's only me here to take any calls. I don't know what to do!' The voice was now almost a plea for help. 'I'll take full responsibility,' said I, from nowhere suddenly achieving a degree of superiority over this hapless trainee. 'All right, but if anything goes wrong, it's your fault,' he snapped before thudding the receiver on the desk.

It crossed my mind that this lad was undoubtedly future editor material, as off he went, leaving me to listen to various mumblings, beeping car horns, a police siren and other background noises on the other end of the line. All the time plunging penny coins into the slots to keep the line open. Eventually, and it must have been at least twenty minutes, I heard a more familiar voice and footsteps getting nearer until Tarelli came on, rasping, 'What is it, Robert? And believe me it had better be good.'

It occurred to me later that I had missed a heaven-sent opportunity to obtain pay-back for all the stress he had caused but, either through a lack of bottle or maybe just selfish smugness that me, Bobby Cass—the kid he wanted out of the door—was giving him one of the best stories he had ever come across, all I blurted out was, 'There's been a double murder in Lansdowne Street.' And that, apart from passing on what details I knew about where and when, was the last I had to do with the tale. The boys lined their pockets that day with tip-offs that produced front page splashes in every popular national newspaper. Thanks would have been nice.

CHAPTER TWENTY SEVEN
TRAINING DAYS

Brilliant pay-backs transcend even the best bullshit, and there have been none better in my experience than that concocted by a superbly talented former Northern Echo chief sub-editor called Frank Peters. It was with sadness that one day I noted a paragraph in the paper mentioning that Frank had passed away, the profession would have been worse off without him.

I first got to know Frank on one of the weekend schools which Westminster Press trainees attended during the indenture period. He was very much a senior junior coming towards the end of his three years; I was just beginning and in a circle of rookies who regarded him and others like him with some awe, while they tended to dismiss us with utter contempt. Boisterous horseplay was frequent, especially after the older lads had inhaled too much of any barmaid's apron, and on one occasion Frank and his cohorts thought it hilarious to wrap me in toilet paper, mummy fashion, and set it alight. Such fun, and you entered into the spirit of things by laughing off the third-degree burns. Respect was not generously bestowed; you had to earn it.

Some years later, after Echo editors such as Harold Evans had come and gone, I was back in the North-East working on The Sun following spells in Manchester with the now defunct racing daily, The Sporting Chronicle and then The Daily Mirror. My attention was drawn to the Echo's front page. The first column below the fold was where the paper featured one paragraph news shorts with one-line headings which began with a dropped capital letter, but never like on Saturday, January 16th, 1982. From the top, this was how the headings read:

Freeze ending
Up and up
Child saver
'Keep off'
Plane 'iced up'
Inflation steady
Feathered find
Everybody out
Rolling on

The capitals, read from top to bottom, formed a message from Peters to the then editor, Frank Pifer; a magnificently contrived parting shot to end what had apparently been a stormy relationship between the pair before the chief sub moved to The Times. At least a couple of editions had rolled off the presses before it was spotted and changed, but those few thousand that made the newsagents are now collectors' items.

Great friendships were struck up on those training weekends. Many, regrettably, have been lost either by time or travels. I rejoice in the fact that two in particular stayed strong for over fifty years. The first was with my mentor, the dearly departed Vince Wilson and the second with Jim Mossop, whose talents have taken him to every great sporting event throughout the world, latterly with The Sunday Telegraph and before that The Sunday Express. Their demeanour never changed; down to earth, genuine, ever helpful, always up for laugh and a good boozing session—but always professional and spot-on when it came to doing the job.

There is currently a small but significant breed of self-praising sports journalists around who might just be worthy of the highly-inflated opinions they have of themselves had they achieved a fraction of the success of Vince, Jim and people like them in terms of contacts and stories. Another of the older brigade Jim Lawton, a brilliant sports journalist I first met in Manchester in the early sixties, once epitomised the difference in attitude with a rapier-like put-down of a younger scribe who caught James propping up a bar in typical convivial mood. 'Your problem,' observed the smart-arse, 'is you don't take the game seriously.' 'Wrong,' replied Lawton. 'What we don't do is take ourselves seriously.' Enough said!

There was no room for egoism during our formative years with tyrants such as Professor A.P. Duncum, Westminster Press Group Training Officer, around to call the shots. He was a portly man with thinning dark hair, owlish glasses and an expression that fluctuated between sneer, frown and dark fury. What he didn't do, especially in front of minions like myself, was smile. Everybody, save for a few brown-nosed swots with plummy accents, fell foul of Duncum, often through no fault of their own.

I remember during one particular weekend school in Weetwood Hall on the outskirts of Leeds; the mission put before us was simply to go out and get a story. A bus dropped us off somewhere in the city; we were given a notebook and pencil and a time limit of three or four hours. Obviously, you were hoping you would happen on to a bank robbery, a serious accident—even a drunken brawl just to make things easy, but life could never be as simple as that.

Anyway, after meandering aimlessly through the streets without a thought in my head and time running out, I found myself passing in front of an official looking building with steps leading up to it. At the entrance, there were a number of different signs, one of which said, 'Lost Property'. Feeling increasingly desperate, I walked through the door to be greeted by a bespectacled man standing behind a huge counter wearing what was obviously a brown city council uniform.

After explaining what I was all about, I asked whether he'd had any unusual lost property handed in. 'Funny you should ask that,' he laughed. 'We've just had a donkey brought in.' My initial inclination, of course, was that he was taking the piss, but then he added, 'Do you want to see it?'

Scepticism was quickly followed by amazement and then excitement as he led me into a backroom, where standing amongst the boxes of junk and all sorts of other paraphernalia, there was indeed a rather moth-eaten donkey chewing contentedly on a dish of cornflakes. The animal had apparently been found wandering on some waste ground not far from the city centre and had become a potential threat to traffic. I noted all the details and then realised, after all that, I didn't have enough to stretch the article to the required 500 words. That was when, bless him, the lost property man patted the donkey's neck affectionately, smiled and whispered: 'I bet you would have a story to tell, old chap!'

Inspiration clanged like a morning alarm call. That's it! I would do an imaginary interview with the donkey. It would allow me a deal of poetic licence but the bottom line would be based on truth. As it happened, I didn't think I did too bad a job; the article had pathos, humour and human interest. I described the donkey's early life as a children's pet to rides on Scarborough beach and donkey derby races; kindly treated and whipped by cruel taskmasters alike—it had the lot. I submitted it with not a small amount of confident satisfaction. It might not have been Vincent Mulchrone, but it would do.

Then came judgement time, and Duncum handed out the usual praise to his cronies followed by measured compliments to some and mild criticism to others, until there were just two left; Mossop of the Barrow Evening News and Cass of The Northern Echo. Jim got it first.

'This may or may not be a very good story, Mr Mossop. I wouldn't know because I can't read a word of it—your handwriting is atrocious,' lashed Duncum. Fatally, Jim opted to protest. 'But I have no desk in my room. I had to put my case on my knees and use that to rest on,' he said weakly. The eyes narrowed behind the glasses; the lips curled into that familiar sneer. 'Oh,' said a now mocking Duncum, performing superbly for his bunch of brown-nosing worshippers. 'So, you want to be a journalist.' Jim nodded meekly. 'Perhaps go on to become a war correspondent.' Jim kept nodding. 'I take it then you would refuse any assignment in any war zone that did not have a desk, a comfortable chair and a telephone.' Jim stopped nodding. Duncum had made his point.

Then he turned to me, flinging the six or seven pages of my masterpiece in my general direction and, in doing so, scattering them everywhere, he announced, 'And as for Mr Cass and his rubbish about a lost donkey, I don't believe a bloody word of it.' More sniggers from the cronies, profiting from Jim's put-down. I just gathered the pages together in absolute silence. Amazingly, Jim and I returned to Weetwood Hall recently, although now of course the former halls of residence is a luxury hotel where we stayed after taking part in a charity golf day for Sir Steve Redgrave.

Well, Mossop and I managed to see off most, if not all, of those brown-noses and, until he was handed summary redundancy by The Sunday Telegraph, we were both still covering some of the world's great sporting events together more than fifty years after those days when we were just raw recruits. Major football events such World Cups, European Championships and Champions League; golf tournaments like the Open and the Masters; although I have to say his passport has twenty times more stamps on it than mine. And the Barrow boy and I are still managing to mix pleasure with business, as we have always done.

I remember one particular occasion when we travelled to Bari, Italy, at the end of May in 1991 to cover the European Cup final between Marseille and Red Star Belgrade, the special attraction for ourselves and the other gathered English-based hacks being the appearance of England international Chris Waddle in the Marseille team.

The social portents did not seem encouraging when, almost coinciding with our plane touching down around lunchtime on the day before the game, the good burghers of Bari declared their city tee-total. The bars in Bari were as dry as a vulture's crotch, not even a glass of Chianti was to be had in the restaurant where we had dinner. Consequently, Mossop and myself, in company with Jeff Powell of The Daily Mail and the aforementioned Jim Lawton of The Independent, emerged from the eating house desperate for a nightcap but bereft of hope of getting one. Secretly I wasn't that bothered. A few months earlier I had been diagnosed with an angina condition and been ordered by my cardiologist to go easy on the drink, among other things.

We were just about to hail a taxi when someone spotted a couple of groups of blokes entering what looked like a bodega, which had a dimly lit window and a flickering red neon sign above the door. After a short discussion, the general consensus was 'Let's see what the place is all about; if its crap we'll call it a night.' We could certainly never have anticipated what was happening on the other side of the door. The place was packed to the rafters with locals—all drinking out of tiny coffee cups, and all as pissed as proverbial newts!

It transpired that to get around the drinking ban, they ordered coffees and then topped them up with scotch, brandy, gin—anything they fancied. And we needed no invitation to join them. Four times four rounds later—sixteen large ones; myself on whisky, the others on brandy—we were ready to be taken away. Mossop and I staggered to the hotel where we were sharing a twin-bedded room which was seriously worse for wear. And that's when it began. First of all, the room started spinning like a merry-go-round, then came nausea and the feeling I was about to throw my insides up, followed by what I thought was a tightness in the chest but was probably just a guilty conscience at having completely disregarded any of the medical advice I had been given. Mossop on the other hand was comatose, having gone out like a light. 'Jim, Jim,' I moaned, reaching over to shake him awake. 'I don't feel at all well.'

'You'll be all right, pal. We've had a bit too much to drink. Try to sleep, you'll feel better tomorrow.' It was a pathetic attempt to offer some comfort when all he wanted was to remain undisturbed, but I began to feel really terrible. 'Jim, the pains are getting worse. I think I'm having a heart-attack.' I was shaking him again not even thinking about what he could or should do about my condition. 'Look, I'm not so clever myself,' he said with growing impatience. 'You'll have a touch of indigestion with all the food and drink. Trust me, everything will be fine after you've had a good kip.'

But I couldn't sleep, and the pains and panic were increasing. 'Jim,' I implored again. 'What am I going to do? I think I'm dying.' Mossop sat up, switched on the light and offered the hand of true friendship. 'Well die, you bastard, and let me get some sleep.' It was some morning after. At least for three of us. Mossop, Powell and myself vowed never to touch another drop. Lawton, who must have had the constitution of a rhinoceros, was as fresh as paint. We declined his offer to revisit the scene of the crime for a lunchtime pick-me-up.

I can't let mention of Mossop pass without poaching his great story of what happened when he and the late Frank Clough turned up in Cyprus in May 1975 to cover an England international; a story expertly told by him (with slight adjustments) at Frank's funeral. Cloughie, a bluff, down-to-earth Yorkshireman, invited Jim to accompany him on a trip to the army camp he was stationed at during his national service. Off they went to find a place much changed; the barracks were now in the hands of the United Nations and, standing guard, rifle across his chest, was a giant of a man; clearly Scandinavian, wearing green battledress, yellow cravat and blond hair poking out beneath a powder blue steel helmet. Not overawed in the slightest, Cloughie walked up to the guard and began speaking in slow, deliberate fashion. 'Excuse – me. My – name – is – Frank – Clough. I – am – from – England. I – am – a journalist – covering – England's – football – match – over – here. I – was – here – in – the – army – during – the – troubles. I – have – brought – my – friend – James – Mossop – who – is – also – journalist – to – show – him – where – I – was – stationed. Is – it – all right – if – we – have – a – look – around? Looking straight ahead and without changing his expression, the guard replied, in the broadest Yorkshire accent, 'Fuck off.' Dumbstruck, Cloughie and Mossop looked at each other in disbelief before Cloughie responded, 'Great! You're English. Where are you from?' 'Heckmondwike, Yorkshire,' declared the soldier. 'Bloody hell, what a coincidence. I'm from Cleckheaton,' said Cloughie, to which the guard retorted, 'Tha can still fuck off!

I have digressed back to the characters who shaped my youthful career, and there were more than a few. An obligatory part of the three-year indenture programme with the Westminster Press, owners of the Echo and Despatch, the Darlington-based morning and evening papers respectively, was a six-month spell learning how to sub-edit. The nuts and bolts of it were to do with typefaces, shaping stories to fit the pages and writing headlines. The regular subs knew their job all right—newspapers are all about reacting to news as it happens and, when necessary, these lads could change a front page in a heartbeat.

There was a late morning ritual on the Despatch that was so comical at times you had to keep reminding yourself it was a serious item on the daily agenda. The deputy chief sub was a guy called Hector Thompson, a heavily-built theatrical character with a booming Churchillian voice which he used when he felt the need to make pronouncements on any world-wide topic from the perils of communism to the price of potted meat. It was also Hector's responsibility to phone the despatch room, which was the area where the papers came off the presses to be wrapped in bundles and loaded into the vans for distribution, and dictate the main headlines for the placards that were posted at various selling points throughout the town.

Unfortunately, more often than not, on the other end of the line was a chap called Alf who was a little short in both the hearing and intelligence departments. The resultant confusion often bordered on farce with Hector bellowing at ever-increasing decibels to make himself understood. Then one day, it all went wrong in spectacular fashion. Hector was about to dictate a headline about a serious house fire in the town with the words 'Holocaust razes Darlington bungalow.' Alf dutifully picked up the phone in the despatch room. 'Are you ready, Alf?' boomed Hector, and began repeating each word slowly and louder until, perspiring with the effort, he finally got the message across. An hour later we were informed there had been an unprecedented demand for the early edition of the paper in response to a placard which read 'HOLY GHOST RAISES DARLINGTON BUNGALOW!'

The experience gained working in the Bishop Auckland district office was invaluable. There were two senior reporters and a junior, me, who had to cover the whole of South-West Durham. You were in at the deep end reporting breaking news as well as handling the diary jobs such as courts and councils. But they were also even more mundane parochial tasks which are vital to the lifeblood of any local paper— like school speech days, for example. I mention that because it was one such event which provided certainly the most embarrassing moment of my fledgling career.

At 18, I started to smoke a pipe. Why? I don't know, but looking back it had to be some prattish attempt to appear more sophisticated and grown-up— being five feet six inches, still with an outsize head and comparatively skint, it would have taken more than a deerstalker and an ounce of St Bruno to work that magic. Anyway, the chief reporter, a super bloke called Doug Meek, pencilled me in to cover Wolsingham Girls' School speech day. My attempt at a young man about town image was severely tarnished by the mode of transport—the service bus from Bishop Auckland to the picturesque little town of Wolsingham in the heart of Weardale—but, having been put off at the gates, undaunted I strode up the drive, through the entrance, introduced myself to the headmistress and was shown to a table in the school hall adjacent to the stage and rows of chairs, occupied by girls of all ages from eleven to 18.

Nodding and smiling at any who caught my eye, I sat down and nonchalantly placed my notebook, pen and pipe on the table. I gave it ten minutes of trying to look totally cool before loading up the bowl and lighting the tobacco, puffing away like a seasoned John Arlott. Now and again occasions like this one produced good local stories, especially if a principal, an MP, mayor or other civic dignitary spouted on about stuff like the degeneration of youth or the perils of promiscuity or the dangers of rock 'n' roll.

That could well have happened on this occasion, I wouldn't know. I was beginning to feel a little queasy as Ms Whatshername began to drone on about the school's marvellous academic year, but the next thing I was aware of was staring up into a sea of faces from my flat-out position at the side of the chair from which I had tumbled in a dead faint. After reassuring everybody that I was all right and didn't need an ambulance, I made myself scarce long before the ceremony was over. Needless to say, I have never touched the pipe from that day to this.

The three years I had in Bishop Auckland helped to set me up as a journalistic foot-soldier. Some are cut out to be editors and sports editors, others get there more through ruthless ambition than qualification— you can usually spot these by measuring their voices on the Richter Scale; their bullshit blends into bullyshit. There was a time when people in executive positions led by their examples of honesty and integrity; check your facts, don't break confidences, make sure your quotes are attributable.

Nowadays, ninety-nine times out of a hundred, 'a source', 'a close friend', 'a family contact' are just convenient aids to fabrication. 'Never let the facts spoil the story' was once a trite but unjustified comment; sadly, not any more. The best story-getters are the reporters with the best contacts, and good contacts are borne out of trust. I was taught the basic value of trust by journalists like Doug Meek and another former Echo colleague; lifelong friend and subsequent groomsman, Ray Robertson, who had the pleasure of covering Bishop Auckland in their magnificent heyday of amateur football. It was their way—I have tried to make it mine.

CHAPTER TWENTY EIGHT

THE KING OF SPORT

To my cost I have had a lifelong devotion to the sport of kings and, without dwelling on the consequences of being a mug punter, I have to say cost is the appropriate word.

It stems from the days Granny Park, daughter of great Granny Harburn and my mother's mother, took me racing around local northern tracks such as Stockton (before it became the now defunct Teesside Park), Catterick, Redcar, Thirsk, Sedgefield and especially York. She would pile me on to the Scotts Grey bus from Darlington, push me through the turnstiles and then I would watch while she collected information from so-called turf agents who, in reality, couldn't tip coal. But I loved—and still love—going racing, especially having graduated to becoming a regular visitor to courses such as Cheltenham for the fabulous four-day festival in March.

I remember winning a poem prize at school for one I composed about Arctic Prince's Epsom Derby triumph in 1951. I know how it started, 'The sun shone bright in a deep blue sky; 'twas Derby day in the isle.

The cars and buses to Epsom went to see the half and mile.' If I remember the last line, 'But Arctic beat the lot,' and little of what went in between, it's enough to reflect on the fact that I was hooked on racing from a very early age.

Such devotion to the sport sparked an ambition—which I held throughout my journalistic apprenticeship—to become a racing journalist. After I re-joined the Echo and Despatch from doing National Service to cover Darlington, a notice in the Sporting Chronicle advertising a vacancy for a racing sub editor/writer, persuaded me to take the plunge. Anticipating the competition would be fierce, I travelled with trepidation to Manchester for an interview with the editor, Bill Clarke, a lovely chap who had been in charge of the paper since it was an all-sport publication.

Bill, bless him, was a dyed in the wool football man, whose brother Alf worked for the Manchester Evening Chronicle and was one of eight journalists killed in the Munich disaster in February 1958. But what Bill did not know about horse racing was an awful lot. I think his interviewing technique was limited to which horses had won the latest Derby and Grand National; when I answered those correctly, the job was mine.

I worked alongside some top racing men on the Chron: Fred Shawcross, Tim Richards, Ollie Chisholm, Dickie Onslow, Dick Adderley and Maurice Healey; but it didn't take long for me to realise prospects of getting out of the office and actually meeting and writing about the people involved in the sport were virtually nil. It was time to move on and the straw that broke the camel's back came on a day at Haydock Park when I was asked by the late Claude Harrison, one of racing's most idolised media personalities, to leave the press room because I was not wearing a tie.

Such elitism may be the exception rather than the rule these days with the accent more on journalistic ability than the old school tie, although there are still a few turned up noses, as in most specialist sports when the press room is invaded by general renegades there to cover the big occasions such as those at Cheltenham, Epsom and Aintree.

But I have had my moments, particularly when I was asked to ghost a series of articles for The Mail on Sunday by the greatest jockey of all time, Lester Piggott, which necessitated me interviewing the Long Fellow in his Newmarket home. It was a labour of love. We spent time in his lounge festooned with memorabilia from his magnificent career; visiting stables and looking at various horses in their paddocks.

And I must have made an impression. A few weeks later I was in Marbella writing a feature on Sir John Hall, the owner of Newcastle United who had a villa in that spectacular Spanish resort.

Sir John, his daughter Alison and I were dining in Silks, a horse-racing themed restaurant in Puerto Banus, when in walked Lester with a few friends. It did my ego no harm at all when he walked over to our table and was introduced to my two companions.

Unfortunately, Sir John had to leave because his wife Lady Mae had been feeling unwell but Lester stayed for a while, concentrating, it must be said, on chatting with Alison more than myself.

Then it was time for him to re-join his friends, but not before, with that typically nasal-voiced pronunciation, he mumbled something which I took to interpret as 'got one for Saturday'. 'Did you say you've got one for Saturday, Lester?' I inquired. He nodded before uttering something that neither I nor Alison, by now close to apoplexy, could understand. 'Sorry?' I said, shaking my head. He repeated the name of the animal, again completely unintelligibly and again prompting the same quizzical reaction from the pair of us. And then, with his weather-worn features wreathed in the most wonderful smile, he retorted, quite plainly this time, 'Suppose you want me to write the fucking thing out for you.' The three of us just fell about. The name of the horse he wrote on a napkin was Hal's Pal. It lost!

And thereby hangs my tale of losing bets which at times has bordered on the sublimely ridiculous. The consolation for one particular hard luck story is its retelling became part of my after-dinner repertoire. I still get pressed to repeat it.

It starts with me, many years ago now, getting a call from a mate wondering how my luck was. As it happened, I was going through a bad enough patch to leave the turf alone and that is what I told him. 'Pity,' he said. 'I've heard there's a Northumberland permit holder sending a horse down to Fontwell Park for a selling chase. It will be a big price but he thinks they can't kick it out of the first three. Don't go mad but if you fancy a little each-way, the horse is called Pongee Boy.'

This was long before televised races in betting offices. Race information was provided by commentaries, usually via a female voice on what was called the blower. I wasn't that bothered about having a bet but, since I passed a bookie on the way back from a press conference at Sunderland's Roker Park, I decided to pop in.

Pongee Boy was on the boards at 33-1 with a very short odds-on favourite looking the likely winner. Suddenly, the price shortened to 25-1 and I invested £2 each way. It looked good value when it plunged in stages until it was around 12-1 on the off.

There was less than a circuit left of the two-mile chase when the blower deigned to give it a first mention in fifth or sixth place behind the runaway favourite. I got excited when Pongee moved up to fourth with three fences left, muttering 'get third' under my breath. It did; then second, and I'll confess to punching the air in delight when it passed the odds-on chance between the last two with the blower voice declaring, 'Jumping the last, Pongee Boy has gone clear'.

I was counting the £60 plus I was going to pick up (a tidy sum in those days) and wishing I'd been a little more adventurous when the voice crackled again, 'Pulled up Pongee Boy.' 'What?' I found myself addressing the speaker high on the wall in the betting office. 'Pulled up? How can the horse be pulled up?' The words fell on deaf ears; the disembodied female voice and the rest of the shop's punters, most of who looked at me dismissively with a familiar 'don't tell me your troubles mate' expression. Sympathy is in short supply in those situations.

But what had happened to Pongee Boy? That's what I wanted to know. I couldn't wait to get the following day's Sporting Life and read the summary of the race. It went something like this, 'Rear early; made progress on second circuit to lead last; collapsed on run-in; died!' I did try to rustle up some sympathy for connections of the unfortunate animal. I really did!

But you win some and lose a lot more and, if one is fortunate to land a big 'un, the thrill and excitement is something you never forget. I once staked £5.50 on a 50p Yankee (six doubles, four trebles and an accumulator). Paying the then ten per cent tax would have cost me an extra 55p, but I didn't. That decision cost me over £200 when all four horses won, but I still picked up a little more £1,492, an amount I remember because of the year Columbus discovered America.

My winnings enabled me to pay cash and have a little change for a brand new top of the range Ford Cortina GXL, like the one used in the TV detective thriller Life on Mars—that's how long ago it was.

I'll never forget the name of the horse which completed the four-timer; 'Kirwaugh'. In fact, so taken was I by its success that, after a heated discussion with my wife Janet, I managed to persuade her to name our house after the animal. Unfortunately, the good fortune which I hoped would continue to embrace our rather grandiose naming ceremony—Veuve Clicquot; Beluga et al—was rather short-lived. When we moved to a smaller house some time later, the board name found its way to the council rubbish tip; such are the vagaries of the sport of kings.

CHAPTER TWENTY NINE
QUEEN AND COUNTRY

Not many outside blue-blooded aristocracy and their hangers-on can brag about getting a wedding present from the Queen, especially one which if I'd had my own way would have been immediately marked 'return to sender' with a polite 'thanks, but no thanks, Ma'am.'

Such was my lot on February 11th, 1960, when a large brown envelope with 'On Her Majesty's Service' in the top right hand corner dropped through the letter box. I am a bit hazy about full text of the wordy document inside, but suffice to say I was ordered to present myself at Royal Army Service Corps Willems Barracks in Aldershot on March 1st to begin two years in the service of Queen and country.

The summons was final confirmation that all my considerable efforts to avoid something for which I was utterly unprepared—a life in the military—had ended in abject failure. I had entertained notions of escape after receiving my first call-up papers some time earlier. Then, as my three-year indenture period as a trainee journalist was judged to be the same as if I was involved in an industrial apprenticeship, I was deferred until my indentures were completed.

Fast forward almost three years when I was working in Bishop Auckland and playing football for a local team in a Wednesday league. We were a spirited bunch and had our talent matched our enthusiasm we might have been invincible. Sadly, that was not the case, a factor never more emphasised than on the day we played an away match against top of the league Sunderland GPO. These postmen, with first class stamped all over them, quickly put us to the sword, scoring five goals without reply before half-time. Indeed, it was in the dying minutes of the first half when, for me personally, a bad afternoon got even worse.

We had to defend a corner and, adopting my role as a creative right-half albeit a shade short of stature, I lurked around the penalty spot waiting to pounce on any loose ball ready to launch a counter attack. Sure enough, I was ideally placed to pick up an attempted clearance which came to me at waist height. I raised my right foot to bring the ball down and, at the same time, turning to attempt a 20-yard pass to a team-mate waiting on the flank. That was when the sky fell in. Some burly postie came crashing in, sending my body one way and my leg the other. Those who have suffered broken legs will know about the excruciating pain and sickening nausea.

An X-ray at Sunderland Orthopaedic Hospital revealed a double fracture of the right tibia which necessitated four months in plaster. Insult was added to injury somewhat when I discovered later, this being in the days before there were substitutions, our ten men had fought back so bravely in the second half that we only lost 5-1. Digressing slightly, this was the first of two occasions when I suffered broken limbs, albeit in very different circumstances. Some years later I was playing dominoes when my chair collapsed causing me to fall awkwardly and break my ankle. A broken leg playing football; a broken ankle playing dominoes—such is life.

Anyway, back to draft-dodging. As luck would have it, while I was recuperating from the football injury, my leg in plaster up to the top of the thigh, I received my second call-up notice. It came when, because the Government had announced they were gradually phasing out conscription, I believed there had to be a great chance I could miss out if I contrived to swing the lead a little longer—or indeed if I managed to slip under their radar. While all this was going on I was making plans for another not insignificant occasion in my life: my wedding!

Janet and I had already fixed February 20th as the big day. It wasn't quite 'love on the dole' but I would have preferred a much more salubrious affair. Unfortunately, Northern Echo trainee pay was minimal and Janet's salary as an office worker was equally so. And neither of our sets of parents were in a position to help us out financially. It would have helped considerably if I could have avoided the draft and moved on to better wages as a fully-fledged journalist.

I'm not blaming the postman, you understand. After all it had been one injudicious tackle by one of their number which raised my hopes of remaining in Civvy Street. And I hadn't given up hope of failing the medical which was arranged after call-up papers number three duly arrived. I thought about turning up on crutches; as it was I probably over-played the walking stick routine. The examiner had clearly seen it all before and his 'we'll be in touch' parting shot had a 'sorry pal, you're hooked' expression all over his rather smug countenance.

And so it came to pass; 19 days before my nuptials Her Majesty's advisors decided I was vital to the safety of the nation and I became S/23767004 Private R.S. Cass attached to the 2nd Training Battalion of the Royal Army Service Corps.

Astonishingly I was initially regarded as officer material. This meant being selected for a Potential Officers Course which meant ten months of intense drills: weapons training and exercises designed to test a candidate's initiative and leadership qualities before either qualifying to become a second lieutenant for the remaining 14 months of the service or, indeed, signing on as a full-time soldier. While I have nothing but respect for the men and women who put their lives on the line in the service of their country and remembering that, fortunately, there was no need to fire a rifle in anger during my National Service, I resolved to do my time, make the most of it and enjoy the company of others similarly situated.

Were it not for the fact that, after my contribution to Janet's marriage allowance, I presented myself at the weekly pay parade to pick up the princely sum of today's equivalent of £1.50 which rendered me permanently skint, I would probably have enjoyed it a good deal more. Because there were good times. Using my initiative to remove myself from the POC, I ended up as one of only two NCOs in the RASC Officers School where I was employed as the CO's shorthand writer. I rarely did a parade; in fact, I was not even required to wear boots.

Wednesday afternoons were spent on recreation which in my case meant playing football. Although I was only on the fringe of the battalion team, I still got to train with its star players; professional footballers who were invariably allowed time off to play for the respective clubs. In my case, that meant mixing with three of the best known players of their day—Ronnie Yeats, who had a distinguished career as Liverpool's towering centre-half and captain and later headed their scouting staff; Chris Crowe, who was good enough to win an England cap and at the time was with Blackburn Rovers; and last but certainly not least Alex Young, an Everton idol, who was tagged the Golden Vision because of his silky skills by no less a person than the late great Danny Blanchflower. Even our cookhouse corporal was a professional goalkeeper, a Scot by the name of Jimmy Rollo.

But rubbing shoulders with household football names is one thing, appearing in a movie with a cast list which included the world's finest actors, it has to be said, was a bit of a step-up, even something of a quantum leap!

It all started with a message posted on the barrack notice board which declared that the company had been asked to provide 24 squaddies to act as extras on a movie called Tunes of Glory which was being shot at Shepperton Studios. The barracks were suddenly buzzing with budding Laurence Oliviers. Sadly, it was the crucial addendum to the message which immediately cast serious doubt on my chances of making the selected two dozen. There was to be an inspection parade and the final choice would come down to those judged to be the best turned out. That meant battledress and trousers cleaned and pressed until the creases were razor-sharp; webbing brushed and blancoed without showing so much as a speck, brass that glinted like gold; berets shaped until they hugged your skull, and finally, boots polished to such a degree of sheen that you could see your reflection in the toe-caps.

To say it presented a problem was the understatement of the decade. I was always smart enough when I turned up for work at the Officers' School but dress discipline was no great requirement and, having a special dispensation which absolved me from wearing them, my boots had never seen a lick of polish for months.

A despairing acceptance that I and celluloid would remain total strangers had begun to set in. And it was precisely at that moment that inspiration hit me in the shape of a fellow squaddie busily ironing his shirt into what could only be described as a work of art. Clearly, Billy regarded turning himself out in pristine fashion as a labour of love. Over the next two hours he worked on his BD, his webbing, and finally his boots, applying coat after coat of polish followed by constant rubbing with the handle of spoon. At last he lashed a final dollop of spit on the toe-caps, buffed them with his rag and then held them up to the light in triumph. They were immaculate; there was no two ways about it.

Clearly, Billy was earmarked for the movie industry, and furthermore, I decided there and then I was going with him! The question was what would I have to do to persuade him to turn me from a comparative sow's ear into a military silk purse. As it turned out, it was a lot easier than I expected. I caught him over lunch in the St Andrew's Club (known to everybody as the Jock Club) in the barracks and a short discussion revealed that he really loved all the bullshit; the ironing, polishing, brass-rubbing. And for five bob (which I could hardly afford), he would get to work on my kit—strictly on the QT of course. If I say it myself I dressed up as smart as a carrot, and that's why Billy and I and 22 other immaculately presented squaddies found ourselves on the coach to Shepperton—my appearance receiving a particularly favourable observation from the Regimental Sergeant Major at the inspection parade.

I have to say; our contribution was hardly pivotal to the success of what was a great movie. Our roles were to perform parade and exercise duties as a backdrop to conversations between actors such as Sir Alec Guinness and John Mills in the foreground in what was a studio mock-up of Stirling Castle, the regimental headquarters. Of course, we never picked up a penny for being there—our reward was a once in a lifetime experience of stepping briefly into a land of make believe and receiving cursory 'what a fine body of men' comments, not only from the likes of Guinness and Mills and the others in the Tunes Of Glory cast, but also, as predictably we marched in formation everywhere, from stars such as Cary Grant and Robert Mitchum who were shooting a film called The Grass Is Greener while we were there.

We could, however, embrace one claim to fame which made up for our indiscernible screen time when the movie eventually hit the cinemas. Actually, that's not quite correct, having obtained a DVD when it was once given away free with the Mail On Sunday, I did manage to freeze it for that one nano-second to spot me in the front line of one of the drill sessions (I think!). Not so with Gerald Harper's dramatic farewell salute as the Guinness character was driven away at the end—that was all our own work. Harper played one of the officers and his original salute resembled something between John Wayne and Les Dawson. He needed expert advice, 'It's the longest way up and the shortest way down,' we told him. And after a few practices he got it just right.

And that was about it as far as the army was concerned. Life became a lot more bearable when I was allowed off barracks after Janet and I moved into a flat in Aldershot, but the only drama after that was when it was mooted that the last remnants of national service would have to do an extra six months to make up the shortfall between conscripted and regular soldiers. Fortunately, I just missed that, although one of the officers suggested I signed on because he thought I would make an excellent sergeant. As undercover reporters with The News of the World used to say, I thanked him, made my excuses and left. I was glad when it was all over. We said our goodbyes and, apart from the odd rare meeting, I never came across any of my fellow squaddies again.

CHAPTER THIRTY
END GAME

On his 70th birthday, I remember my father observing, 'That's it, three score years and ten. I am now stealing time from somebody else.' Well, Dad's larceny continued for another 19 years before he was taken after a stroke.

Without doubt, in my case, reasonable longevity has been possible thanks initially to Granny Harburn and latterly to the skills of two brilliant surgeons. The first, Jonathan Darke, performed a quadruple by-pass in August 1999.

The second, Bryon Jacques, redeemed the incompetence of a botched gall bladder operation with life-saving stomach surgery in July 2012, for which I will ever be indebted to The Mail On Sunday editor, Geordie Greig, and managing editor, John Wellington, for footing the bill for the operation when waiting my turn on the National Health could have been fatal.

So, in making it beyond the aforementioned three score years and ten and remembering those friends and acquaintances who, tragically, have lowered the average, there's one bloke in particular whose premature passing I will ever mourn. When cancer took away Joe Melling at the tender age of 57, that awful disease also robbed me of my best friend.

I have already many times alluded to his gifted talents as a football journalist but what I remember most about Joe was his companionship and his humour, qualities which were reflected perfectly in three taxi journeys we shared—two in London and the other in Rome.

The latter episode saw the pair of us in the Eternal City in March 1973 covering Roma v Newcastle in the Anglo-Italian Cup. It was a case of when in Rome on a Wednesday, do what left-footers like myself, Melling and the Newcastle Journal's John Donoghue do, and that is attend the weekly Papal audience which, since it was in the morning and the kick-off was in the afternoon, we felt could be done with time to spare.

Leaping the language barrier with breath-taking verbal persuasion, Joe effected our admission into the vast auditorium alongside St Peter's Basilica where we found ourselves standing behind around 5,000 seated pilgrims. On the raised platform in the far distance were large groups of ermine-clad cardinals perched either side of a solitary white-robed figure—Pope Paul VI.

And there we stayed all morning. In fact, deciding not to leave until we had a close-up of the Holy Father being carried out on his papal chair, our visit stretched into the early afternoon, in spite of warnings that taxis, especially after such events, were like gold dust.

Whether or not divine providence was on our side, we did get as close as a couple of yards as the Pope departed hence, allegedly with Cass punching the air and shouting 'you'll do for me'. And we waited all of a minute in the square outside before a taxi pulled up and out clambered three attractive American females. We decided to tempt fortune no further.

Travelling in a London taxi, swapping stories with the back of someone's head has been a regular source of amusing anecdotes and not inconsequential information. However, neither was forthcoming when, because of tube problems on the Metropolitan line, Melling and I were persuaded to grab a cab from Kensington for a match at Wembley. Not a trip which should have taken an eternity—unless you fell foul of a driver who was not only allergic to the accelerator pedal but also contrived to find every traffic jam en route.

And while Joe and I were getting increasingly hot under the collar as the clock—on his meter as well as the time—ticked on, he compounded his contrasting mood of utterly infuriating serenity by singing along to his radio, especially when Ruby Murray came warbling Softly Softly. When she finished, turning his head slightly towards us, he observed, 'How great was that? Let me tell you, they don't write songs like that anymore.' Joe's riposte was swift. 'And let me tell you, mate. When we got into this fucking cab, that was number one!'

The ride we took to Kensington after a Bell's Managers' lunch, then traditionally held the day before the FA Cup final, was infinitely more pleasurable. Suitably pissed and buoyed by the cheery chat with the cabbie, Joe and I launched into a succession of jokes which had him in hysterics. He was still laughing when we got out of the cab and gestured to pay the fare. 'Forget it, lads,' he said, waving away our offer

317

to pay. 'This one's on me. Never enjoyed a ride as much in my life.'

It didn't stop my pal bidding farewell to the driver in the time-honoured way, 'Don't suppose there's a chance of a couple of blanks, my friend!'

Such are the memories of a joyous life in sports journalism.